ENGLISH ANTIQUES 1700-1830

ENGLISH ANTIQUES 1700–1830

Donald Wintersgill

To Henry

With love,

Ann

Xmas '83

William Morrow & Company, Ltd.,
New York

For my mother

Published in Great Britain under the title
The Guardian Book of Antiques 1700–1830

Printed in Great Britain
Library of Congress Catalog Card Number 75–4162
ISBN 0–688–02931–0
1 2 3 4 5 79 78 77 76 75

Preface

This book is largely based upon articles which have appeared in *The Guardian*, under the general titles 'Auctions and Collections' and 'Collector's Guardian'. They have often brought a remarkable response from readers, to judge from the letters that have come in. Indeed, several readers suggested that the articles should be published in a more permanent form. A newspaper article and a book are however, very different both in scope and in aim; accordingly, much of the original material has been rewritten and expanded and much fresh material has been added.

The history and characteristics of the styles of the period 1700–1830 are recounted in the earlier section on furniture and are summarized in the glossary. Guidelines on more detailed reading, and the sources of the quotations, are given in the bibliography.

I would like here to emphasize the assistance given to me by Sotheby's and Christie's of London in compiling the illustrations for this book, and to thank them for their generosity in giving permission for so many pictures to be reproduced.

Donald Wintersgill

Acknowledgements

The author particularly wishes to thank for their help Mr Michael Archer, of the Victoria and Albert Museum; Mr Graham Childe, of Spink and Son; Mr Paul Clarke, of Asprey's; Mr Anthony Coleridge, of Christie's; Mr Arthur Grimwade, of Christie's; Miss Susan Hare, of the Goldsmith's Company, London; Mr Martin Mortimer, of Delomosne and Son; Mrs Sue Rose, of Christie's; and Mr Sebastian Whitestone, of Asprey's.

He also acknowledges with much gratitude the help he has received from Mr Stanley Clark, of Clark Nelson Ltd. and of Sotheby's; Miss Margaret Conlin, of the *Guardian*; Miss Lynn Daniels, of the Wedgwood Museum, Barlaston, Staffordshire; Mr Geoffrey Godden, of Godden of Worthing; Miss Emma Holland-Martin, of Sotheby's; Mr John Forbes, Deputy Warden, Goldsmith's Company, London; Mr John Herbert, of Christie's; Mr Paul Kelvin, of the *Guardian*; Mr Edmund Laird-Clewes, of Spinks; Mr George Levy, former president of the British Antique Dealers' Association; Mr Henry Sandon, of the Dyson Perrins Museum, Worcester; Mr Bruce Tattersall, of the Wedgwood Museum; and Mr Ben Weinreb of B. Weinreb Ltd.

The staffs of Sotheby's and Christie's – and especially the staffs in the press offices – have been most generous with their knowledge and time. Permission to reproduce material was kindly given by Mr Alastair Hetherington, editor of the *Guardian*; Dr Hugh L'Etang, editor of the Practitioner; and Dr Stuart Maxwell, editor of History of Medicine.

Picture credits

Christie's and Sotheby's have most generously allowed the author access to their incomparable files of photographs, catalogues, and other material for the preparation of this book. Most of the photographs are from the two firms and grateful acknowledgement is made. Other photographs were generously given by:

Asprey's: Many of the pieces of furniture and clocks
Bonham's: Victorian papier mâché
British Museum (Natural History): Furniture beetle
Chartered Insurance Institute: Fire mark
Cinzano UK Ltd: Beilby goblet from the Cinzano Collection
Cooper-Bridgeman Library: Several colour plates
Delomosne and Son: Many of the items of porcelain
Dyson Perrins Museum, Worcester: Portrait of Dr Wall;
    Worcester porcelain
Mr Geoffrey Godden, of Godden of Worthing: New Hall porcelain
Goldsmiths' Company: Examples of forgeries, fakes, and alterations
    in silver. Records of Hester Bateman's marks. Wine fountain
    by Peter Archambo. Wine cooler by Digby Scott and
    Benjamin Smith. Wine cooler by Paul Storr. Table
    candlestick by George Wickes. Device for holding playing
    cards, by Benjamin Smith and his son, also named Benjamin.
    Basin by Paul de Lamerie
Harvey and Gore: Sheffield plate
Leeds Art Galleries: Several colour plates
Middle Temple: Tureen by Peter Archambo and Peter Meure
National Maritime Museum: Harrison's chronometer (on loan from
    Ministry of Defence, Navy); prisoner-of-war ship models
National Portrait Gallery: Likenesses of Lord Burlington,
    Matthew Boulton, William Kent; silhouettes
Private collection: Salt cellar in Sheffield plate.
Spink and Son: Many of the pieces of furniture. Some silver
Victoria and Albert Museum: Papier mâché tray; samplers;
    silhouette by Francis Torond (Crown copyright)
Wedgwood Museum: All the items of Wedgwood
Mr Ben Weinreb: For use of an original edition of Hepplewhite's
    Guide
Wartski: Snuffboxes

Contents

Introduction

The story is told of a beginner in collecting Chinese jades who paid a large sum of money to a Chinese expert for a course of lessons in how to detect the pieces that are 'wrong'. He complained bitterly at the end of the course to a friend: "All that happened was that the expert came into the room with a carving, bowed, put it on a table, bowed, and went out. After an hour he came in, bowed, took the jade, bowed, and went away. I was just left alone with the carving for the whole time. And do you know – for lesson number seven he brought in a fake . . ."

The moral is that experience and study are the best guides and protection. One of the experts in ceramics in a big London firm sometimes disagrees with his staff on the authenticity or otherwise of a particular item. His method then is to put it on his desk for a few days so that he can observe it from time to time. Soon the answer to the problem comes to his mind.

'Study' pieces are worth acquiring: for example, a badly broken and heavily restored porcelain figurine – genuine, but of little commercial value. Observation of such a figurine for a while in your own home can teach you a lot.

Museums can be a great help. The staff should be willing to discuss problems and points with members of the public, and it is generally possible to get special permission to handle pieces which are usually locked up in showcases or stored in the cellars.

Auctions are another source of instruction. Viewing days just before the sale give everyone a chance to hold a china bowl against the light to see if it has been cracked or mended; to examine the wood of a table for its age and patina; to find out if the hallmarks on a silver candlestick have been worn down by generations of polishing, thus detracting from the value of the piece. Auctioneers can be helpful, although they are often busy people: they are, of course, closely in touch with prices. They do, however, act on behalf of the seller, and not, as it might sometimes seem, on behalf of the buyer.

Forming a collection can be done in several different ways. Going around junk shops, antique shops, and auctions, picking up items and experience all the time is fun, but snags can arise. Millionaires can afford mistakes, although they are probably as money-conscious as anyone, if not more so. Nobody else can afford to pay too much, or get something that is going to be an ugly and useless embarrassment. So it is essential to keep a clear head at auctions: see

A contemporary caricature of Christie taking a sale

the goods at least once before the day of the sale, fix an upper limit on what to pay, and stick to it.

The legend that going one bid above a dealer at an auction will mean a fair price is not necessarily true. The dealer himself may be making a mistake. Or he may have in mind a rich and dedicated client who is willing to pay above the odds. Or he may be acting on such a client's instructions.

Auction catalogues do not usually give more than a bare description of the lots, without mentioning defects. A porcelain figure may have been broken and given a new head; a silver teapot may have suffered from years and years of daily use. The buyer must beware – although some firms of auctioneers will refund cash if an object is proved, within 28 days, to be an out-and-out forgery.

On the other hand, auctioneers are as fallible as the next man, and a valuable lot may be misdescribed. This kind of mistake can happen at every level in the trade, and bargains can sometimes be picked up by the knowledgeable. Another point to remember is the cost of repairs. A table which is cheap at £20 is dear if another £100 has to be spent on replacing a worm-eaten leg and polishing a badly scratched and dented top. It is a sad truth that craftsmanship has been in decline since the Industrial Revolution, and this situation has serious results for the heritage. Repairs, restorations, and conservation must be done, but young craftsmen do not seem to be attracted to the life. A damaged piece may have to wait years before a craftsman gets round to tackling it. A botched job by a semi-skilled worker is worse than none at all. The craftsmen who can do a good job – often men in their sixties and seventies – are fewer every year. Their names are even kept secret by their lucky clients lest 'outsiders' lure them away.

Dealers can be of enormous help to the beginner, and even to the well-established collector. It all boils down to trust and friendship. A reliable dealer gives advice of all sorts on price, condition, suitability, and taste. The customer pays, not only for the pieces, but for the good dealer's knowledge; in every part of the country are dealers who are true connoisseurs.

The profit motive is not always to the fore. A dealer will keep choice goodies on one side for his favourite clients and fix fair prices. He likes to feel that he is enriching the lives of people with whom he is in sympathy.

He will act 'on commission' at an auction. This means that the client who sees something in the catalogue and on viewing days can go to the dealer and say "What do you think of this? Is it genuine? Is it in good condition? Has it been restored, and if so, how much? What would be a fair price?". If all is well the dealer will bid, and if he is successful, the piece will go to the client. The dealer gets a commission from the client, perhaps ten per cent of the price. The dealer does not own the piece, nor have capital locked up.

What are the snags? An unscrupulous dealer could tend to advise a purchase and suggest a high price, simply to get the business and a larger commission: but this seldom happens, because sharp practice is bad for business, whatever the short-term advantages are.

Mistakes are bound to crop up, either over the quality and price of an object or over its suitability for the home or the collection. Millionaires may call in an interior decorator or dealer, and say: "Fix me up with the best you can buy – I want it finished six weeks from now." Lucky for both. But people with less ample means will want the pleasures of the hunt, and the learning that goes with it, and they will want to shop around for exactly what is right for them. Patience is necessary or else the collection acquires wrong things which have to be weeded out at a later stage.

It is not necessary to restrict buying to one period: a Queen Anne japanned cabinet and a late Victorian sideboard can be blended harmoniously and successfully. Variety and contrast are the key-words. A stately home, for generations in the same family, has a kind of unity, although the contents may have been gathered together over hundreds of years.

Selling antiques gives many people anxiety, in case a treasure is sold for a song. The first rule is never to sell to dealers who come to the front door and offer cash on the spot. These are people with little knowledge but a rough idea of some values; they will of course tend to offer low prices. A refinement of the practice is to gain entry, look around, and make offers for various items. Some of the prices named are exceedingly generous; others very low. The householder is impressed by the generous offers. The next step is for the dealer to say: "I can't take all the stuff away with me now. Let me have that and that and I'll come round for the rest tomorrow." The owner agrees and the dealer pays cash – but the things he takes away are the ones for which he has offered the low prices, not the high ones. The next day he fails to appear for the 'costly' items – his bluff has worked and the owner has been diddled.

Someone who wants to sell can go to a museum and ask one of the staff for an opinion on an object's condition, age, origin, and so on. But the rule is that museums do not give estimates of prices. With this information the owner is well armed for the next step: the choice of going to a dealer or an auctioneer.

A constant argument goes on between the two professions about the merits of each method of selling. The dealers say that they give the straight market price, as far as that can be judged by anyone. They also point out the expense of selling at auction – commission of between ten and fifteen per cent of the price made, insurance, perhaps charges for illustrations in the catalogue. Dealers also claim that they can give a better deal than the auctioneers because an auction is in a sense a gamble. Prices depend on odd factors. A foggy day or a transport strike can keep buyers away, reduce competition, and push prices down.

On the other hand the auctioneers give publicity to sales – in the case of the big London auctioneers, international publicity. London has been the centre of the international art market since the Second World War. Other places are important, however – notably New York and to a lesser degree Geneva. There are many reasons for London's dominance. Sotheby's and Christie's have very high standards of expertise and probity – something that cannot be said about all auctioneers on the Continent and elsewhere. Broadly speaking, no taxes are payable by the seller or the buyer (the exceptions are minor and in any case do not apply to goods which are later exported). In many other countries taxes are payable. Britain has no import or export duties on antiques and works of art.

London is a convenient meeting point for buyers from the United States, Japan, the Continent, Australasia and the Middle East. Some goods may be brought from the United States, auctioned in London, and sent back to the United States again. Firms of packers and shippers make everything fairly easy. Dealers can charge their travelling and other expenses against tax.

People from outside Britain who send their goods for sale in London are paid in the currency of their choice – a considerable attraction and a system that helps to make art and antiques a kind of international currency.

Sotheby's took over New York's premier auction house, the Parke-Bernet Galleries, in 1964: a highly significant move for both firms and for the art market. The great New York auction houses were at one time the American Art Association and the Anderson Galleries. They were bitter rivals but combined in 1929. A secession from the AAA-AG took place in 1937 and was led by Hiram H. Parke, the most remarkable auctioneer the United States has ever produced. One by one his rivals were vanquished. His partner was Otto Bernet – the name is Swiss-German and the final 't' is pronounced. Both men were dead by the time their firm was taken over by Sotheby's.

The Parke-Bernet Galleries have a notable history. One famous event was the sale in 1961 of Rembrandt's *Aristotle Contemplating the Bust of Homer*, which went for $2,300,000 to the Metropolitan Museum of Art, New York. But Sotheby's was at this time becoming

A
CATALOGUE
OF THE GENUINE
Houſhold Furniture,

Jewels, Plate, Fire-Arms, China, &c. And
a large Quantity of Maderia and high Flavour'd Claret.

Late the Property of

A Noble PERSONAGE,

(D E C E A S ' D,)

The Furniture Conſiſts of Rich Silk Damaſk, mix'd
Stuff ditto, Cotton and Morine in Drapery Beds,
Window-Curtains, French Elbow and back Stool
Chairs, a large Sopha with an Elegant Canopy over
ditto, Variety of Cabinet Work in Mahogany Roſe-
wood, Japan, Tortoiſhell, inlaid with Braſs, &c.
Large Pier Glaſſes, a curious Needle-work Carpet 4
Yards by 5, Turkey and Wilton ditto, ſome valu-
able Jewels, and Plate, &c. Uſeful and ornamental
Chelſea, Dreſden and Oriental China,, a Muſical
Spring Clock and Eight-day ditto, ſome fine Bronzes,
Models, Pictures, &c. &c.

Which will be Sold by Auction
By Mr. CHRISTIE,

At the Auction Room, in PALLMALL, on Fryday
next, and the Four following Days.

The whole to be view'd on Wedneſday next, and 'till
the Time of Sale, which will begin each Day at
Twelve o' Clock.

Catalogues to be had at the Great Room as above, and
at *Mr. Chriſtie's, Caſtle-Street, Oxford-Road.*

The first of Christie's sale catalogues: December 1766

CATALOGUE

OF

IMPORTANT OLD MASTER PAINTINGS

The Property of THE RT. HON. THE VISCOUNT COBHAM, K.G., P.C., G.C.M.G., T.D.

The Property of THE HON. COLIN TENNANT

The Property of SIR GEOFFREY HARDY-ROBERTS

The Property of THE NORTON SIMON FOUNDATION, LOS ANGELES

The Property of THE LATE DR. AND MRS. A. V. McMASTER

The Property of THE LATE MR. PHILIP LINDSTEDT, OF GOTHENBURG

AND OTHER OWNERS

INCLUDING

Christ's Descent into Limbo BY ANDREA MANTEGNA

Marchesa Lomellini-Durazzo BY SIR ANTHONY VAN DYCK

The Painter and his Wife BY THE MASTER OF FRANKFORT

Jacob's Journey BY JACOPO BASSANO

A Landscape with a Shepherd piping BY CLAUDE

A Landscape with the Flight into Egypt BY DOMENICHINO

A Painter in his Studio BY GERARD DOU

The Doge's Palace and the Molo and *The Entrance to the Grand Canal* BY CANALETTO

A pair of Caprice Landscapes BY FRANCESCO GUARDI

The Four Seasons BY GIUSEPPE ARCIMBOLDO

A Pavilion in a Garden and *View in Cologne* BY JAN VAN DER HEYDEN

A View of Tholen BY JAN VAN GOYEN

ALSO PAINTINGS BY

NARDO DI CIONE, SEBASTIANO DEL PIOMBO, JACOPO AMIGONI, PIETER BRUEGHEL THE YOUNGER, JAN BRUEGHEL THE ELDER, DAVID TENIERS, BALTHASAR VAN DER AST, PHILIPS WOUWERMANS, JAN DAVIDSZ. DE HEEM, CORNELIS DE HEEM AND ABRAHAM VAN BEYEREN

WHICH WILL BE SOLD BY AUCTION BY

SOTHEBY & CO.

P. C. WILSON, C.B.E. (*Chairman*) A. J. B. KIDDELL C. GRONAU P. M. H. POLLEN G. D. LLEWELLYN
R. P. T. CAME M. J. WEBB LORD JOHN KERR THE EARL OF WESTMORLAND, K.C.V.O. J. L. MARION (U.S.A.)
P. M. R. POUNCEY J. M. LINELL M. J. STRAUSS D. J. NASH T. E. NORTON (U.S.A.) A. T. EELES P. D. THOMSON
D. ELLIS-JONES R. J. DE LA M. THOMPSON D. E. JOHNS M. D. RITCHIE A. M. KAGAN (U.S.A.)
A. HOLLOWAY D. J. CROWTHER SIR PHILIP HAY, K.C.V.O., T.D. C. H. HILDESLEY G. HUGHES-HARTMAN
E. L. CAVE (U.S.A.) V. ABDY J. M. STOCK J. BOWES-LYON
Associates:
A. R. A. HOBSON H. A. FEISENBERGER T. H. CLARKE N. MACLAREN
A. MAYOR P. J. CROFT J. F. HAYWARD C. C. H. FENTON
JOHN CARTER, C.B.E.

NEW YORK: SOTHEBY PARKE BERNET INC.

Auctioneers of Literary Property and Works illustrative of the Fine Arts

AT THEIR LARGE GALLERY, 34 AND 35 NEW BOND STREET, W1A 2AA

Telephone: 01-493 8080

Day of Sale:

WEDNESDAY, 11TH JULY, 1973

AT ELEVEN O'CLOCK PRECISELY

On View at least Two Days Previous (Not Saturdays)

Illustrated Catalogue (68 plates) Price £2.25

A Printed List of all Prices and Buyers' Names at this sale can be supplied for 15p and for all sales at low subscription rates.

A modern saleroom catalogue. Thousands of copies of such catalogues are sent to collectors, dealers and museums all over the world

more and more active in seeking out business in the United States and posed a serious threat to the 'family-run' Parke-Bernet Galleries.

The atmosphere at the Parke-Bernet auction house in upper Madison Avenue is quite unlike the atmosphere in any other establishment of the same kind. Parke-Bernet has showmanship, drama, even flamboyance: other places tend to be formal and rather dull. Only the most remarkable auctions in London are ever honoured with applause from the people present.

Geneva is another centre for the never-ceasing buying and selling of treasures. Christie's began to sell jewels there in the late 1960s: British law imposed a heavy duty on jewels brought into the country and it made sense to set up shop in a strategic centre outside Britain for this branch of the business. Soon the scope was expanded to include silver, furniture, icons and other articles.

The two great international auction houses have agents, representatives, or offices all round the world – from Los Angeles to Madrid, from Hong Kong to Rio de Janeiro, from Sydney to Stockholm. Rivalry between them is strong. A standing joke is the way in which the staffs sometimes avoid naming the other firm. People at Christie's in London talk about the organization 'up the hill' (that is, the gentle rise in the ground between St James's and Bond Street); people at Sotheby's talk about the organization 'down the hill'. The publicity machinery of both houses is complex; Sotheby's, for example, send hundreds of thousands of their catalogues every year to collectors, dealers, and museums. The auctioneers advise their clients on a minimum price at which an item should be sold – the reserve price. If bidding does not reach this level the item is withdrawn and stays in the owner's possession – it is 'bought in.'

A peculiarity of the trade applies to the buying-in of lots, in some firms of auctioneers. If the bidders knew that lots were failing to reach the reserves, confidence would be lost and bidding would become even less keen. So the man in the rostrum pretends to knock the item down and gives a fictitious name as the 'buyer'. Sometimes only one person in the room is really interested in buying and is in the bidding. The reserve has not been reached. So the auctioneer pretends to take bids from elsewhere in the room, to keep the really interested buyer in the running. As soon as the reserve has been reached, and if the last bid was one from the genuine buyer, the lot is knocked down. All this sounds an odd system but it is the custom of the trade and the auctioneers are acting in the seller's interest.

'Quality' newspapers in their reports may say that a sale totalled £100,000; but in the case of Sotheby's and Christie's this figure includes the amounts 'made' for bought-in lots. In theory none of

A watercolour by Rowlandson of a sale at Christie's

A famous modern auction: the portrait by Velasquez of his assistant Juan de Pareja at Christie's in November 1970. It was sold for £2,310,000 to the dealers Wildenstein, who were bidding on behalf of the Metropolitan Museum, New York. In the rostrum is the Hon. Patrick Lindsay, a director of Christie's

the lots offered may have been sold at all, and all may have been withdrawn. The auctioneers point out that the figure at which a lot is bought in is one bid above the amount offered in the sale and thus reflects the market price. The auctioneers are discreet about how many lots have failed to reach their reserves – again, in order to preserve confidence in the market.

Acute competition in the saleroom happens from time to time, to the benefit of the seller. Perhaps two people decide that they must have the lot at all costs; perhaps a feud is going on between rival dealers and each is determined to conquer the other. The other side of the coin is the illegal practice among dealers of holding a 'ring' – a particularly unpleasant racket. A ring works in this way. Several dealers get together before the auction and agree among themselves that certain of them will bid for certain lots and the others will keep out of the running. If all goes well the selected lots go to members of the ring at unnaturally low prices. The conspirators hold a meeting after the auction and conduct another 'sale'. The items bought on the ring's behalf are allocated to individual members, who pay a more realistic price into the kitty. The last step is for the kitty to be divided among the conspirators.

The result is that the original seller gets a low price, the auctioneer gets a smaller commission, and the members of the ring emerge the richer. But as the saying goes there is no honour among thieves. It has been known for a ring to be formed within the ring. A few members of the ring with specialized knowledge may be aware that one or two items are especially valuable and the other people may be ignorant of it. So the same operation is gone through – bids at the second 'auction' are kept low by the fresh set of conspirators who cheat their fellow cheats.

'Ringing' was exposed by the *Sunday Times* in the 1960s and has since then been substantially reduced. But in certain cases it still goes on at auctions outside London. And even in the glamorous London establishments some 'petty ringing' is known. This does not have the elaborate organization of the other kind. What happens is that two or more dealers will have quiet discussions during viewing days, and decide that Mr A. will not compete with Mr B. for certain things if Mr B. does not compete with Mr A. for others. The system cannot work for headline-grabbing masterpieces because competition from wealthy collectors and museums is too intense.

One form of joint bidding is quite legal. Two or more dealers pool their resources to bid for something which is particularly valuable and which might be too costly for one dealer to buy alone. They share ownership, risk, and profit if any is made.

What are the advantages and disadvantages of selling to a dealer? One advantage, as has been mentioned, is that one avoids auctioneers' commission and other charges. Another is that one avoids the risk of the item being bought in at auction: a commission still has to be paid in such a case, although on a lower scale.

A rough idea of the market value is essential. An inkling can be had about authenticity, condition, and so on, from a museum. An auctioneer will give a quick off-the-cuff valuation for nothing. Advice can be got from one of the salerooms in London. Queues of hopeful people carrying boxes and brown paper parcels can sometimes be seen at Sotheby's and Christie's. If a personal call is difficult because of distance, a letter with a full description and a photograph may do instead.

The danger is in going to a reputable and honest dealer with, say, a silver tankard and discovering that he knows a lot about Ming porcelain but nothing about silver. A good alternative to an outright sale to a dealer might be to get him to sell on one's behalf – 'on commission'. What happens is that the pieces of furniture, silver, or whatever, are put in the dealer's shop with an agreed price tag. When – or if – they are sold, the dealer takes a cut, but he does not at any point own them. This system has some advantages for both the seller and the dealer. The seller may get a better price, and he does get the advantage of the dealer's contacts with his regular private clients and with the trade. The dealer does not have to tie up capital and does not take any risk.

The British Antique Dealer's Association publishes a list of its members, their specialities, and their addresses. The association has certain standards which candidates for admission must reach – skill, financial soundness and probity. But nobody is perfect, and even a member of the association might in certain circumstances be tempted to offer an unfairly low price. It is in everyone's best interest for a seller to do a lot of homework.

The trouble is that no one can ever safeguard himself completely against mistakes. What appears to 99.9 per cent of people as mere junk could possibly be worth a fortune. This 'junk' is quite likely to be recognized by someone, sometime, because of the way the antique trade works. Take, for example, a Ming vase which has for years and years been unrecognized and used to hold flowers in a home in the countryside, far from the museum experts, the posh auction houses, and the dealers of Bond Street. It comes up for auction when the owner of the house dies or moves away. The vase is bought by a local dealer who handles all kinds of goods. He sells it with several other items of pottery or porcelain to another dealer who is more of a specialist; this man sends it to an auction in

London or to one of the bigger auction houses outside London. Or he takes it to the Portobello Road market in London, or to a really expert dealer. A vast amount of buying or selling in the trade is between dealers, and not members of the public. As the Ming vase goes from hand to hand the chances of its discovery become more and more likely.

Dealers sometimes feel themselves maligned. It can, in fact, be a risky trade in which mistakes are easily made, and losses thus heavy. One distinguished dealer in London tells how he travelled to the United States for a sale of good furniture. He arrived suffering from fatigue and 'jet lag', went straight to the auction, and paid more than £3000 for a table. When he arrived back in Britain, he realized that it was 'wrong' – a hotchpotch of several different bits cobbled together. He could not possibly cheat a customer by selling it in his shop. So he sent it to one of the smaller auction rooms where it made £300.

Dealers also make mistakes in the excitement of the auction room, even if they have had many years of experience. Getting hold of good stock is from time to time as hard as selling it. Deciding on what to buy and at what price is full of pitfalls. The fact is that no firm rules apply: the monetary value is simply what someone, somewhere is willing to pay. This is especially true when the market is going up or down quickly. Inflation made one dealer cry out in despair: "It's not that the paintings aren't worth these huge sums of money. It's the money that isn't worth the money any more."

Investing in art and antiques became a fashion from the early 1950s when the market began to take off. Up and up went the prices. Graphs later appeared in the newspapers showing that the Old Master drawings had increased in value by x per cent, and violins by y per cent, and English oak furniture by z per cent. Record prices were announced almost daily by the big salerooms. Confidence bred confidence. Old fashioned collectors and connoisseurs were shocked. The heritage of the past, they said, should not be treated in the same way as cotton futures and shares in ICI and gilt edged securities. Dealers, it is said, disliked all the brouhaha: the public was getting too well informed about prices and, because of that, the dealers were finding that bargains were scarcer.

Moreover, the graphs were questioned. The art market is not a scientific business, and does not lend itself to scientific treatment. Prices depend on rarity, condition, and fashion. Freakish results can happen.

Another much criticised aspect was the claims by the salerooms of record prices. An object sold in 1920 for £100 and resold 50 or more years later for £400 has not really gained in price: in the intervening period the value of the pound has collapsed. A good example was the sale in 1974 of a manuscript of Chaucer's *Canterbury Tales,* produced about 1445. It fetched £90,000 at Christie's. This was claimed to equal the record price for an English manuscript. But the comparison was with a manuscript sold in 1968, Caxton's translation of Ovid's *Metamorphoses.* The purchasing power of the pound had changed considerably in the meantime.

The 'dividend' from an 'investment' in art and antiques is really the pleasure (and perhaps the use) to be had from day to day. If a monetary gain is made at the same time, that is just an extra bonus. Monetary gain is not necessarily to be forgotten, and it does enter what has been called 'excuse' buying. A man may come home with a purchase which knocks a hole in the family budget for a week or a month. He calms his wife with: "Yes, but it is such a good investment."

The boom in art and antiques has been stimulated by talk of investment, by the publicity machines of the big salerooms and the trade in general, by some tax advantages to be gained, and by flights from devalued money into tangibles. But all this could not have happened without people's love of old and beautiful objects, and their desire to have them in their homes. Important, too, are nostalgia for the past and a wider appreciation of what is worthwhile.

One of the peculiarities of the upper end of the auction trade – the stuff worth five or six figures – is that 'tired' goods do not generally fetch the prices they deserve. Tired goods are those which have appeared fairly recently on the market, say in the last two or three years. They do not have freshness and interest for the potential buyers. This is something to be borne in mind by the lucky who have plenty of money, and who seek a short term investment.

Furniture

The accession of Queen Anne in 1702 coincided roughly – but not exactly – with a break in fashion and taste. Furniture for the upper and middle classes had been made, since the Restoration of the monarchy in 1660, in walnut and beechwood. This was still being used, but in a quite different way.

Fashionable furniture of the late seventeenth century tended towards fussiness, with elaborate carving and with legs and other parts turned on a lathe to form twisted ornaments like sticks of barley sugar (see illustration on page 35). Now, foreign influence had been strong for nearly half a century. The future Charles II, during his exile, saw on the Continent a luxurious style of living. The Restoration in 1660 opened the door for craftsmen and designers from the Continent and the accession of 'Dutch' William in 1689 confirmed the trend. The court of Queen Anne may have been one of the dullest in history up to that time; but it did give a chance for buyers and makers of furniture to break away from foreign influences. The Queen Anne style had an elegance, simplicity, and sense of fine proportion, and it has been imitated again and again by designers and craftsmen. Along with this went greater comfort and convenience in houses and in many pieces of furniture.

The new elegance and comfort are displayed in the shape of chairs. Late seventeenth-century chairs were elaborately carved with high, straight backs – the backs being sometimes two and a half times the height of the seat from the floor. By about 1700 the backs were beginning to be curved, to fit the body, and the great innovation of the time had appeared; the curved and flowing cabriole leg. It was sturdy on chairs, slender and light on tables because of the different weights these items had to bear.

Cabriole legs were at first made with stretchers (horizontal bars of wood joining the legs and giving the whole structure extra strength). Soon, however, the stretchers were done away with and the flowing lines appeared in their uncluttered beauty. Usually only the front legs of chairs were in this shape and the back ones were straight; but costly and luxurious specimens had all four. Hogarth wrote in his *Analysis of Beauty* (1753): "The waving line is more productive of beauty than any of the former [i.e. circular and straight lines] for which reason we shall call it the line of beauty. The serpentine line hath the power of super-adding grace to beauty." The cabriole leg was perhaps introduced by an architect and designer, Daniel Marot, who was trained in France. He was a

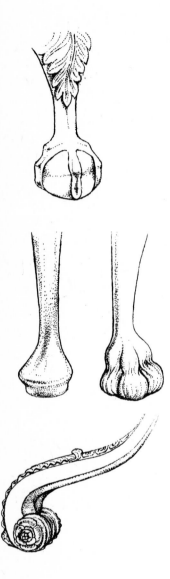

Top, claw and ball foot; *middle left*, pad foot; *middle right*, paw foot; *bottom*, scroll foot

Huguenot and left France after the revocation of the Edict of Nantes in 1685 (see also page 72). Marot entered the service of the Prince of Orange, later William III of Britain. Several convenient kinds of furniture appeared at this time and some of them have been with us ever since.

A chest, for example, is useful, but if it is full and if you need something from the bottom of it, you have to rummage around. Thus the chest of drawers was invented in the later years of the seventeenth century. A variation of the chest of drawers is the tallboy – two chests of drawers, one on top of the other. Seeing what is in the upper drawers is difficult: you have either to stand on a chair or take the drawer out entirely. Putting it back again can mean bumping it against the framework and marking the surface.

Cabinets were originally prestige pieces and were used for storing the 'curiosities' collected by the rich. 'Curiosities' might be Greek and Roman coins, shells, miniature portraits, and so on.

From cabinets evolved writing bureaux on chests of drawers, called escritoires or scriptors. A flap comes down to form a surface for writing on. The bureau also has useful drawers and pigeon holes, and often secret compartments. A refinement is a chest of drawers with bureau and a bookcase as well, beneath a single or double domed hood. The bookcase has doors, sometimes with mirrors on the fronts.

A craze for gambling gripped society at all levels during the early eighteenth century and card tables were made for the now forgotten games of ombre, picquet, and quadrille.

Another invention of the Queen Anne period was the claw-and-ball foot, for chairs, settees, and tables. Its origin is obscure but it may have been devised from a favourite decoration of Chinese porcelain – a dragon with claws pursuing the pearl of wisdom. The claw-and-ball foot is found on cabriole legs but other types of feet are common until much later in the century.

Materials and techniques

The great material was walnut, used for the more costly and sophisticated pieces, but it is a favourite target for woodworm because it is softer, for example, than oak, and the losses from woodworm have been enormous.

Walnut was used in two ways: as solid wood or as a veneer – thin slices applied to a less expensive type as deal or oak. Veneering eked out supplies and enabled the craftsman to display the attractive grain to the best advantage. This, too had its snags: veneer is apt to warp and split in dry conditions.

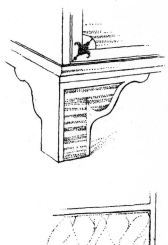

Top, bracket foot; *bottom*, bun foot

It is said that vast numbers of the trees were planted in the reign of Elizabeth and that they came to maturity in the mid-seventeenth century. Demand was so great, however, that supplies had to be imported from the Continent and the east coast of North America. Houses were being built bigger than before and needed bigger, more modern furniture. Isabella, Lady Wentworth wrote to her son Lord Raby in 1711: "Your lodgins ar excessif cold, the rooms soe large and soe high if the fyer be never soe great one syde freesis while the other burns."

Walnut, attractive though it is, was given extra decoration – marquetry. This is a 'picture', in wood, of flowers, foliage, birds, and butterflies. It is built up, like a jigsaw puzzle, from tiny pieces of veneer. Marquetry in the age of Queen Anne was of dark and light woods only; in the seventeenth century other materials were also used, such as ivory and tortoiseshell. Special colours were produced

Bureau bookcase in burr walnut of about 1710. Several secret drawers are behind the series of small drawers where the flap comes down. At the sides are carrying handles; the piece is in three sections. 85 inches (216 cm) high; 43½ inches (110.5 cm) wide (opposite page)

Bureau in walnut of the Queen Anne period. A well-mannered object relying on good proportion and matched veneers highlighted by brass handles. The design is traditional and has remained popular: it is good sense to keep to a well-tried form

by staining or scorching the wood. Parquetry is a geometrical pattern of woods of different colours.

Another form of veneering was oysterwork. The smaller branches of olive, walnut, kingwood (sycamore or maple stained green) and laburnum – particularly where they spring from the trunk – were sliced like salami and fixed on the surface of the furniture. The slices have a fanciful resemblance to oysters.

The best sort of walnut veneer was from malformations in the tree, which gave a veined and tangled appearance to the wood. It is called burr walnut.

Veneering called for special skills; and the tendency during the eighteenth century was for makers, at least in London, to specialize in particular branches of the trade, such as chairs. Some areas of London were noted for certain kinds of work – either expensive or inexpensive – just as Hatton Garden is nowadays

Side table in walnut; George I period. For the bedroom. The legs are plain except for C-scrolls. Also called, in the United States, a lowboy

the centre for the wholesale jewellery trade and Bond Street has some of the most expensive shops. The capital had about a million inhabitants in 1700; the next largest towns such as Bristol and Norwich had only about 30,000. The London trade was therefore dominant. As communications were appallingly bad until the arrival of turnpike roads, canals, and railways, however, fashions changed only slowly in many parts of the country. Tall and narrow chairs with canework were made everywhere for a long time after the curvilinear or cabriole kind was invented.

A vast amount of ordinary furniture was being made, throughout the eighteenth century and later, by village joiners and by town craftsmen. They worked in traditional ways, with traditional tools, and used oak, elm, yew, beech, ash, and so on. Their customers were not interested in the vagaries of London fashion. Changes did percolate through, but these took time. Dressers, settles, chests, and corner and hanging cupboards were the bread and butter work of the joiners.

Japanning

Japanning is a British imitation of Oriental lacquer. It was done by craftsmen but was also considered a suitable hobby for ladies of leisure.

Lacquer is one of the most accomplished arts of the Orient and was especially admired in the West during the periodic crazes for *chinoiserie* (the Europeans' own version of Chinese art). Lacquered screens and panels from the Orient were incorporated into European furniture.

Lac is the syrupy juice of the lac tree, which was cultivated in plantations. It is a remarkable substance, resisting heat, water, acids, and the rigours of time; it is vulnerable only to strong light. The process of manufacture was painstaking. Layer after layer was applied to a base, which was almost always of wood. Sometimes as many as 30 layers were given. Each was allowed to dry in special atmospheric conditions and was rubbed smooth. The next stage was to carve, paint, gild, or inlay the surface. A whole range of colours was achieved by dyes – red, yellow, green, black, and reddish brown.

Lacquer was expensive in China and Japan and even more expensive when it was brought to Europe. Lac, the raw material, does not travel well because it reacts with air. So a substitute was devised in Europe, made in a quite different way. Resin dissolved in alcohol, size made from boiled parchment, and whitening were applied to a base of wood. The surface was then polished and ornamented. This process, called japanning, was fairly easy to do.

John Stalker and George Parker published in 1688 an illustrated *Treatise of Japanning and Varnishing,* which spread the message. The 'treatise' complained that some people had made "new Cabinets out of old Skreens. And from that large old piece, by the help of a Joyner, made little ones such as stands or tables, but never consider the situation of their figures, so that in these things, so torn and hacked to joint a new fancie, you may observe the finest hodgpodg and medley of Men and Trees turned topsie turvie."

Chest on stand, japanned in the manner of Stalker and Parker; about 1710. For the living room or best bedroom. The shape is English and the decoration chinoiserie. It has original brass fittings. 61½ inches (156.8 cm) high and 41 inches (104.5 cm) wide

The revival of chinoiserie in the mid-eighteenth century (see page 38) brought japanning back into favour too. The *Ladies' Amusement or Whole Art of Japanning made Easy* was published in 1760. The foreword warned ladies against placing any "exotic or preposterous object" in their European-style designs. Greater liberties could be taken with the Indian or Chinese "for in these is often seen a Butterfly supporting an Elephant or things equally absurd."

This book had more than 1500 plates, many of them by the French artist Jean Pillement. Japanning in the later years was done with less care than at the beginning. The European imitation of the Chinese art proved to be fairly perishable, and many of the pieces now suffer from flaking.

Gesso

Another specialized technique was the use of gesso (pronounced jesso). Chalk and parchment size were mixed and applied to a shaped or roughly carved piece of furniture. Up to 20 layers were put on. The gesso, when it had hardened, was carved with decorative fancies and gilded. This technique was used for tables, the frames of mirrors, chests, chairs, and torchères (large stands for candelabra). It was quite expensive and the furniture was not particularly robust, so gesso was used mainly for state rooms of large houses.

Most scope was available in decorating the tops of tables, which were given geometric patterns, flowers or foliage. Patrons could have their coats of arms incorporated. Gesso is vulnerable to damp and heat, which makes the layer of gilding peel or crack.

Two notable makers during the first quarter of the century were John Gumley and James Moore, who at one time were in partnership. They are unusual not only for the quality of their work but because Gumley is mentioned in literature and journalism of the time and Moore put his name on some at least of his gilt gesso furniture. Gumley made a fortune and married off his daughter and sole heiress, Anna Maria, to William Pulteney, Earl of Bath. The earl may have made the worse bargain because she was described as a vixen. Sir Richard Steele wrote of Gumley's gallery over the Royal Exchange as "a place where people may go and be very well entertained, whether they have or have not a good taste." Moore evidently worked for William Kent, a leading architect and designer. Some of Moore's surviving output is in Hampton Court, Buckingham Palace, and Blenheim. These two makers are distinguished for creative design and outstanding craftsmanship, and their furniture was just right for mansions in the current mode.

A splendid armchair in gesso of about 1720. The arms end in eagle's heads and the legs have Indian masks with plumes

The arrival of mahogany

Britain's sea power gave her access to woods from the Americas, Africa, and the East Indies; mahogany especially was taken up with enthusiasm.

The term 'Queen Anne' can be stretched to cover not only her reign (1702–1714) but also the period up to the mid-1720s. What changed the scene was the arrival of mahogany and the influence of William Kent, the first British architect to design furniture.

Mahogany is a marvellous material for the cabinet maker's skills. It is hard and strong, does not readily warp, resists woodworm, and is very suitable for carving. The massive and ancient trees yielded wide planks which were ideal for large table tops. Some species of the wood have rich natural patterns; others are plain.

It also varies in colour, according to the species, from light reddish to dark brown; it darkens with age and generations of polishing, and acquires a pleasing mellow surface or patina.

Mahogany comes from the Caribbean and from tropical regions

Opposite page
Chair of about 1755, in mahogany. The design is from Thomas Chippendale's *Gentleman and Cabinet-Maker's Director.* (Montacute House, Somerset)

Rent table in mahogany; of the 1760s. The top has a section which comes out to reveal a well. Round the top are 11 drawers with letters of the alphabet. The pedestal has a cupboard. The theory is that the tenant paid over his rent which was dropped into the well. But many pieces called rent tables may have been for gentlemen's libraries or studies; the rent would have been handed over in the estate office

of the American continent. Parliament abolished in 1721 almost all import duties on timber from British possessions in North America and the West Indies. The aim was to increase the amount of timber available for shipbuilding, but the cabinet makers seized their chance. Walnut was scarce in France because a hard winter in 1709 killed many trees; and in 1720 the French Government banned exports of the wood. Supplies could be had from Virginia but that variety is darker than the European and quite unlike it. So, from the removal of the import duty onwards, mahogany became more and more popular and gradually ousted all other woods for fashionable furniture. The value of mahogany shipped in 1720 was £43 and in 1750 was almost £30,000. Demand was so great that the ancient forests were ruthlessly exploited and by the end of the eighteenth century supplies were almost exhausted.

The first mahogany to be imported in quantity came from San Domingo and Jamaica. It is dark, heavy, and without figuring. In about 1750 it was superseded by the Cuban variety, which is of a rich colour and with attractive figuring and is suitable as a veneer.

Opposite page
A mahogany armchair of the George II period with attractive back and simple, pleasing leg. The back show some of the fashion for chinoiserie. (Sotheby's)

Kneehole desk in mahogany; about 1765. The top has tooled crimson leather. Another form which has always been popular. Perhaps made outside London

Secretaire bookcase in mahogany; about 1765. The 'drawer' below the doors comes down to form a writing flap. A somewhat dull item. 90 inches (229.5 cm) high; 46 inches (117.3 cm) wide

The Honduras variety, lighter in weight and colour than the others, was used in the second half of the century; it was also called baywood from the Bay of Honduras. Species which were not strictly speaking mahogany but which were similar, such as padouk, came to be used and were sometimes described as mahogany.

Early mahogany furniture was in exactly the same style as walnut pieces: the cabinet makers did not yet realize the fresh scope the material offered.

Kent and Burlington

Apostle of Palladianism and Apollo of the Arts.

William Kent (1684–1748) was born in Bridlington, Yorkshire, and was apprenticed there to a coach painter when he was 14. He left for London five years later and went in for portrait and historical painting. Some patrons sent him to Rome, and when he was there in 1716 he met Robert Boyle, third Earl of Burlington. This resulted in a long friendship and collaboration. The two propagated the Palladian style of architecture, an attempt to restore what was thought to be the true classical style. Their reputation and influence were powerful.

Lord Burlington helped Kent to get commissions from the wealthy, especially in portraits and murals and ceiling paintings with allegorical and historical themes. Horace Walpole, diarist, connoisseur, and son of the Prime Minister Sir Robert Walpole, thought that Kent had genius in other branches of art but that his portraits "bore little resemblance to the persons who sat for them, and the colouring was worse;" and that "in his ceilings Kent's drawing was as defective as the colouring of his portraits, and as void of every merit." William Hogarth thought that neither England nor Italy ever produced a more contemptible dauber and caricatured him mercilessly. Kent got his own back: he used his influence to prevent Hogarth doing a portrait group of the royal family.

Burlington, the other great name in the Palladian movement, was called the Apollo of the Arts. He was a patron of artists and men of letters and an architect in his own right. Walpole of course wrote about him and said: "He possessed every quality of a genius and artist except envy" and that he "spent large sums in contributing to public works, and was known to choose that the expense should fall on himself rather than that his country should be deprived of some beautiful edifices." Burlington supplied designs for, among other buildings, the dormitory at Westminster School and a house

Chair, of the late 17th century

for General Wade in Cork Street, London. Of this house Walpole wrote: "It is worse contrived in the inside than is conceivable, all to humour the beauty of the front" and Lord Chesterfield suggested that "as the general could not live in it to his ease, he had better take a house over against it and look at it."

Kent did package deals for his clients, the wealthy élite – house, garden, and furniture as an integrated whole. The furniture was a version of the rich and ornate baroque style he studied in Italy. He used large and elaborately carved festoons, masks, mouldings, architectural motifs, and a lot of gilding. The effect was theatrical and the interiors seemed hardly suitable for the comfort of the people who lived in the houses. But Kent had a huge success. Walpole wrote: "His oracle was so much consulted by all who affected taste, that nothing was thought complete without his assistance. He was not only consulted for furniture, as frames of pictures, glasses [i.e. looking glasses], tables, chairs, etc., but for silver plate, for a barge, for a cradle. And so impetuous was fashion, that two great ladies prevailed on him to make designs for their birthday gowns. The one he dressed in a petticoat decorated with columns of the five orders [of architecture]; the other like a bronze [statue], in a copper-coloured satin, with ornaments of gold."

But Kent's work had little influence on pieces made for people outside the élite. His furniture when removed from its proper setting sometimes appears ponderous and unattractive.

The 1740s saw a growing influence of French fashions. One

Left:
William Kent, by an unknown artist

Right:
Lord Burlington, by Jonathan Richardson, painted in 1717

Side table in gilt gesso in the style of Kent, 45 inches (112.8 cm) wide. The top is carved in low relief; below it is a frieze with swags of flowers and a head; the legs have Red Indian masks and end in feet in the shape of cloven hooves

Chest in the style of Kent; 55 inches (140.2 cm) wide. The top is in mahogany; the lower part is carved in high relief and is painted in white on a pale green ground. The carving includes flowers, leaves, berries, lion's paw feet, and ornaments in imitation of the classical style

writer said: "The ridiculous imitation of the French taste has now become the Epidemical distemper of this kingdom, our cloathes, our furniture, nay our food too, all is to come from France." But the British translated the styles into their own language.

Interest in the Palladians and Kent was shown as late as 1744 by the publication of *Some Designs of Mr. Inigo Jones and Mr. Wm. Kent,* by John Vardy, an architect. It is likely that a family firm was in existence – Vardy, his brother Thomas who was a carver, and John Vardy's son, also called John and an architect. Or it is possible that the elder John put business for furniture in his brother's way.

The rococo style

Fantasy, exuberance, and whimsy, in the French, Chinese, and Gothic tastes.

Rococo was the thing now: a decorative, light style with asymmetrical lines but still with balance. It used the themes of rocks, shells, flowers, leaves, fishes, fountains, water, and icicles. Rococo had its origins in early eighteenth-century France and spread all over Europe and to America. The French Regent, Philippe d'Orléans, commissioned work from Gilles-Marie Oppenord (1672–1742), a Dutchman who excelled at designs for interiors. His work contained the seeds of Rococo. Another pioneer was Juste-Aurèle Meissonnier (1675–1750), who was born in Turin but became a goldsmith for the French court. The style was disseminated by the publication of engravings.

The outstanding interpreter of the rococo in Britain was Matthias (or Matthew) Lock, a carver who published books of designs in the 1740s but of whose life almost nothing is known.

Rococo is at its best in carving – for example on chimney pieces, mirror frames, wall lights, and stands for candelabra.

At this time also Chinese and Gothic taste was revived. One writer complained: "The simple and sublime have lost all influence almost everywhere, all is Chinese or gothic; every chair in an apartment, the frames of glasses, and tables, must be Chinese: the walls covered with Chinese paper filled with figures which resemble nothing in God's creation, and which a prudent nation would prohibit for the sake of pregnant women."

And another wrote, in 1753: "According to the present prevailing whim everything is Chinese, or in the Chinese taste, or as it is sometimes more modestly expressed, partly after the Chinese manner. Chairs, tables, chimneypieces, frames for looking-glasses and even our most vulgar utensils are all reduced to this new-fangled standard; and without doors so universally has it spread, that every gate to a cow's yard is in Ts and Zs and every hovel for the cows has bells hanging at the corner."

Sir William Chambers (1726–1796), a distinguished architect, actually visited China, and in 1757 published *Designs for Chinese Buildings, Furniture, Dresses, etc.* It was compiled from the drawings he made on the spot. He thought that the *chinoiserie* of the time was just a passing craze and protested against the "extravagant fancies that daily appear under the name of Chinese."

Gothic has had amazing staying power in the British scene. Even Sir Christopher Wren used it occasionally although he disliked it. The eighteenth century took an antiquarian and romantic interest in the middle ages. Sham and picturesque ruins appeared in the parks of stately homes, and a fashion for the Gothic was established by the 1740s. The most famous building of the time in this manner was Strawberry Hill, Middlesex, which was built for Horace Walpole.

Side table by Matthias Lock; painted and gilded and made about 1744. It is 60 inches (153 cm) and 31 inches (79 cm) high. Lock designed it to the order of Lord Poulett (1708–64) and it was for Hinton House. The drawings have survived. Knowledge of the history of an object adds to the interest – and price

Walpole, son of the great Prime Minister, went into Parliament. He did not make his mark in politics but as a wit, letter-writer, and leader of the fashionable world. The first phase of Strawberry Hill was completed in the early 1750s, so in this Walpole was not a pioneer. But he did incorporate in what he called his 'prettiest bauble' of a house some faithful and scholarly versions of genuine Gothic.

Pointed arches, stained glass windows, and fan vaulting are all very well for architects but are not easily adapted for pottery and porcelain: the materials are just not suitable. Silver can be used with a little more success, as medieval chalices and some Victorian silversmiths' work show: the metal is marvellously adaptable.

Furniture makers did their best, with carving and with adaptations of the pointed arch. But the style never really caught on in the applied arts during the eighteenth century and Regency.

Chippendale

These three styles were given an impetus by the most famous of British furniture makers, whose name has become a household word: Thomas Chippendale. The curious thing is that he was not, to his contemporaries, the outstanding craftsman of all. He had a fair number of rivals of at least equal status and he probably never had royal patronage. He won his renown and lasting reputation through his genius for publicity.

Chippendale was born in Otley, Yorkshire, in 1718, the son and grandson of joiners. It is possible that he studied drawing in London as a young man – little is known about his life. Few references are made to him in writings of the time, which seems to imply that he never achieved acceptance in high society. Even someone of his ability could not have gone as far as he did without a patron – but the mystery of who it was has never been cleared up.

He was running a small cabinet-making business, with specialist workmen, by the time he was 35. His name was made in 1754, when he was 36, by the publication of his *Gentleman and Cabinet Maker's Director . . . . a large collection of the most Elegant and Useful Designs of Household Furniture in the Gothic, Chinese, and Modern Taste*. The first edition came out in 1754 and was followed by others in 1755 and 1762. The first was dedicated in the fulsome manner of the time to the Earl of Northumberland, who was spending prodigally on five mansions and castles. The dedication was an astute move. Chippendale, who longed for royal patronage, tried to dedicate the third edition to Prince William Henry, but the Prince or his advisers forbade it. Some copies were printed with

Ribbon-back chair, from the *Director*. One of Chippendale's most successful and charming designs

the dedication; the rest do not have the offending page.

The *Director* (for short) had 161 plates and was the first book of its kind to be published by a cabinet maker; its predecessors were by architects. Some of his designs were quite traditional. His attempts at Chinese and Gothic were a long way from their originals. The Chinese style had pagodas, mandarins, dragons, and fabulous birds, imitated from porcelain and wall hangings. The Chinese would have been astounded by it. Chippendale's ideas were taken up in Europe and North America, except for the Gothic.

The *Director* cost £2 8s when it was first issued – equivalent to at least £40 in modern money. It was a pattern book and anyone could use it as he pleased; so a piece of furniture closely resembling one of the plates is not necessarily by Chippendale. An item which can be proved to be by him – for example by means of a bill or other document – is worth a great deal more than it would be otherwise.

The rococo never took deep root in Britain, although its influence is sometimes felt even now. Only the smart and rich were interested in it: they constantly demanded novelty and exotic materials. The cult of conspicuous consumption, before the invention of cars and electrical goods, was concentrated on furniture, silver, porcelain, houses, and gardens.

Time and again British fashion goes in for fanciful and even excessive styles but time and again returns to simplicity and restraint; and so it happened with rococo.

Mirror to go above a fireplace; in the 'Chinese Chippendale' style. The frame is elaborately carved with trees, foliage, and animals; in the centre is a pagoda. Carving gave the cabinet maker the best chance for fanciful use of exotic styles; he was much more restricted by his material than the potter. 36 inches (91.5 cm) high; 65 inches (165 cm) long

Rococo was swept aside in the late 1760s by neo-classicism, whose high priests in Britain were the four Adam brothers and especially Robert, the oldest. Chippendale, astute as ever, switched to the neo-classical and held a sale of his stock in 1766. It was becoming out of date and would soon be useless to him.

He made, under Adam's influence, furniture which was not only in mahogany but gilded, painted, lacquered, or ornamented with marquetry. He achieved, in this last phase of his career, a brilliance of technique unsurpassed in Britain and bearing comparison

Secretaire in satinwood of about 1775. Probably by Chippendale and his partner Thomas Haig after a design by Robert Adam. It is crossbanded in kingwood and inlaid with marquetry of very fine quality. 38 inches (96.8 cm) high, 34½ inches (87.8 cm) wide

with the best work of the great French cabinet makers of the eighteenth century. The last and the finest of his work was for Harewood House, Yorkshire. By 1775 his bills for Harewood amounted to £6326 – an immense sum.

For all his genius and drive, Chippendale's business practices seem to have been lax. He was in trouble with the Customs in 1769 for importing unfinished French furniture without declaring its proper value. He appears to have acted in a highly improper way when a client went bankrupt: he with three others arranged

A superb piece of furniture about 1760. The quality of the carving and design are remarkable. The back and arms are of limewood and the legs and seat rails of pine; they are all gilded. Matthias Lock was the maker and he may have been influenced by some of the designs of the 'French chairs' in Chippendale's *Director*. This chair was once owned by the artist Richard Cosway who used it for his sitters and it appears in some of his portraits

for the bankrupt's property to be sold off in one lot to an associate. The other creditors complained that a higher price could have been obtained and that they had been cheated.

Chippendale died of consumption in 1789. For all his reputation, he was not the greatest cabinet maker during the early part of his career. That honour goes to William Vile.

Vile, who died in 1767, was for a time in partnership with John Cobb, who died in 1778. Vile's known work, dating from the 1760s, is exceptionally good and he charged correspondingly high prices. It is superior to anything known to have been done by Thomas Chippendale's firm in the Rococo style, although it is

Lady's writing table and bookcase of about 1760. The writing drawer pulls forward on two legs. Design based on one in Chippendale's *Director*. 87 inches (221.8 cm) high; 49 inches (124.8 cm) wide

'Chippendale' which is a household word. Vile also worked in the restrained classical manner. His rich and exuberant designs have been compared with the most creative work of Paul De Lamerie, the great silversmith (see page 79).

Vile and Cobb were appointed cabinet makers in chief to George III. Cobb was a 'singularly haughty character' and 'one of the proudest men in England.' He always appeared 'in full dress of the most superb and costly kind, strutting through his workshops giving orders to his men.' George III, for whom he did work, 'smiled at his pomposity.' Cobb left a sum of £20,000, "never to be broke into . . . my intent being that there should always be

'A lady's writing table and bookcase', from Chippendale's *Director*

the interest . . . to support the name of Cobb as a private gentleman." The furniture of which he alone, without Vile, is known to be the creator is in the classical style and is decorated with marquetry.

William Ince and John Mayhew published a book meant to be a counterblast to Chippendale's – their *Universal System of Household Furniture*. This had 300 designs and the notes were in French and English: they wanted to get a share of the export market.

Robert Manwaring published in 1765 another book with a longwinded title: *The Cabinet and Chair-Maker's Real Friend and Companion*, with more than 100 designs. Among his ideas were chairs and seats for use out of doors and meant to be made with 'the Limbs of Yew, Apple, or Pear Trees.' He wrote that he had "the Boldness to assert, that should the ornamental Parts be left out, there will still remain Grandeur and Magnificence behind."

William Hallett (1707–1781) reached the peak of his profession, was a clever businessman, and was described in his own time as "the great and eminent." He built himself a mansion and left a substantial fortune. Much of his work was in the Chinese style.

Benjamin Goodison, who worked from about 1727 to 1767, did commissions for Frederick, Prince of Wales, and for Sarah, Duchess of Marlborough 'who employed him in her many houses.' The Prince, when he died, owed Goodison large sums and Goodison also supplied his coffin. His designs were bold and the quality of his metal enrichments was high.

Giles Grendy (1693–1780) had a thriving export business and did both elaborate and simple work. He became Master of the Joiners' Company in 1766 but in June 1769 the clerk of the company was directed to write to Grendy and tell him that he was expected to be more diligent about his duties.

Hepplewhite

The neo-classical style was taken up by the nobility and spread to the middle classes. Satinwood became popular – a light and attractive wood thought suitable for the bedroom, drawing room, and boudoir.

The great name is again of a shadowy figure, George Hepplewhite. The term 'Hepplewhite' is applied to furniture made from 1775 to 1790, roughly speaking. Neo-classicism was the rage.

The towns of Pompeii and Herculaneum, buried by lava from an eruption of Vesuvius in AD 79, had been excavated from 1738 onwards. What was found was a revelation. Ideas about classical architecture, decoration, and furniture were dramatically changed. It was suddenly realized that previous knowledge was far from accurate. Educated people, soaked in the literature of Greece and

Fire Screens

Fire screen or pole screen, from the *Director*. Chippendale has here mixed rococo and chinoiserie themes. An impractical design

Tripod table in mahogany of about 1765. The feet are slightly asymmetrical. 23½ inches (59.8 cm) high; 17 inches (43.3 cm) across. This is a fine example, but many tripod tables now about are fakes. They have been converted from pole screens, which have the necessary tripod feet and stem. Pole screens were to protect the ladies' complexions from the direct heat of open fires (above)

Secretaire bookcase in satin-wood; about 1780. It is cross-banded in kingwood and has a secretaire drawer and three graduated drawers. Elegance personified; restraint, proportion and beautiful timber. 84 inches (214.1 cm) high (left)

Rome, took up the neo-classical movement with enthusiasm.

Robert Adam (1728–1792) became the most fashionable architect of the day. His father, William, was an Edinburgh architect. Robert and his brothers John, James, and William were all trained in the same profession and Robert studied in Italy from 1754 to 1758.

Connections with influential Scots in London were a springboard for his career. He was also skilled at publicity, was unhampered by false modesty, and knew how to exploit the fashionable world's obsession with change and fresh ideas – keeping up with the Lord Joneses. His system was fully thought out by the mid-1760s. He and James published in 1773 *The Works in Architecture of Robert and James Adam,* in which they wrote: "The massive entablature, the ponderous compartment ceiling, the tabernacle frame, almost the only species of ornament known in this country are now universally exploded, and in their place, we have adopted a beautiful variety of light mouldings, gracefully formed, delicately enriched and arranged with propriety and skill . . . we flatter ourselves, we have been able to seize with some degree of success, the beautiful

Opposite page
A small and pretty mahogany writing table of the George III period, 36 inches (91.5 cm) high and 31½ inches (80 cm) wide. It has gilt metal mounts in the neo-classical manner. The desk has a roll top which comes down to cover the pigeon holes and writing space. (Sotheby's)

Card table of about 1785, 26½ inches (67.4 cm) high. It is in rosewood and is crossbanded in kingwood. The marquetry is of fine quality. On the top is a fan design of a kind that was fashionable from the 1770s onwards. A three-dimensional effect was achieved by staining and scorching the wood

THE

CABINET-MAKER

AND

UPHOLSTERER's GUIDE;

OR,

REPOSITORY OF DESIGNS

FOR EVERY ARTICLE OF

HOUSEHOLD FURNITURE,

IN THE NEWEST AND MOST APPROVED TASTE:

DISPLAYING

A GREAT VARIETY OF PATTERNS FOR

Chairs	Tea Caddies	Hanging Shelves
Stools	Tea Trays	Fire Screens
Sofas	Card Tables	Beds
Confidante	Pier Tables	Field Beds
Duchesse	Pembroke Tables	Sweep Tops for Ditto
Side-Boards	Tambour Tables	Bed Pillars
Pedestals and Vases	Dressing Glasses	Candle Stands
Cellerets	Dressing Tables and Drawers	Lamps
Knife-Cases	Commodes	Pier Glasses
Desk and Book-Cases	Rudd's Table	Terms for Busts
Secretary and Book-Cases	Bidets	Cornices for Library
Library Cases	Night Tables	Cases, Wardrobes, &c. at large
Library Tables	Bason Stands	Ornamented Tops for Pier
Reading Desks	Wardrobes	Tables, Pembroke Tables,
Chests of Drawers	Pot Cupboards	Commodes, &c. &c.
Urn Stands	Brackets	

In the PLAINEST and most ENRICHED STYLES; with a SCALE to each,
and an EXPLANATION in LETTER PRESS.

ALSO

THE PLAN OF A ROOM,

SHEWING THE PROPER DISTRIBUTION OF THE FURNITURE.

The Whole exhibiting near THREE HUNDRED different DESIGNS, engraved
on ONE HUNDRED and TWENTY-EIGHT PLATES:

FROM DRAWINGS

By A. HEPPLEWHITE and Co. CABINET-MAKERS.

THE THIRD EDITION, IMPROVED.

LONDON:

Published by I. and J. TAYLOR, at the ARCHITECTURAL LIBRARY,
No. 56, HOLBORN, opposite GREAT TURN-STILE.

MDCCXCIV.

Opposite page
Bachelor's chest of about 1720, veneered in walnut. It is $33\frac{1}{2}$ inches (85 cm) wide. The top has a flap which folds out to form a little table. (Stourhead, Wiltshire – the National Trust)

Title page of the 1794 edition of Hepplewhite's *Guide*

spirit of antiquity, and to transfuse it with novelty and variety, through all our numerous works."

Adam did not design furniture for the public at large, but the cabinet makers took up his ideas. Hepplewhite showed that the aristocratic Adam style could be used for the middle-class home. Hepplewhite's reputation comes from his *Cabinet-Maker and Upholsterer's Guide,* published in 1788, two years after his death. Almost nothing is known of his life. He was apprenticed to the firm of Gillow's in Lancaster, migrated to London, and set up a small business in Cripplegate. His widow, Alice, who must have been enterprising, kept the business going and published the *Guide.* It has engravings of about 300 items, was an instant success, and was reissued in 1789. A revised edition was published in 1794.

Hepplewhite loved the typical neo-classical shapes – urns and vases – and foliage. But he was neither an architect nor an antiquarian. He aimed, as the preface to the *Guide* says, "to unite elegance and utility and blend the useful with the agreeable." The preface also says: "We designedly followed the latest or most prevailing fashion." In other words the *Guide* was to summarize taste rather than spread the gospel of a new style. Hepplewhite's designs were probably very like what was being done by other firms such as Gillow's of Lancaster and Seddon's of London and some of the designs were of a type popular for a decade.

Mahogany, with its masculine air, was used for furniture in the dining room and library; satinwood, more light and feminine, was for the bedroom, drawing room, and boudoir. The term 'satinwood' covers a great variety of species from the West and the East Indies; they are all a golden yellow.

It is uncommon to find a piece of furniture which corresponds exactly to one of the published patterns. A customer would look at the *Guide* and pick out something he or she fancied but would modify it – perhaps a different set of legs for a chair, or a back from another pattern.

Hepplewhite was fond of shield-backed chairs and his book has several variations on this theme. The shield encloses the Prince of Wales's feathers, or a classical urn, or festoons of drapery. The legs were usually straight and tapering. Painted or japanned furniture from this time onwards was quite the rage.

Prices at this time do not seem particularly high, even allowing for the difference in the value of the pound. The *Cabinet-Makers London Book of Prices,* published in 1788, illustrates more than 200 designs for furniture of good quality. Wardrobes were from £1 14s to £3 15s; card tables from 7s 6d to 15s; library bookcases from £3 12s to £5 15s. But furniture for stately homes would be con-

Dumb waiter in mahogany of about 1790. This type of furniture was a British invention. The dumb waiter – or sometimes two – enabled diners to have their food near the table, dismiss the servants, and talk in private. This one is unusual: the tiers fold so that it does not take up too much room when they are not being used

siderably more, being perhaps designed by the architect and thus specially made.

The largest firms had huge stocks. Seddon and Sons, of Aldersgate Street, London, had at the beginning of 1790 stock worth more than £100,000. The firm had 400 employees in 1786 – gilders, mirror workers, locksmiths, carvers, seamstresses, and sawyers as well as joiners.

But another designer wrote in 1791 of Hepplewhite's book: "If we compare some of the designs, particularly the chairs, with the newest taste, we shall find that this work has already caught the decline, and perhaps in a little time, will suddenly die in the disorder." The author of these words was possibly suffering from jealousy. He was Thomas Sheraton, the last of the three great figures who have become household words.

Sheraton

Genius, innovator, lay preacher and eccentric.

Sheraton was a man of paradox. He epitomizes for many people the most technically accomplished era of Georgian furniture, yet he lived in poverty and sometimes squalor and his mind became deranged in later years. He was a cabinet maker but gave up that work and scraped a living as publisher, author, and teacher of drawing. As in the case of Hepplewhite, no piece of furniture made by him has been identified and his reputation depends on his published designs. He seems to have found comfort in religion, for he became a Baptist lay preacher and wrote on devotional subjects. The style he evolved was a refinement of the neo-classical, sometimes verging on the effeminate.

His influence was through *The Cabinet-Maker and Upholsterer's Drawing-Book,* which he issued in 49 separate parts between 1791 and 1794. The first sections are on geometry and perspective and are not very practical; they also show his preoccupation with theology and learning. But the third section is useful and informative. His skill in drawing is remarkable; he was an innovator; and he sometimes delighted in complicated and ingenious devices.

Sheraton was born in 1751 in Stockton-on-Tees, Co. Durham, and almost certainly learned his craft in the district. His humble origins gave him a sense of social inferiority. He went to London about 1790 and it seems that he soon gave up making furniture. Instead, obsessed by his lack of education in childhood, he set up as a teacher. His business card of about 1795 says that he "Teaches Perspective, Architecture, and Ornaments, makes Designs for

Design by Hepplewhite for a chair, from the third section of the *Guide* (top)

An armchair in the Hepplewhite style with its original painted decoration of old English flowers in colour on a dark green ground; about 1790

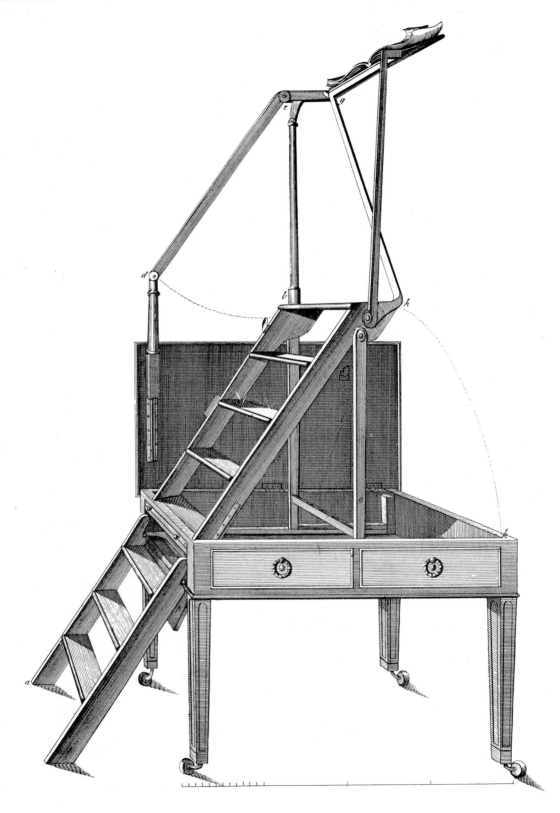

Cabinetmakers, and sells all kinds of Drawing Books &c." He left London in about 1799, returning to the North of England, but again went to London and in 1803 published the *Cabinet Dictionary*. This has sound information on the trade and has 88 engraved illustrations but shows that his powers were failing.

Many of the designs in the *Dictionary* reflect ideas of the newest style, now called Regency, and the *Dictionary* was the first book of its kind to do so. But at this stage Sheraton's work was inconsistent in quality and he could not come to terms with the great changes that had happened in the ten years between the publication of the *Drawing-Book* and the publication of the *Dictionary*.

Adam Black, founder of a publishing firm which is still in business, worked for Sheraton in 1804 when Sheraton was engaged in his last effort, *The Cabinet-Maker, Upholsterer and General Artists' Encyclopaedia*. Black wrote: "He lived in an obscure street, his house half shop, half dwelling-house, and looked himself like a worn-out Methodist minister, with threadbare black coat. I took tea with them one afternoon. There were a cup and saucer for the host, and another for his wife, and a little porringer for their daughter. The wife's cup and saucer were given to me, and she had to put up with another little porringer. My host seemed a good man, with some talent. He had been a cabinetmaker, was now author and publisher, teacher of drawing, and, I believe, occasional preacher. I was with him for about a week, engaged in most wretched work, writing a few articles, and trying to put his shop in order, working among dirt and bugs, for which I was remunerated with half a guinea. Miserable as the pay was, I was half ashamed to take it from the poor man."

Black also said of Sheraton: "He is a man of talents, and, I believe, of genuine piety . . . he is a scholar, writes well; draws, in my opinion, masterly; is an author, bookseller, stationer, and teacher. We may be ready to ask how it comes to pass that a man with such abilities and resources is in such a state? I believe his abilities and resources are his ruin, in this respect, for by attempting to do everything he does nothing." The *Encyclopaedia* was issued in instalments and ran from 'Astronomy' to 'Canada.' It is verbose, rambling, and in parts has nothing much to do with its title.

Sheraton died at his home in Soho, London, in 1806, of phrenitis (inflammation of the brain with delirium and fever). He was aged 55. A contemporary account said that he left his family 'in distressed circumstances.'

The first edition of the *Drawing Book* had more than 700 subscribers; very few were private individuals and the rest were cabinet makers, upholsterers, carvers, chair makers, and so on. More than half lived in London. His work had therefore a wide indirect

Armchair in painted beech-wood; the decoration is in the manner of George Seddon. About 1790 (above)

This set of library steps, from the *Drawing-Book*, folds up and forms a table: a good example of ingenuity and the way in which one item of furniture could be made to serve two purposes (opposite page)

influence; but the drawings are not a direct reflection of what was actually made. He was full of fresh and original ideas.

Indeed some of Sheraton's designs verge on the bizarre. One, in the *Drawing Book*, is for a library table. It is oval; drawers pull out, one at each side, and from the drawers emerge folding stands to hold books or maps. It is rather like a conjuring trick. A 'secretary' or writing table has a cupboard for a chamber pot and slippers; the flap for writing on is 3 feet 7 inches from the floor and the person who uses it has to do so standing up. 'Kidney tables' were popular at this time. Sheraton has a design for one, saying that it gets its name 'on account of its resemblance to that intestine part of animals.' His kidney table has drawers at the curved ends – not an easy place to fit them in.

A very popular type from about 1790 to 1810 was a writing or library table called a Carlton House table, which has small drawers curving round three sides of the top.

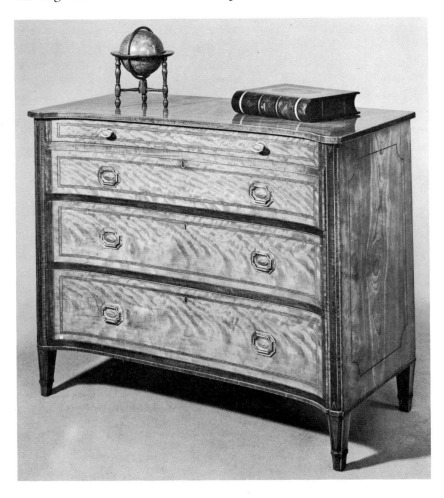

Dressing chest veneered in highly figured satinwood. 42 inches (107 cm) wide and 20 inches (51 cm) high. Similar to the design in the *Drawing-Book* on the opposite page

The tendency to make one piece of furniture serve two purposes is shown in 'writing fire screens.' They are to protect ladies' complexions from the heat of the fire and also to use as a desk: a flap comes down and reveals small drawers and pigeon holes. These were often only eighteen inches or two feet wide and three inches deep. Mahogany continued to be used, both as a veneer and in the solid. A French visitor wrote: "It is indeed remarkable that the English are so much given to the use of mahogany; not only are their tables generally made of it, but also their doors and seats and the handrails of their staircases . . . their tables are made of the most beautiful wood and always have a brilliant polish like that of the finest glass."

Cuban mahogany was a rich reddish brown and some parts of the tree had beautiful figuring which was excellent for veneering. But Sheraton wrote that Honduras mahogany or baywood was mostly used. It came in larger sections and was easier to work with.

Dressing chest from Sheraton's *Drawing-Book*

Sheraton said: "The grain of Honduras wood is of a different quality from that of Cuba, which is close and hard, without black speckles, and of a rosy hue, and sometimes strongly figured; but Honduras wood is of an open nature, with black or grey spots, and frequently of a more flashy figure than Spanish. The best quality of Honduras wood is known by its being free from chalky and black speckles, and when the colour is inclined to a dark gold hue. The commonest sort of it looks brisk at a distance, and of a lively pale red; but, on close inspection, is of an open and close grain, and of a spongy appearance."

Satinwood was highly prized. It was suitable for inlaying and painting. Harewood was used for veneer; it is actually sycamore or maple stained with oxide of iron and greenish-grey. The colour tends to disappear with age unless it is in a part protected from light.

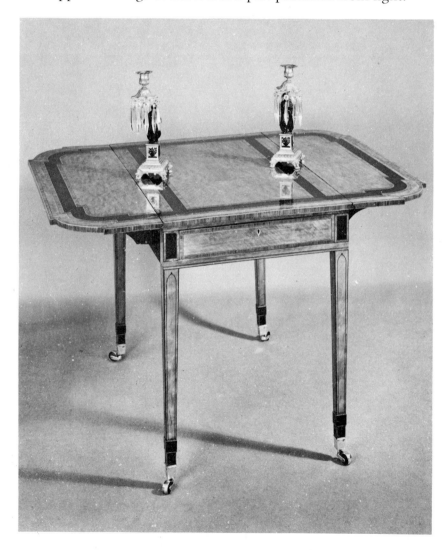

Pembroke table veneered in richly figured West Indian satinwood and crossbanded in purpleheart and tulipwood. The legs are solid satinwood with inlay. 28 inches (71 cm) high; 43 inches (109.6 cm) wide with the flaps raised. A very beautiful object

The Regency

Reaction against neo-classicism, a search for the true Roman manner, and a turning towards past styles.

Adam's brilliant successes did, of course, bring him some criticism. Horace Walpole wrote in 1775: "We have . . . very good architects; but . . . Adam, our most admired, is all gingerbread." Walpole saw in 1785 the work on the Prince of Wales's residence in London, Carlton House, and wrote: "There is an august simplicity that astonished me. You cannot call it magnificent; it is the taste and propriety that strike . . . How sick one shall be after this chaste palace of Mr Adam's gingerbread and sippets [fragments] of embroidery." The architect for Carlton House was Henry Holland. Holland had married the daughter of the great landscape architect 'Capability' Brown and Brown helped his career with introductions to the top people.

    The term Regency is a bit odd. It is a convenient label for the period from the 1790s to 1830, but the Prince of Wales was Regent only from 1811 to 1820 when his father George III was mad. It includes what one might almost call a rag-bag of different styles.

Cabinet in Brighton Pavilion taste. Lacquered; the door has summer pavilions and flowering trees. Remote from real life; more like a stage prop than a thing for use (above)

Couch in mahogany of about 1805. The head is in the form of a scallop shell and the feet in the form of dolphins. On the sides are small panels carved with nautical themes. Pieces such as this were made in celebration of Nelson's victories. The couch is stamped twice 'C Munro'; the only C Munro recorded at this date worked in Edinburgh from 1808 to 1812. It is 78 inches (198.8 cm) long.

The Prince was wildly extravagant, reasonably handsome when young, able to charm, generally good-natured, and a patron of the arts. His spending, especially on his palaces, was enormous. Carlton House (pulled down in 1827), the Pavilion at Brighton, Buckingham Palace, and Windsor Castle were built or remodelled; Windsor Castle alone, not the biggest project, cost about £1 million in the 1820s. His debts were a perpetual worry and brought him unpopularity. His position and spending made him one of the leaders of fashion but the Regency styles did not invariably follow his taste.

The neo-classical style of Adam tried to capture the spirit of antiquity but Regency antiquarians and historians sought a more accurate reproduction of the Roman manner – an academic correctness.

Holland admired the French furniture of the age of Louis XVI (1774–1792); the Prince bought French furniture and in 1795 owed £15,000 to one dealer for it. French craftsmen and designers came to Britain.

Lord Burlington was the 'Apollo of the Arts' in the first part of the eighteenth century. Thomas Hope played the same part in the early nineteenth. He came from a very rich Dutch family of mer-

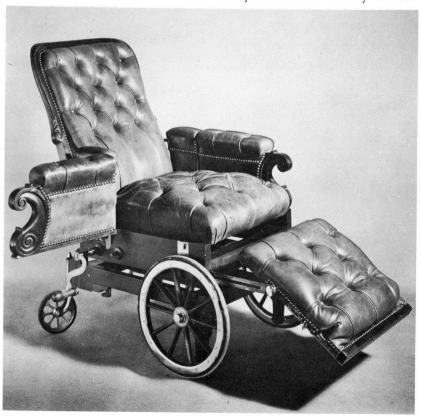

Mechanical chair for an invalid, early nineteenth century. It adjusts to many positions and shows the delight of that period with ingenious devices

Table for a library or hall in rosewood, of about 1810. It has brass mounts. 28½ inches (72.5 cm) high; 48 inches (122 cm) diameter (opposite page, left)

chants and bankers, and in his youth spent eight years studying architecture in Greece, Egypt and other parts of the Middle East, Sicily, Spain, and elsewhere. He was a writer of fiction, collector of Old Masters and other treasures, and amateur architect. He published in 1807 *Household Furniture and Interior Decoration*, which for years was used as the yardstick of accuracy in the Greek, Roman, and Egyptian styles. All this might seem only scholarly – but Hope's book did have a considerable influence on upholsterers and cabinet makers.

The next publication took Hope's work and made it practicable for the more ordinary person: *A Collection of Designs for Household Furniture and Interior Decoration* – the title an echo of Hope's. This was issued in 1808 by George Smith, a cabinet maker and upholsterer of London. It had 158 plates in colour. Smith's work was a common-sense application of all the Regency ideas up to that date. He also, unlike Hope, tackled Gothic and Chinese styles.

Well-off people at this time had an equivalent to our glossy magazines such as *Vogue* and *House and Garden*. This was Acker-mann's *Repository of Arts, Literature, Commerce, Manufactures, Fashions, and Politics* – or *Repository* for short – which appeared,

A curiosity: a crutch of the Regency period, in mahogany. It has a leather padded top and weighted hemispherical base. One of a pair. Nobody quite knows their purpose. Perhaps they were for propping up a drinker, or for someone who had lost both legs. 39 inches (99 cm) high (above)

Standing desk in mahogany about 1810. It was probably made to special order and is in the style of Gillow of Lancaster. Paintings and drawings show that people sometimes liked to stand when they were reading or writing. This desk is 51 inches (129.5 cm) high

usually monthly, from 1809 to 1828. Especially interesting are the coloured illustrations of women's fashions, because the models are posed on pieces of furniture which must have been characteristic of the time, and not merely gimmicky.

An extraordinary craze for the Egyptian manner followed Napoleon's expeditions to Egypt and Syria from 1798 to 1801 and Nelson's victory at the Battle of the Nile. Napoleon took with him about 160 archaeologists and artists: their reports started the ferment of interest. Furniture acquired ornamental sphinxes, lotuses, crocodiles, and suchlike. Sphinxes, male in ancient Egypt, changed their sex when imported to Britain – years ahead of their time, it would seem.

Chinoiserie popped up again. Carlton House had a Chinese room, but the Prince's architectural fantasy, the Brighton Pavilion, was nearly all in the Chinese taste. He bought vast amounts of Chinese furniture, porcelain, and curiosities and also commissioned new pieces in what was hopefully thought to be nearly the authentic style. Bamboo was imitated in European woods and furniture was decorated with lacquer or japanning. Pagoda shapes were used for chairs and sofas. Chinese ideographs, real or fanciful, were inlaid in brass on some pieces.

Sofa table in mahogany; Regency. It is in the style of Gillow of Lancaster. Sofa tables were to go in front of sofas and were for books or needlework. This one has brass cappings on the feet. 44 inches (112 cm) wide, unextended

French fashion was steadily imitated. The Prince Regent loved especially *boulle*, an inlay of tortoiseshell and brass. It originated in Italy and was perfected by André-Charles Boulle (1642–1732) who did much work for Louis XIV. After the Prince became George IV in 1820, a diarist wrote: "The King had talked of going to Hanover, but the Duke of Wellington says there is not much chance of that unless we allow him to take his eating & drinking money, his money for buhl furniture, & for buying horses, which we could not think of doing."

Gothic, which had last flourished at Walpole's Strawberry Hill and at the time of Chippendale, began to reappear in Sheraton's *Dictionary* and *Encyclopaedia*. Ackermann's *Repository* said in 1827: "No style can be better adapted for its decoration [the Library] than that of the middle ages, which possesses a sedate and grave character, that invites the mind to study and reflection. The rays passing through its variegated casements cast a religious light upon the valuable tomes on either side, the beautiful arrangement of its parts combining to produce an impressive grandeur in the whole design." Gothic fitted in well with the horrific 'Gothic' novels of the day and with the historical novels of Sir Walter Scott, who wrote: "Our national taste has indeed been changed, in almost every particular, from that which was meagre, formal, and poor, and has attained, comparatively speaking, a character of richness, variety, and solidity." He added: "Profusion of ornament is not good taste," prophetic, for the Victorians were often guilty of over-elaboration.

A trademark of the Regency period is the way in which the legs of chairs are curved. This idea was taken from the painted Greek vases discovered at Herculaneum and Pompeii and the result was an object of great beauty and refinement. Sometimes only the back legs were curved; sometimes all four. One type, the 'Trafalgar' chair, has ornament like a rope, to celebrate and commemorate Britain's naval victories. The best designs of chairs are especially accomplished and satisfying: the lines of legs, arms, and backs flow into one another. Trafalgar chairs usually have caned seats and were fitted with cushions; the wood is often painted beech.

Some chairs have animal or semi-human figures forming the front legs or the supports for the arms.

Windsor chairs, an established pattern at this time, began to be manufactured around High Wycombe, Buckinghamshire, in 1805 and the town has been a centre for the furniture industry ever since. Men called 'bodgers' turned the legs on simple lathes in the woodlands of the district and immense quantities of the chairs were made. Windsor chairs can be comfortable without cushions or upholstery. They were made to fit the body – the seat was shaped and hollowed.

Hall chair of the Regency period with a painted heraldic emblem. The class consciousness foreshadows the Victorian obsession with respectability

Social manners permitted people to lounge about; the *Repository* said in 1809; "Amongst the various decorations of a library, a sofa is an indispensable article of furniture; it not only ornaments, but becomes a comfort when tired and fatigued with study, writing, and reading – the exhausted mind can only be recruited by rest . . . in no other country in the world is such complete convenience and comfort to be found as in England." Sheraton said settees were also essential in the drawing room. Lolling on a couch was in imitation of the Greek philosophers. Sofa tables – long, and designed to be used by ladies sitting on sofas – are among the most attractive of Regency designs and seem to have been invented in this country. They gave a lot of scope for the designer and decorator. The sofa table could have a section in the middle which turned over and the piece then became a leather-topped writing table or a chequered games table.

The Regency cabinet-makers tended to rely on exotic veneers for effect. Rosewood was especially popular – a dark purplish brown with variegated figure, heavy and durable. The term rosewood is applied to many species. Other woods were amboyna (rich, dark brown, from the West Indies); maple (white, stained); and zebra wood (light brown with striking dark brown stripes, from Guyana). The veneers were especially beautiful when combined with inlays or mounts of brass. Marquetry was out of fashion.

Small cheveret in satinwood of about 1795. A cheveret was to carry books from room to room. This one, delicate and dainty, was for a lady. It has painted garlands of flowers. $41\frac{3}{4}$ inches (105.5 cm) high; $16\frac{1}{4}$ inches (41 cm) wide (left)

A jardinière or plant holder of about 1815, in rosewood with brass mounts. The top is a Chinese bowl of the early nineteenth century. This piece shows both the way in which classical forms were interpreted and the inventiveness of the period. Rooms of the eighteenth century were sparsely furnished compared with our own time; chairs, for example, tended to be placed against the wall and the centre of the room was kept clear. But during the nineteenth century new forms of furniture were being invented and the glorious clutter of the middle class Victorian house was on its way (right)

Miniature furniture

For the dolls' house and nursery.

Very grand families in the late seventeenth century and the first part of the eighteenth sometimes owned sumptuous dolls' houses, designed by architects and furnished by craftsmen. They were then called 'baby houses,' but they were for the adults to play with, not the children. They were expensive and the children no doubt had their own cheaper versions. The houses and furnishings have survived because they were costly and valued; letting the children play with them would have been too risky.

Swift wrote in *Gulliver's Travels* (1726) that when Gulliver was in the land of the giants he had "a set of silver dishes and plates . . . not much bigger than what I have seen of the same kind in a London toyshop for the furniture of a baby house."

Horace Walpole recorded in 1750: "The Prince of Wales is building baby houses at Kew." This was Frederick Prince of Wales, then in his early forties.

Not all miniature furniture was for baby houses. Some was made as samples, says one theory, to show to customers in a craftsman's shop or to take to a customer in his own house. An ordinary shop or workshop would not carry much stock since the business would be mainly special orders and a customer would not get a good idea of what he might like from a half-finished article. But this function of miniatures as samples – if it ever was the case – must have come to an end when in the mid-eighteenth century practical pattern books began to be published.

Another use was perhaps as trade signs or as eye-catching items to put in a shop window. It is also thought that apprentice cabinet makers, before they became journeymen, may have made miniature pieces to show their skill. This must have been done in their spare time, after long hours in the workshop.

Another type was for the actual use of children with their dolls. Cradles and tea tables are among the commonest; they are often of simple, even rough construction, and were made by carpenters or skilled amateurs. Child-size chairs are found, sometimes incorporating pewter chamber pots. 'Baby walkers' are frames on castors; the child was locked in and could not sit down but supported himself on the frame. Most of the furniture made for the use of children in this country is plain, but the American equivalents are sometimes magnificent – almost as if they were symbols of the parents' pride.

Points of quality to look for are the same as with full-size furniture: good joins between the parts, well-fitting drawers, skilful veneering if there is any. Also desirable is correct proportion, never easy to achieve in miniature work.

A certain style of old dressing table had built into it a small chest of drawers on each side of the mirror; these have been removed in some cases and passed off as miniatures. But they can be identified for what they are because the wood is thicker than in the genuine article.

Fakes: worming: care of furniture

Furniture is, perhaps more than any other type of antique, fraught with difficulties over restoration, faking, and forging. The dividing line between necessary restoration and downright deception is hard to draw. Centuries of use may mean that heavy restoration is essential if the object is to survive, have a useful life, and give pleasure. On the other hand, what pretends to be eighteenth-century furniture in the United States has been estimated at many times the quantity actually made. Another difficulty is that the Victorians and Edwardians were fond of reproducing the styles of previous ages. Good materials and much skill and labour were put into these reproductions; regular use and the passing of time have added the appearance of age.

Some of the points to watch are:

Marriages: two sections of one piece of furniture were not made for each other but were brought together later in life with perhaps unfortunate results. Examples might be a chest and a stand; or a small bookcase and a bureau forming a bureau bookcase. The danger is when parts fail to match in colour of wood, size, or style.

Divorces: large and cumbersome articles tend to be less saleable than small, so they are split up. This applies more to Victorian than to eighteenth-century and Regency pieces; but Regency furniture was thought of as second-hand junk until the 1940s and was ill-treated. Examples of divorces are tallboys (high chests of drawers) divided into two small chests of drawers; huge Victorian sideboards divided into corner cupboards, cabinets, and chests. The faker here runs into trouble, as usual, because some of the surface has to be made good.

Alterations: simple and ordinary pieces are ornamented with fancy fittings. An ordinary chair is given arms. An armchair is expanded into a settee, the extra wood being hidden by the upholstery and one new leg being supplied.

Five chairs can be made into a set of six. The five are dismantled, some new arms, legs, and so on are made, and from all this material the six are assembled. The new pieces of wood are discreetly distributed around all six chairs.

A bureau bookcase in walnut may have solid wooden doors on the upper part. But it becomes more valuable if instead it has mirrored panels. Similarly, cabinets with solid doors have been converted into china cabinets with glazed doors.

A bachelor chest is a small low chest of drawers, with a folding top which forms a table. It is a popular object nowadays and ordinary small chests are inclined to acquire folding tops.

Old wood can be pressed into service: a piece of panelling becomes the back of a settle, balusters from a staircase the legs of a table. The variations are enormous.

Patina: this comes from many years of use and polishing, and is one of the most difficult things to falsify. We might in fact be taken aback if we could see an old piece in its condition when new, because we value and have become accustomed to the mellow richness of age. French polishing removes this and gives a far less pleasing effect. This was often done to old furniture during the nineteenth century when the compound was first used.

Wear and tear is normal. People tip up chairs and strain the joints. Feet scuff the stretchers (the rails between the legs of some chairs and tables). Table tops get marked by all sorts of accidents. On the other hand some antique furniture is in very good condition indeed; it may have spent part of its life in a church, it may have been thought unfashionable and banished to a spare room or an attic for generations, or it may have always been in the little-used state rooms of a palace or large country house.

Stretchers, then, will usually show wear in the places most likely to be scuffed by feet. Edges of tables will be in general rubbed and rounded, not sharp. There is similar wear to the arms of chairs which will be smoothed by sleeves.

Carving can be added, to increase the attractiveness. Ordinary pad feet have been re-carved as ball-and-claw feet; plain cabriole legs have been given shell and other motifs. Shallow carving is suspect: it may mean that the craftsman was working on a portion of original and plain wood and was limited in what he could do by the small depth of the wood already there. Carving is expensive, and something is wrong if an otherwise modest item has a lot of it. Early fakers could not resist over-embellishing furniture.

Materials: these present the faker with a big problem. Modern machine-made screws are quite different from the original hand-made type; so are brass handles, castors, and the glass of mirrors.

Worming

Woodworm is one stage in the life-cycle of the furniture beetle or *Anobium punctatum*, a creature for which hardly anyone has a good word. It does, however, sometimes help fakers and forgers and it gives work to restorers and pest exterminators. The beetle is dark brown and shiny and about a quarter the size of a house fly. The worm or maggot is about a third of the size of the maggots found in peas and has a small black head and heavy jaws.

Wormholes are generally taken as a sign of age and so fakers have sometimes deliberately taken wormy wood and incorporated it into false pieces. The deception is revealed if the tunnels are exposed lengthwise, for the insect emerges from the wood through a simple hole, never a furrow. An exposed tunnel means that the wood has been cut at a later date. No craftsman would use wormed wood, so the faker as well as the worm has been at work.

Legend says that even the wormholes have been faked by the firing of a shotgun at the wood; the pellets, it is claimed, make the right kind of hole. The idea is unlikely in the extreme. Affected wood is plentiful enough, and how do you get the pellet out?

Restoration of severe damage is desirable not only because the condition is unsightly but also because the tunnels weaken the whole structure. It is a tricky process and not to be undertaken by a novice if the furniture is valuable. The dust left behind by the worm as it eats its way along is blown out. A synthetic substance, epoxy resin, is injected in a liquid form, sometimes with a hypodermic needle. This swells and hardens, and strengthens the wood. Then the holes are stopped up with beeswax and turpentine, mixed to the consistency of butter and stained to match the wood. Or beeswax and resin are used. The piece is polished and with luck and skill the holes will be almost invisible.

So much for damage already done – but the living *Anobium punctatum* is always with us. Understanding its incredibly boring life cycle is the key to tackling the menace. Its natural habitat is dead trees and it can fly short distances into buildings. It is, however, more likely to arrive in infected wood or wickerwork, which should be banned from every well-regulated household.

The life cycle is:

The female lays tiny eggs – oval, white, and visible to the naked eye – in crevices and on rough surfaces of wood. Within four weeks they hatch into grubs. The grubs bore into the wood for food and shelter and live there for at least one year and as many as five.

Then the grub moves to just below the surface, excavates a cell, and becomes a pupa. Within a few weeks the pupa is an adult beetle; it burrows free (leaving the telltale hole) and goes in search of a mate.

The woodworm beetle *Anobium punctatum*

This usually happens in May to August. The female lays its eggs . . . and the cycle starts again. Within a few weeks of mating the adults are dead.

The presence of wood dust on or below a piece of furniture means that the pest is active. Two methods of treatment are used:

Fumigation: poisonous gases penetrate the tunnels well. Hydrogen cyanide, deadly also to man, must be handled by experienced operators. Carbon disulphide mixed with air is explosive.

Applying fluids: this has an advantage over fumigation because the fluids not only kill the grubs but also leave behind a deposit of poisons which prevent more attacks. Liquids may, however, harm upholstery.

Late spring and the summer are the best times for treatment because that is when the pupae are near the surface, the beetles are emerging, or the eggs have recently been laid.

Signs of active infection – wood dust or freshly made holes – should be taken seriously. The infected object should be removed from other wood or at least wrapped up in paper or polythene so that emerging beetles cannot fly free.

Furniture beetles are not the only enemy. The Powder Post Beetle attacks the outer layer (the 'sapwood') of hardwoods. Treatment is the same. The death watch beetle and the longhorn beetle attack construction timbers and woodwork but not furniture.

Temperature and humidity

Central heating can severely damage furniture, paintings on wood, objects of ivory, and other valuables. It can also affect the health of people suffering from bronchitis, asthma, sinusitis, and similar diseases; shrivel pot plants and flowers in vases; build up static electricity in carpets so that when someone in the house touches a light switch he or she gets an unpleasant electric shock; warp modern doors, window frames, and skirting boards made of poorly seasoned wood; dry out paper, parchment, and leather; and harm carpets, curtains, and upholstery.

The reason is that warm air can hold much more moisture than cold air. The warm air from a central heating system sucks out moisture from anything in the room of animal or vegetable origin. The answer is to instal a humidifier, which disperses into the air the moisture that is lacking. Many types are available and expert advice should be taken on the one suitable for each room. Extra safeguards are a hygrometer, which measures the relative humidity; and a humidistat, which automatically controls an electric humidifier.

Veneered furniture is particularly vulnerable. Dry air makes the glue loosen, and it makes the veneer and the basic body of the article – the 'carcase' – shrink; but they may do so in different degrees. Wood also shrinks more in one direction of the grain than in another. All this can result in the veneer splitting and coming away from the carcase. The same can happen with parquetry and marquetry.

A Louis XV writing table of marquetry was sold at Christie's in 1958 for £35,700. This was for many years the highest price paid at auction for a piece of furniture. The table was stored during the Second World War in a garage – admittedly a well-built garage – but came to no harm because the atmospheric conditions were right.

Some furniture is inlaid with brass or mounted with ormolu (gilded brass or bronze). If the wood shrinks, the metal is almost bound to buckle or come away.

Many factors affect the degree of damage. The surface of the wood may be waxed, varnished, painted, gilded, covered in gesso, or treated in some other way; all these affect how the wood reacts to low humidity. Thin panels tend to suffer more drastically than thick ones.

The natural process of ageing makes wood brittle and less able to adapt to sudden changes of humidity. Timber was formerly seasoned but is now kiln dried. The old process left in the timber a higher percentage of moisture; so antique furniture suffers even more than modern.

Old houses provided comfortable homes for furniture if not for people, with plenty of draughts to counter the effects of open fires. Curtains, upholstery, and potted plants – such as the Victorians loved

The top of a Louis XV marquetry table which was stored in a garage during the Second World War. It was unharmed because the atmospheric conditions were right.

– also helped, by acting as a 'buffer' against the drying effect. Removing a piece from a cold and draughty church or country house to a warm shop, house, or museum can result in disaster. Even switching on and off the light in a showcase may alter the temperature, and therefore the humidity, and harm the contents.

Some collectors are a little wary of buying, for example, Queen Anne furniture veneered in walnut; solid walnut is a better bet.

A superb example of Queen Anne walnut: chair of about 1720. The legs are finely carved with acanthus scrolls; the seats have their original needlework covers; the feet are 'paw and ball'; the central splat of the back is veneered in burr walnut and has cross-banding. This splat is slightly curved to fit the user's back and the combination of veneering, banding, and the curve show technical mastery.

Silver

Antique silver was scarcely collected before the early years of the nineteenth century, while the system of hallmarks, which gives us an enormous amount of information, was understood by hardly anyone except the trade until the publication of monumental works of scholarship by Victorians.

Until this change came about, pieces of old silver were merely regarded with sentiment and affection as heirlooms or as benefactions to colleges, livery companies, and churches; or were thought of as a way both to keep capital and to use it at the same time. When cash was short the silver could be sold for the melting pot. The beauty of the craftsmanship and design hardly mattered much. Indeed, pieces that were old-fashioned tended to be scrapped and more up-to-date ones made from them. Banking as we know it and limited liability companies for keeping money and for investment, are comparatively modern inventions. Fear of a bank's failure encouraged people to put some at least of their assets in coin or plate.

All this, from the collector's point of view, had both disadvantages and advantages. The disadvantages were that enormous amounts of silver were melted down, especially after the dissolution of the monasteries to satisfy the greed of Henry VIII, and during the Civil War to pay for troops.

The advantages were that people were encouraged to order work from the silversmiths. Coin, instead of being kept in an iron-bound chest under the bed, was sent off and made into things for everyday use, for ostentatious display, and for enjoyment of its appearance. Moreover, in the age of faith, churches were given silver for use in rituals and for adornment: chalices and patens, tankards, cups, candlesticks, processional crosses, and so on. Even domestic pieces were, after the Reformation, sometimes given to churches. Many millions of pounds worth of silver is owned by the Church; much anxiety and soul-searching are caused when a congregation, faced with death-watch beetle in the roof and cracks in the spire, and with unused silver tarnishing in a safe, thinks of selling.

Silver has remarkable qualities. It is easily hammered into shape; it is brilliant when polished, reflecting a high proportion of the light; it does not readily tarnish except when exposed to certain chemicals, or salt, or yolk of egg; it acquires with use a delightful patina. It can be rolled to a thickness of 0.0005 inches; an ounce of silver can be drawn out into a mile of wire.

The hammer was one of the main tools of the trade. A sheet of silver was beaten into the proper shape on a wooden stake or anvil.

A simple bowl or beaker could be made entirely in this way. More complex articles, such as an octagonal coffee pot, were made from separately shaped pieces soldered together. Solid parts, such as a handle in the form of a human figure, were cast from moulds.

Roughness and imperfections were removed by a smooth hammer (the 'planishing hammer') and by polishing. Castings were filed and finished.

The craftsman can ornament silver with engraving (lines cut into the surface with special tools), chasing (marks made with a hammer but without taking out any metal), embossing (raising the surface by blows from a hammer on the reverse side).

Gilding is done by several processes. One of the old methods is to melt gold and mix it with mercury. The amalgam is spread on the surface to be gilded and the article is heated. This leaves a film of gold fixed to the silver, and the mercury comes away in poisonous fumes. A safer method is to soak a linen rag in a solution of chloride of gold, dry and burn it. The ashes are rubbed on to the surface to be gilded and the gold remains. Modern techniques use electrolysis. (One technical point: the phrase 'parcel-gilt' means partly gilded.)

Queen Anne

The craft reached a peak of achievement – some would say *the* peak – with the Queen Anne style. But 'Queen Anne' is a misnomer. The style really appeared a decade before she came to the throne and continued well into the reign of George II.

Politics and economics played an important part in the story. The political event was in France: the Revocation of the Edict of Nantes in 1685. The Edict, granted in 1598, gave the Huguenots the right to worship according to the Protestant way. But France under Louis XIV was not prepared to tolerate an independently-minded minority whose loyalty, it was thought, might be suspect. Persecution followed and the Edict was repealed. An example of the cruelties imposed on the Huguenots was the billeting of unruly soldiery, especially the Dragoons, in their districts. Women were raped, men beaten. It has been calculated that 400,000 people left France within a few years.

France's loss was other countries' gain. The Huguenots took with them their skills. Britain welcomed them as unfortunate fellow Protestants and substantial funds were raised for their relief.

Silversmiths were among them. But immigration caused stresses and the silversmiths of London feared for their livelihoods. A petition was submitted to the Goldsmiths' Company, in 1711, ostensibly about a member who was in trouble for allegedly using

A chocolate pot by William Penistone, 1711. It is 10¾ inches (27 cm) high. Hot chocolate was at the height of its popularity in Britain between about 1675 and 1725. The pear-shaped body of this example is rare for such an early date. Chocolate pots have generally a hinged or sliding finial on the top of the cover so that a rod could be inserted and the contents stirred. The rods were of ebony or hard fruitwood, sometimes with flanges at the bottom to make the stirring more efficient. Silver rods are very rare; in any case, few chocolate pots have their original rods

All the pieces of silver illustrated in this chapter are made in London, unless another town is specifically named

too much solder in his work. It said: "Partly by the general decay of trade and other ways by the intrusion of foreigners, several of the workmen of the . . . Company have for the support of their families been put under the face of underworking each other [i.e. doing jobs at cut rates] to the perfect beggary of the trade and at length under the necessity of loading their work with unnecessary qualities of solder to the wrong and prejudice of the buyer and the great discredit of the English workmen . . . by the admittance of the necessitous strangers, whose desperate fortunes obliged them to work at miserable rates, the representing members have been forced to bestow much more time and labour in working up their plate than hath been the practice of former times, when prices of workmanship were greater."

Not only price cutting worried the silversmiths of London. The immigrants were also in many cases more skilled, for example at casting and engraving. Their arrival pushed up standards both of craftsmanship and design. Moreover, they could do work in the French style which was in demand by persons of fashion: the splendour of the court of Louis XIV was imitated all over Europe.

So two styles were being used side by side: the English, which relied for its effect on sobriety, good proportion, elegant outline, and plain surfaces; and the Huguenot, which was more ornamental and magnificent. Curiously, the immigrants came mostly from outside Paris and their work did not have the richness of the Parisian craftsmen. The Parisian Huguenots in many cases did not emigrate, believing that 'Paris was worth a Mass.'

The silversmiths worked mainly to order; the raw material was so costly that keeping a stock was impractical. The success of the

Teapot by Humphrey Payne, of 1717. Payne worked at the sign of the Hen and Chickens in Cheapside and made many excellent tea and coffee pots and jugs and, indeed, specialized in these items. He died on the same day as De Lamerie. The pear shape appeared early in the Queen Anne period and lasted until about 1720; sometimes such teapots were octagonal in plane. The bullet shape replaced the pear shape. Silver teapots were made less often after the 1740s because porcelain ones were available instead and were fashionable (left)

Coffee pot by Samuel Wastell, 1703; $10\frac{5}{8}$ inches (27 cm) high. The spout is shaped like the head of a swan (right)

Huguenots depended on the patronage of the clients; the country was ready for their skills. At the same time a Huguenot would accept a commission for work in the plain English style; the English silver-smiths adopted the new fashions; and by the 1720s the two streams were merging.

Economic factors were another influence. More wealth was about, at least for some classes. Demand for silver was strong – for example, people needed pots for the newly fashionable drinks, tea, coffee, and chocolate. The metal used was in a thicker gauge than before. During the second half of the seventeenth century embossing was popular, and the metal for embossing has to be comparatively thin: but this kind of ornament was less favoured for the Queen Anne style and thinness was no longer necessary.

Reform of the coinage in 1560 laid down that silver coins had to be of the Sterling standard of fineness: 925 parts of silver in 1000. This lasted until the Coinage Act of 1920. The purity was the same as for the raw material of the silversmiths. It was convenient because the family plate could be easily sold when money was needed, and the silversmiths had, in the coin of the realm, a source of metal. But in the 1690s so much coin was being melted down that commerce was disrupted. Coins were also being clipped at the edge for the sake of the metal. Worn and clipped coins of Elizabeth were still circulating towards the end of the seventeenth century. Trading was made difficult when many coins had to be scrutinized and tested for weight. New coins of the proper weight tended to be hoarded or themselves

A rare and curious piece: a miniature porringer of the Queen Anne period, in gold. It is 1½ inches (4 cm) in diameter and weighs 13 dwt. No marks, but is 24 carat gold (above)

A toy tea and coffee service of about 1725; some pieces are by David Clayton and some by John Cann. The coffee pot is 2¼ inches (6.7 cm) high (right)

to be clipped: bad money drives out good. Severe penalties against clipping, such as branding or hanging, failed to stop the practice. Things were so bad that the Government called in the old coinage and declared that it would not be legal tender after 4 May 1697. Furnaces were set up near Whitehall, London, and huge amounts of worn and clipped coins were collected and melted down. Many people hung on until the last minute and just before the deadline the army had to be called in to control the vast crowds of people who gathered in the area of the furnaces. Even the recall of the coinage was not the complete answer, for the issuing of the new was extremely slow. Parliament had to act to stop the melting down of coin, and decreed that silversmiths were to use from 25 March 1697 only metal of a higher standard of purity – 958.3 parts of silver to a 1000. Bullion from coins needed to be refined. The Act was called the 'Act for encouraging the bringing in of wrought plate to be coined,' or the Wrought Plate Act for short. The real purpose was quite different from the one suggested by the formal title.

The Act also said that the marks punched on plate were to be changed. To distinguish between the old standard and the new, the mark of a seated woman was to be struck on the new. This gave the name Britannia standard to the purer form. Opinions varied about the technical merits of the change. Some people said that the old standard was more durable; others that the new was a finer colour.

The Wrought Plate Act did not apply to Scotland because the Union of the two Parliaments had not taken place; nor did it apply

A monteith made in London in 1706 by John Jackson. The body is chased with bands of flutes, is matted, and has punched motifs. The rim is detachable

to Ireland where the Britannia standard was never used.

The Act of 1697, by a strange oversight, did not mention the English assay offices outside London and another Act had to be passed in 1700 to sort out the anomaly. It said: "The goldsmiths, silversmiths and plateworkers of this Kingdom remote from London are under great difficulties and hardships in the exercise of their trade for want of assayers in convenient places . . ." And it authorized offices to be set up at York, Exeter, Bristol, Chester, and Norwich.

The difficulties of the Mint were in time solved. The Bank of England's notes became more acceptable and banking in general better organized, so that coin was not so vital in commerce. Another Act was passed in 1719 which made both standards legal from the following year. The Act of 1719 also put on a tax of sixpence an ounce and future Governments were to raise revenue in the same way, to the annoyance of the trade.

Rich people could afford massive silver objects such as wine cisterns, which were in fact for cooling bottles of wine. They were as big as a baby's bath. One made in 1701 by Phillip Rollos for the

Cruet frame, three castors, and two bottles for oil and vinegar by Fleurant David, a Huguenot; 1725. Such items appeared in the Queen Anne period and were made by a long line of specialists in the eighteenth century

Wine fountain by Peter or Pierre Archambo, of 1728. It is no less than 27½ inches (70 cm) high and is a most lavish object. It was made for the second Earl of Warrington and has on top an earl's coronet and at the sides the Earl's armorial devices of boars. This piece is a duty dodger (see page 107)

Duke of Marlborough is 17 inches high and 3 feet 10 inches wide.

Smaller than the wine cistern was the monteith, a large bowl. An Oxford antiquarian, Anthony à Wood, wrote in 1683: "This year in the summer came up a vessel or bason notched at the rim to let drinking glasses hang there by the foot, so that the body or drinking place might hang in the water to cool them. Such a bason was called a 'Monteigh' from a fantastical Scot called 'Monsieur Monteigh' who at that time, or a little before, wore the bottom of his cloake or coate . . . notched."

Sometimes the notched ring was detachable, and from this the punch bowl seems to have evolved.

The British tea ceremony dates from Queen Anne's reign. Addison wrote in 1711: "All well-regulated families set apart an hour every morning for tea and bread and butter."

Tea was first known in England in about 1660 and was thought of then as a medicine: the equivalent of liver salts for over-indulgence. Pepys recorded in 1660 that he "did send for a cup of tee, (a China drink) of which I never had drank before." Coffee houses sprang up during the reign of Charles II and tea was taken there as well. In the Queen Anne period it was a fashionable drink but expensive: green tea was more than £1 a pound and bohea was even more. Containers were thus small and were provided with locks to

A tankard made in London in 1700 by Isaac Dighton. It holds 3¾ pints and weighs 57 oz. Not visible in the photograph is an engraved coat of arms; it is repeated on a shield at the bottom end of the handle.

The lion adds to the magnificence of this notable piece. Sometimes lions were added to tankards after they were made – even soon after – but this one is original.

The leafy decoration is cut card work. This technique was done by cutting a pattern from sheet silver and soldering it to the body of the object. Sometimes the aim was to give strength. The metal used when this tankard was made was of the Britannia standard, softer and not as durable as the sterling standard (left)

Tea kettle by Joseph Ward, of 1719. It has contemporary engraving. The tea kettle was for replenishing the teapot and had a spirit burner to keep the water hot. The utensil first appeared about 1685 but did not become common until the end of the seventeenth century. Kettles and pots were sometimes made to match; the kettle is distinguished by the handle over the top. Tea kettles began to be superseded about 1765 by tea urns. (The example shown here is a duty dodger – see page 107) (right)

prevent theft by servants. Swift wrote in his satirical *Directions to Servants* that the "comforts and profits" of the waiting-maid were reduced by "the invention of small chests and trunks with lock and key wherein they keep the tea and sugar, without which it is impossible for a waiting-maid to live . . . there is no other method [for the maid to get at the delicacies] but by a false key." Sugar was expensive, too. A women's magazine said a "tea table cost more to maintain than a nurse with two children."

Tea caddies were then called canisters; the word caddy did not appear until the late eighteenth century. (It was derived from the Malay *kati*: a unit of weight, equivalent to $1\frac{1}{3}$ pounds, used in the tea trade.) Canisters sometimes come in sets of two for the different sorts of leaf which the hostess blended on the spot. A third matching box was for sugar, or perhaps for the blending. These sets were sometimes put in boxes, as Swift pointed out; they were of shagreen, tortoiseshell, or wood with mounts of silver.

Teapots of the Queen Anne period were either pear-shaped or nearly spherical. They were replenished from tea kettles, which are also pear-shaped but are larger and have a handle going over the top of the lid. Beneath the tea kettle was a lamp to keep the water hot.

Coffee and chocolate pots are similar to each other except that chocolate pots have a hole in the lid so that a rod can be inserted to stir up the contents.

A luxurious item of this period was the toilet set. One made for George Treby, MP, in 1724 had 26 pieces and the bill came to the very large sum of £377 13s. 10d. It hardly seems possible that one dressing table could hold the entire set. Paul De Lamerie was the maker.

Paul De Lamerie

The greatest silversmith of the eighteenth century.

The *London Evening Post* wrote on De Lamerie's death in 1751 that he was "particularly famous in making fine ornamental Plate, and has been very instrumental in bringing that Branch of Trade to the Perfection it is now in." His working life spanned 40 years, during which styles changed, and De Lamerie was often years ahead of most of his contemporaries.

He was, as his name suggests, of Huguenot descent. His father, Paul Souchay de la Merie, and his mother, Constance le Roux, were of aristocratic birth. Religious persecution forced them to flee first to the Netherlands, where Paul was born in 1688. The family then moved to London in 1691 and lived in Soho. The father had been an army officer in the service of William of Orange but because of his aristocratic birth a trade or profession would be unacceptable to him. The whole family probably lived at first on the Royal Bounty, a fund for helping the refugees; the family received £6 for the year 1703.

The young Paul was apprenticed in that year to Pierre Platel, another Huguenot and a master of the craft. Platel took on De Lamerie without the usual fee: the Huguenots helped each other out and indeed stuck together to a certain extent well into the eighteenth century.

De Lamerie set up business on his own account, first in Windmill Street and then in Gerrard Street, London. It seems that he not only ran a workshop but also sold jewels and watches, at least by the time of his death. His commissions included objects of the most sumptuous kind and quite ordinary wares. George Treby, whose toilet service for his bride cost so much in 1724, bought a large amount of other plate from De Lamerie between 1721 and 1725, spending a

This gilded basin made by De Lamerie for the Goldsmiths' Company of London in 1741. The arms of the Company, in the centre of the basin, include a leopard's head which is one of the marks of London silver.

total of £2025 4s. 3d.

Among De Lamerie's masterpieces is a salver made for Sir Robert Walpole, the Prime Minister, in 1728. Walpole's official title was First Lord of the Treasury and it was the custom on the accession of a new monarch for the holder of the office to be given the discarded silver matrix of the Exchequer Seal. This happened when George II came to the throne in 1727; Walpole had the seal melted down and from the metal the salver was made. It is square, 19 inches across, and georgeously engraved in the centre with the royal coat of arms; the King enthroned and bearing his crown, orb, and sceptre; a panorama of London; and allegorical figures. The engraving is by Hogarth.

The Goldsmiths' Company commissioned from De Lamerie (and still possesses) a gilded ewer and basin made in 1741. They were to perpetuate the memory of the Company's benefactors, whose presentation plate had been melted down in 1667 and 1711. The ewer is nearly 15 inches high; its handle, huge in proportion to the rest, is in the form of a sea god. The basin, 31 inches across, has in the centre the Company's coat of arms and round the rim has putti (little naked boys) holding the symbols of Minerva, Hercules, Mercury, and Vulcan.

Minutes of the Company for 9 December 1741 state: "All the new plate lately made for the Company having been now viewed by the several Members present at this Court it was the General Opinion that the same is performed in a very curious and beautiful manner." These pieces are a virtuoso performance and form a spectacular and lavish display, but they are quite impractical as vessels. At the same time De Lamerie was willing to turn his hand to perfectly plain and modest things such as salt cellars, knives, forks, and spoons – or at least his apprentices and craftsmen did them.

He worked at first in the obligatory Britannia standard. Although the Wrought Plate Act of 1719 restored the ordinary standard, as an alternative, De Lamerie stuck to the finer metal until 1732. He then registered a new mark with the Goldsmiths' Company and turned to the old standard. The reason may have been that metal of the old standard was easier to work; and the new rococo style demanded elaborate and even fantastic forms. Details of his life are scanty because silversmiths then had little social standing. Some facts have, however, been gleaned from rate rolls, parish records, and legal documents. He married, in 1717, Louisa Juliott, who was of Huguenot descent and was then 23. They had six children – four girls and two boys – but only three girls survived to adulthood. His father died a pauper in 1735, when Paul De Lamerie was well established; it seems they had fallen out.

A candlestick by George Wickes, 1737. It is silver-gilt and is 10 inches (25.5 cm) high. Candlesticks sometimes were made in sets; they were then numbered so that when stock-taking was held it was easy to check that all were present and correct. Until the middle of the 18th century candlesticks tended to be of good quality, but then mass production and standardization came in for the less expensive pieces

Almost none of De Lamerie's accounts have survived, although they do include the one for the Treby toilet set. Another surviving set of accounts is for silver supplied to Admiral Hawke, later Lord Hawke, between July 1749 and February 1751. The accounts include £23 7s 1d for two square salvers and 4s 4d for engraving them. The salvers and the accounts were sold by a descendant of Hawke at Christie's in 1969 for £20,500.

De Lamerie died in August 1751. He had no surviving son to carry on the business. His will directed that the unfinished stock in his shop should be completed by one of his workmen and sold. "All the genuine and entire stock of curious patterns and tools" was auctioned.

The rococo, 1725-65

Exploitation of the exuberance, magic, and fantasy of the rococo style was pioneered by De Lamerie, always in the forefront of creativeness and skill. Silver was especially suitable for the scrolls, flowers, leaves, dolphins, fish, crabs, scallops, serpents, mythological figures and Chinamen so much liked by the rococo designers.

Boredom is impossible, and the eye is carried from part to part by the vigour and movement of the compositions. Immense sums were spent by the wealthy. Two pairs of candlesticks cost the Earl of Malton £48 14s in the late 1730s – enough to keep a

Tureen made in 1754 by Peter Archambo and Peter Meure; 11 inches (27.9 cm) high. The design echoes porcelain tureens of the period. A wealthy household may have several matching tureens; so that the lids and bottoms were kept together, numbers were scratched on the silver in a place where they would not be noticed. Sometimes the weight was also scratched on; the owner would then know how much the object was worth if it had to be melted down

family for a year in modest style. Another client ran up a bill for £1756 in 1735.

A splendid example of the profusion of ornament is a tea kettle made in the 1730s. The three feet are each in the form of a crouching triton; the body is embossed with Neptune and other watery personages; the spout is another triton blowing a conch shell; two mermaids support the handle. All this can hardly have improved the taste of the tea. The maker was Charles Kandler, of German origin and perhaps related to J. J. Kändler who worked for the Meissen porcelain factory (see page 121).

The greatest surviving example of English silver of the time is a centrepiece for a dining table which was made in 1741 for Frederick, Prince of Wales. The base has shells and sea-foams; fierce dolphins hold up with their tails a boat-shaped tureen and are helped by mermen. The tureen is festooned with shells and surmounted by Neptune holding a trident. It is possible that this piece is one known to have been made for the Prince at a cost of £242 3s 6d. The craftsman was either Paul Crespin, of Huguenot descent, or Nicholas Sprimont, who was born in Liège and who was a founder of the Chelsea porcelain factory (see page 154). Sprimont even gave some crustaceans an extraordinary kind of immortality by making moulds from their shells and casting copies in silver.

Ideas were being exchanged all the time between makers of silver, pottery, and porcelain, and furniture. Elaborate pieces,

A tea caddy by Peter Archambo, 1745. It is 5 inches (12.7 cm) high and is in the chinoiserie style with figures, buildings, flowers, and scrolls. During the rococo period tea caddies were one of the most delightful forms for the silversmith. Some makers specialized in them

verging on the bizarre, were for the wealthy, but all through the period simple and functional objects were being made. Style was decided by the taste of the client and by the amount he was willing to spend. Another consideration was whether the object was to be for display or for everyday use.

Changes took place in the way the craft was organized. Most silversmiths in the 1720s were in a small way of business. Soon, the number of partnerships increased and a single firm would take on a good number of apprentices. De Lamerie, for example, seems to have had at least four apprentices at any one time in his working life except for one year. The apprentices needed skilled men to teach and supervise them. Makers tended more and more to specialize – in spoons, casters, candlesticks, salt cellars, and so on. But individuality was not submerged as it was to be in Victorian times.

The trade was still beset by old grievances and by time-hallowed malpractices. Grumbles about the Huguenots were surfacing as late as 1737, when the Court of the Goldsmiths' Company ordered

Salt cellar by Eric Romer, of about 1760. Romer was Norwegian in origin and specialized in pierced baskets and epergnes. These salt cellars have frames of silver pierced and are chased with a scene of an Oriental garden; the human faces above the feet are Chinamen. The bowls are of glass because salt attacks and corrodes silver. The construction of these is unique, as far as is known: the silver bodies form a frame which is locked together by the rim. Eighteenth century salt cellars took many forms (above)

Silver-gilt dish by George Wickes, of 1739. It is 12 inches (30.5 cm) across and is boldly decorated with the arms of Frederick, Prince of Wales, son of George II and father of George III. Well engraved coats of arms add to the interest and value; so does a royal association. The style of the dish is of interest – the border is typical of work done 30 years before. Usually decoration closely follows current fashion, at least in London, but occasionally old-fashioned features are found

a case to be drawn up "concerning the privilege and touch [marking of silver] of this Company of late years granted to foreigners and concerning the money taken by the Company marking the plate and smallwares of freemen of the Company equal to foreigners, to the great hardship and prejudice of the members of the Company who bear the expensive offices in the Company equal to foreigners and seem to have the only natural right to the touch; and that the committee consider if foreigners may be excluded from the touch; and if not how they may be further charged in money, for the touching of their plate." The proposals came to nothing except that charges for marking were put up by Parliament the next year.

Fraudulent hallmarks, dodging of the duty on plate, counterfeit punches, and metal with too much alloy were prevalent, and in 1743 the Goldsmiths' Company secured the prosecution and conviction of some offenders. No fewer than 39 members of the Company complained in 1750 about the same old abuses but nothing was done "as no method for redressing the abuses is proposed."

Beer jug, executed in the most exotic rococo style by Phillips Garden, of 1754. It is $13\frac{1}{2}$ inches (34.2 cm) high and of exceptional quality. The decoration includes putti, barrels, barley, hop-vines, female masks, insects, lizards and contemporary coats of arms. Phillips Garden was a purchaser of De Lamerie's patterns and tools which were sold on 4 February 1751 (above)

Tea caddy made in London by Fogelberg and Gilbert in 1786. The decoration is highly neoclassical. A matching teapot is in the Victoria and Albert Museum

Punch bowls were in and monteiths were out; punch bowls were also favourite prizes for race meetings. The 1720s saw the appearance at dinner tables of the tureen – a splendid way of displaying the family's wealth and fashion because it appeared so early in the meal and so prominently. They were popular in both silver and porcelain and some were extravaganzas of fantasy. Fish soup gave a chance for the use of the favourite rococo shells, crustaceans, dolphins, and so on. Sometimes a bizarre touch came in with the mingling of odd elements: De Lamerie made in 1736 a tureen with dolphins and crayfish – and vines and foliage.

Epergnes are another invention of the period: they are complicated frameworks put in the middle of the table to hold candles, cruet frames, sauceboats, baskets for sweetmeats, and assorted dishes. Unwanted bits could be unscrewed and the sockets filled in for the time being with fancy knobs. Not all these things were incorporated in a single epergne and indeed the kind made in this country was often fairly simple. It was the French who went in for the truly comprehensive versions with everything except the kitchen sink.

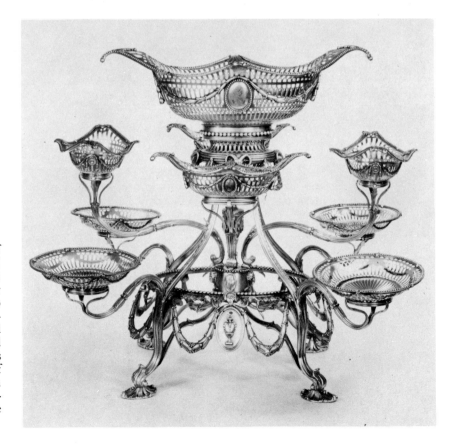

Epergne by Thomas Pitts, of 1775 and with neo-classical details. It is 15¾ inches (39.9 cm) high. Pitts was a prolific maker of epergnes between about 1760 and 1780 in the rococo and neoclassical styles. He supplied many to the firm of Parker and Wakelyn – a firm whose ledgers have survived and which itself continues in the modern firm of Garrards. Epergnes are nowadays especially popular in the United States

The word epergne looks French but is English. The French themselves called the object a *surtout de table*. 'Epergne' may come from the idea that the object was to save *(epargner)* the trouble of passing things at table.

Neo-classical

"The light and elegant ornaments . . . of Mr. Adam, imitated from Ancient Works in the Baths and Villas of the Romans, were soon applied in designs for chairs, tables, carpets, and in every other species of furniture. To Mr. Adam's taste . . . we stand indebted, inasmuch as manufacturers of every kind felt, as it were, the electric power of this revolution in Art." This was how Sir John Soane, architect and connoisseur, described the neo-classical movement in a lecture to Royal Academy students in 1812.

Robert and James Adam drew designs of silver for their clients. The aim was to make sure that everything in the houses was in keeping with the architecture and interior decoration. Ordinary working silversmiths had to follow the trend to neo-classicism. This was inevitable. But the industry itself was changing in several ways.

London's importance as a centre was challenged for the first time since the Protestant refugees started to arrive from France in the 1680s. The makers outside London were angry and frustrated. They had to send their wares to London, Chester, or York so that the metal could be assayed and the objects hallmarked. But at this time Sheffield and Birmingham were thriving centres of production. The craftsmen in these two places were "under great difficulties and hardships in the exercise of their trades, for want of assayers in convenient places to assay and touch their wrought plate."

Goods might get damaged, stolen, or delayed; a craftsman's rivals might be able to see his new designs and pirate them.

Prices in London, said the men in Sheffield and Birmingham, were too high: the London makers had an unfair advantage. Matthew Boulton, owner of a great metal-working factory in Birmingham, added during a campaign for reform that London workmanship was not specially good and that it owed a lot to foreign artists. (He was perhaps referring to the rococo style and to the Huguenot community.) It was also alleged that the London silversmiths used sub-standard metal. The London silversmiths suggested in their turn that the products made outside London were liable to be substandard too. Jealousies abounded. Matthew Boulton wrote to James Adam that the Birmingham factory had many advantages "that are not to be found in any manufacture that is or can be establish'd in a great & Debauch'd Capital.''

Boulton was one of the leaders in the campaign for reform; at last Parliament set up a commission of inquiry. A committee of the House of Commons bought 22 pieces of plate in London and found that 21 of them were considerably below standard. (It should, however, be said that methods of testing were then less exact than they are now).

The upshot was a change in the law in 1773, setting up new assay offices in Sheffield and Birmingham. The marks were to be a crown for Sheffield and an anchor for Birmingham. Much of the business in connection with the bill was done at the Crown and Anchor Tavern in the Strand, London. (The mark for Sheffield was changed in 1975 to a rose.)

Establishment of the assay offices in these two towns reduced London's pre-eminence. Technological advances were being made and were taken up with enthusiasm by the makers in Sheffield and Birmingham, especially Matthew Boulton.

Stamping machines and dies turned out simple repetitive patterns at high speed and efficiency. Rolling mills made possible the manufacture of much thinner and more economical sheets of silver. Mechanical methods are nowadays somewhat frowned upon: craftsmanship is lost and men become the slaves of the production line. This was not the attitude of the eighteenth century. Inventions were welcomed because they were novel and interesting and because of the benefits they brought. Among the benefits was a reduction in the cost of simple articles in silver so that more and more people could afford them: salt cellars, small jugs, teapots, spoons and forks.

Very thin metal did, however, mean that some articles such as candlesticks were not strong and heavy enough to stand on their own, so they had to be strengthened with pitch, resin, or iron rods (this also applied to Sheffield plate.)

Boulton strove towards quality, especially because at that time, as later, the word Birmingham implied shoddiness. The Sheffield makers exchanged dies among themselves; and Boulton sometimes refused individual commissions if the capital investment in dies would mean that the job was uneconomic.

Machines could not, however, compete with the old-fashioned methods in the making of specially imposing or costly pieces such as racing trophies and tureens.

Classical motifs appeared everywhere: festoons of foliage, ram's and lion's masks, key patterns, paterae (a motif in low relief, sometimes resembling a flower), laurel wreaths, and so forth. Classical designs had for a long time been used in Britain but never before with such enthusiasm. The neo-classical 'violent vase

Over page
Opulence in gilded silver: most of these pieces were made in the 1820s when grand silver for formal dinners was popular. They include claret jugs, wine coolers, sideboard dishes, candelabra, and a dessert service. (Christie's)

Opposite page
Soup tureen made in 1737 by John Edwards. It is $16\frac{3}{4}$ inches wide and has lavish decoration with an aquatic theme; shells, bullrushes, dolphins, and the realistic crab on top. The design and execution are brilliant. (Christie's)

Opposite page
A very elegant tureen for sauce or gravy, 10 inches (25.4 cm) across. It was made by the firm of Boulton and Fothergill in 1776 and was hallmarked in Birmingham. Tureens of this kind were often made in sets of four. This example is in the early and robust neo-classical style. (Victoria and Albert Museum)

madness,' as Josiah Wedgwood, the great potter, called it, was based upon the classical Greek vase; Sir William Hamilton, husband of Emma, formed a collection of them. Vase shapes were suitable for racing trophies, casters for sugar and spice, wine coolers, parts of candlesticks such as the nozzles, and tea urns. Tea urns replaced tea kettles in the 1760s. The water was kept warm by a heated iron rod put into a lining in the urn. Die-stamping could be used on straight-sided objects but not on more elaborate and curved profiles.

London makers bought ready-made components from Sheffield and Birmingham and often put their own marks over them. Retailers were coming into their own; a development which tended to break the close connection between patron and craftsman. The London products have in general more individuality than the Sheffield and Birmingham ones mainly because mechanical methods were not so much used; and London, the centre of fashion, was able to react more quickly to change.

'Bright cutting' was much admired and was a new technique. It is a special form of engraving, cut so as to give a different reflecting angle to the main surface. A glittering effect is produced.

Coasters were invented in the 1760s: miniature circular trays for bottles and decanters. They have bases of wood and sides of silver or plated metal and underneath the base is a pad of baize. Their purpose was two-fold: to stop drink from dribbling on to the table and to make it easy to slide the bottle or decanter to the next drinker.

Tankards of this period are less common than of the early Georgian period because people were drinking more wine and spirits and less beer.

Tea services had previously with very few exceptions been bought piece by piece so that the makers and dates were often different and the whole set did not quite match. But in the·Adam period tea sets were made and sold complete.

Stirrup cups were for the hunting set and are in the form of a fox's or dog's head. The rim of the cup is the animal's neck, and because they were used by people on horseback they are not meant to stand upright on a table.

Hester Bateman

One of the well-known English silversmiths, Hester Bateman, is almost a cult among some collectors. Her mark will put up the price of a piece twice, three times, or even more. Yet she was not the only woman who was in the craft in the eighteenth century, and many people think that her work is not of particularly out-

Opposite page
Vase of gilded silver, probably to hold sugar, made by John Arnell of London in 1772; $8\frac{1}{2}$ inches high. It has a frieze of swags and the handles are in the form of bearded and horned faces. The epitome of neo-classical taste. (Victoria and Albert Museum)

standing quality. One of the reasons for her popularity is that she has followers in the United States and this maintains prices. It has been jokingly said that the interest in the United States is because of the matriarchal nature of American society. Another factor in the market is that the tradition of high prices for her work is well established and tends to continue. There is no evidence that she actually manufactured the objects which carry her stamp. She was born in 1709 and married John Bateman, a silversmith and maker of gold chains, in 1732. He died in 1760 of consumption and left his wife the tools of his trade. Hester took up the business in London with her sons John and Peter and an apprentice and later in her career had seven people working for her.

The custom of the time was for the widow of a silversmith to be allowed to be a member of the craft if she had lived with her husband for at least seven years. It was a device to allow her to make a living. But little silver with the Hester Bateman mark is known for the period 1760 to 1774. Most of the output was presumably done for other silversmiths. They would not want their clients to know who the real maker was. Moreover, the Bateman mark is sometimes found to have been obliterated by another maker's, for the same reason.

Her early work is mainly spoons and forks – simple and inexpensive at the time. The range was widened to include small pieces for domestic use such as salt cellars, cream jugs, cups, and wine labels. Wine labels are among Hester Bateman's most attractive pieces.

Rarer are medallions, snuffboxes, seals, chains of office, and communion plate. Much of the work was in the prevailing neo-classical taste. A characteristic decoration is a small beaded edge.

Hester's son Jonathan, the last of her six children, married Ann Dowling in 1769. It seems that she brought some capital into the firm, because soon afterwards private custom increased. Bigger workshops were built in 1786 and the business seems to have done well in spite of the competition felt by all silversmiths from Sheffield plate.

Hester retired in 1790, handing the business over to Peter

Entries in the records of the Goldsmith's Company of London, for Hester Bateman. Her maker's marks are noted as they were changed from time to time. The second last column is for her signature but has only her crude initials and the words 'The mark [i.e. signature] of Hester Bateman.' It seems she was illiterate. The last column is for the signature of a witness (opposite page)

Tea caddy by Hester Bateman, of 1783. It has a bright cut engraving and beading and is 6 inches (15.2 cm) high

Stirrup cup in the form of a fox's mask by Hester Bateman, of 1776 (top)

Cream jug by Peter and Anne Bateman, of 1791. The sides have bright cut engraving and the inside is gilded

and Jonathan, and died in 1794 aged 85. She was probably illiterate, but left about £1250.

The firm continued long afterwards. Jonathan died in 1791 and Peter took his sister-in-law, Ann, as partner. She retired in 1805, suffering from dropsy: Hester's grandson William had become a partner in 1800 and he took full ownership in 1815. Ann left £2000 and other assets; she was as good a businesswoman as Hester. Peter died in 1825, aged 85. William achieved the highest office in the Goldsmiths' Company, the Prime Wardenship, and lived until 1850. His son William took over the business in 1839. The appeal of the name Bateman still attaches to products of the later members of the family and pushes prices up accordingly.

Hester's work has been forged from time to time. A silversmith was sentenced at Sheffield Assizes in 1971 to three years in prison for faking the punches. This was reduced to nine months on appeal. He was caught through a series of coincidences and because several of the spurious objects appeared on the market within a week. It was the worst case of its kind to be detected since the 1930s.

It has been estimated that possibly 11,000 pieces were made in Hester's time, although many will have been lost or, in Victorian times, disfigured by additional ornament. Much is in the United States; other pieces are in churches, museums, and collections in this country. But the large output ensures that items appear regularly on the market. The curious fact remains that Hester's reputation is in the view of many experts overrated.

The Regency and Paul Storr

The Regency style in silver, as in other applied arts, included a huge variety of themes. Britain celebrated in style her naval and military victories, and monumental pieces of silver were ordered in commemoration. Lloyd's Patriotic Fund launched special appeals after victories and the money was spent on presentation swords and plate – for example, after Trafalgar, when the admirals and some of the captains were given large vases of silver valued at £300 apiece.

Britain during this time became the most powerful nation in the world. The landed classes were prospering because rents were going up. The metal was becoming cheaper and more plentiful. The extravagance of the Prince Regent made him highly unpopular at times (a pair of candelabra, 51 inches high, cost him £4003 15s) but he influenced manners and taste.

The feminine style of Adam was superseded by a more ponderous one derived from the later days of Imperial Rome. An influential figure was the architect Charles Heathcote Tatham (1772–1842) who published in 1799 *Ancient Ornamental Architecture at Rome and in Italy* and in 1806 *Designs for Ornamental Plate*. The preface to the second book says, in the ponderous style of the time: "To encourage and facilitate the study of the Antique, in its application to that species of Ornament commonly called Plate, has been my principal motive for this publication. It has been lamented by Persons high in Rank, and eminent for Taste, that modern Plate has much fallen off both in

A silver gilt wine coaster by Paul Storr, of 1818. Coasters are to stop wine spilling on the table and to make it easy to pass the wine to the next drinker. They have wooden bases; underneath the base is a pad of green cloth (above)

A wine cooler, 10¾ inches (27.4 cm) high by Paul Storr, of 1810. It is in silver gilt. The rim has ovolo and dart moulding, the lower part has acanthus leaves, vine tendrils, and bunches of grapes, and the centre has Bacchanalian scenes. The surface is matted except for the foot

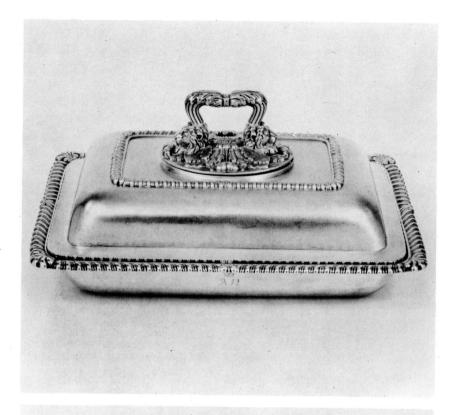

Entrée dish by Paul Storr, of 1814. It is 12½ inches (31.8 cm) high. Large services of dishes and plates were essential to the proper conduct of great houses, but were functional and gave little scope for artistry. The covered entrée dish was an exception to this rule – as is shown in the handle of the one shown here

Cake basket made by Paul Storr, 1817; 11¼ inches (28.5 cm) long. It is a direct copy of a type introduced by De Lamerie in about 1725 and is an example of how some Regency designs harked back to earlier times. Objects like this are called cake baskets but were used for other things too, such as fruit. One is in Hogarth's portrait of the Graham children in the National Gallery

design and execution from that formerly produced in this Country. Indeed, the truth of this remark is obvious, for instead of *Massiveness,* the principal characteristic of good Plate, light and insignificant forms have prevailed, to the utter exclusion of all good Ornament whatever."

The scene is dominated by one maker, Paul Storr, and by one firm, run by Philip Rundell and John Bridge.

Storr was born in 1771, the son of a silver chaser who became a victualler, and was apprenticed about 1785 to Andrew Fogelberg, a Swede of whom almost nothing is known.

He set up his own business in 1793, soon after his apprenticeship was over, but in 1807 took over the manufacturing side of the business of Rundell and Bridge. Orders poured in from the Royal family, the aristocracy, and the gentry. The Duke of Wellington, appointed Ambassador to Paris in 1814, needed a grand dinner service for grand entertaining; Storr made 102 items for it. The present Royal collection has hundreds of articles by Storr, from massive centrepieces for a dinner table to salt spoons. The most expensive royal purchase was a wine cooler weighing 8000 ounces and costing £8500.

Storr had to cope with so much work that he became more or less the head of a large factory. Yet his standards of craftmanship were almost invariably high. Style is perhaps a different matter. Much plate was designed by architects such as Tatham, painters such as Thomas Stothard (1755–1834), and sculptors such as John Flaxman (1755–1826). They did not understand the nature of silver and translating their designs into objects needed great skill. Curiously, the true character of Roman silver was not then known. Buried hoards had been discovered but had been melted down without being properly recorded. More great hoards were to be discovered later – in 1830, 1868, 1883, and 1895. The Regency's attempts at a Roman style in silver were based upon Roman works in stone, bronze, and pottery.

An example of the artist designing objects for the silversmith to make is the Shield of Achilles, which is 36 inches across and weighs 660 oz. It was commissioned in 1818 and several examples of it were made. Flaxman was the artist and Homer's description of the shield was the origin of the design. In the centre is a chariot drawn by four horses; round the border is a frieze of figures. The work is in some people's opinion a failure.

Another is the Wellington Shield of about 1822, which is 40 inches across and was designed by Stothard. In the centre are Wellington and his officers; round them are 12 panels with scenes of battles, inspired by the Elgin marbles.

Gothic fancy: Candlesticks made in London in 1811 by Story and Elliott. They are 4½ inches (11.4 cm) high. They are cast in one piece and unlike some candlesticks are not 'loaded' – i.e. weighted to give them substance and stability

A tea urn by Paul Storr, of 1805. The engraving on the body is of military emblems in a battle-field; the cover has a coat of arms; and on the back is the inscription: 'Presented as a tribute of respect and attachment to Lieutenant Colonel John Smith by the commissioned officers of the second regiment of Loyal London Volunteers for his ability in maintaining the discipline and harmony of the corps and for the honourable friendship that has subsited between himself and his officers. MDCCCV.'

This type of inscription adds to the interest of the piece of plate. Much Victorian plate has, however, been defaced by dealers to remove the inscriptions. The practice also makes the metal thinner (above)

A curiosity: Device for a one-handed card player, by Benjamin Smith and son; of 1817. It is 10¼ inches (26.1 cm) long. The clamp is for fixing to the edge of the table. A full suit of cards can be held. Perhaps it was for someone who lost a limb at Waterloo or some other battle in the wars against France. The mark, of Benjamin Smith and his son, also called Benjamin, is rare; it was only used in 1817 and 1818. This piece shows the adaptability of the metal for all kinds of purposes

Philip Rundell and John Bridge were extraordinary characters, nicknamed by their staff 'Vinegar' and 'Oil.' One account of Rundell, not entirely reliable, speaks of him as being "of a violent disposition, very sly and cunning, and suspicious in the extreme. Avarice, covetousness, and meanness were so deeply rooted in him that it affected every feature of his face and entered into every action of his life." His manners were uncouth. He loved the theatre and the company of actors and actresses. John Bridge was the perfect foil. The same account says he was "naturally of a timid, quiet disposition . . . his back was exceedingly flexible and no man in London could bow lower than Mr. Bridge." He was the firm's contact man and salesman, "beating the bush to drive the game to Ludgate Hill," where the firm had its showroom.

Rundell died a millionaire. His nephew Edmund Rundell, another member of the firm, left half a million pounds. Bridge also made a fortune and was able to buy an estate in Dorset and retire there. Storr shared in the firm's prosperity and had to support a wife and ten children but he left the firm in 1819 to set up on his own. It seems likely that personal relationships between the three men were poor. In any case Storr probably felt that the huge volume of orders he had to cope with was swamping his individuality. He left Rundell in 1819 and set up again on his own, in the area of Gray's Inn Road. He took a partner, John Mortimer, in 1822 but that was a disaster. Mortimer overbought stock for the retail side of the business and in 1826 the firm was on the brink of ruin. An

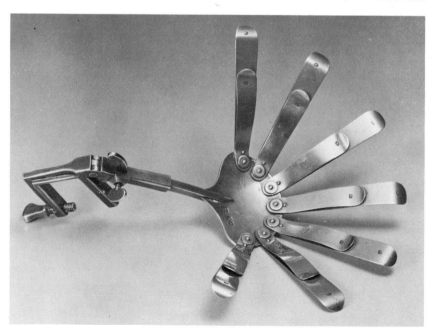

injection of capital saved the day; it came from a relation of Storr's by marriage, John Samuel Hunt, who put up £5000. The business went on under the three men from 1826 to 1838, but Mortimer was always a difficult person to deal with. Storr and Mortimer were involved in a Chancery Court case with each other in 1838 but they seem to have settled out of court. Storr retired to Tooting, south London, the following year and died in 1844. He left £3000 but had no doubt provided for his large family. His firm went through different hands after his death.

Storr's tools, bench, and many of his papers were destroyed by enemy action during the Second World War. His name, like Paul De Lamerie's and Hester Bateman's, adds considerably to the value of a piece.

A silver-gilt wine cooler, 10 inches (25.4 cm) high of 1807, with appropriate decoration. The handles spring from masks of Bacchus; the rim has a band of grape vines. The coat of arms has not been traced. Perhaps it was just made up as a status symbol for the owner.

This piece was made by the firm of Digby Scott and Benjamin Smith, great rivals of Paul Storr. It seems that Scott ran the business side and Smith the creative side. Smith had been trained in Birmingham by Matthew Boulton.

The lavish meals of high society and corporative bodies such as limited companies required sumptuous objects

Scottish Silver

The earlier Scottish silver is especially rare and costly. Invasions, religious strife, civil wars, and the fact that Scotland as a whole was not as prosperous as England all contributed to the scarcity of early silver work. The ordinary collector has to concentrate on the eighteenth and nineteenth centuries. Styles often reflect the character of the nation and a distinct Scottish accent is apparent.

One of the finest achievements was a special type of teapot, beautifully functional and elegant. This is nearly spherical, and is called the 'bullet' teapot. It stands on a foot-rim or flattened base. Decoration is of a very sober sort. Bullet shaped teapots reached their zenith in the 1720s and 1730s; some were made of gold as prizes in horse races.

Bannock-racks are like huge toast-racks and were to hold thick bannocks of oatmeal, hot from the kitchen. The racks, and the bannocks themselves, are now rare – Dr Johnson's dictionary definition of oats as "a grain, which in England is generally given to horses, but in Scotland supports the people", is truly outdated.

Quaichs were originally drinking bowls of wood, either hollowed out or built up from staves in the same way as a barrel. Then they were made with silver mounts and, eventually, entirely of silver. They have two flat handles on opposite sides of the bowl. Quaichs came into favour again in the early nineteenth century

A large quaich, with initials and the date 1714 but with an Edinburgh mark for 1721. The interior is traced with lines in imitation of wooden staves; quaichs were originally of wood, built up in sections like a barrel. They can be quite small, as little as 2 inches (5.1 cm) across

under the influence of the romantic revival and especially the novels of Sir Walter Scott; they are still made as prizes.

Heart-shaped brooches are another form which still survives, this time for the tourist trade. They are called 'luckenbooth' brooches after the 'locked booths' or shops which used to cluster round St Giles Cathedral in Edinburgh. The heart often has a twist at the bottom and sometimes the brooch is of two interlocked hearts. These pieces were made for betrothals and to protect children against the evil eye.

Plaid brooches are circles with long pins across the middle. The pin pierced the cloth and held it in place. They were first made in the Highlands, were imitated by craftsmen in the towns from the late eighteenth century, and in Victorian times were given extra ornament, of cairngorms or other semi-precious stones.

Spoons give the collector a chance to 'bag' the marks of different towns, some of them quite rare. Some places and their marks are:

Perth – a lamb with a banner
Dundee – a pot of lilies
St Andrews – a St Andrew's cross
Montrose – a double rose
Elgin – a woman holding a child

Others are Wick, Tain, Banff, and Aberdeen. The marks of these are usually the name, spelled out or abbreviated.

The far-flung spots offered little work so the craftsmen travelled about doing their orders on the spot. Some of the makers can have been little more than tinkers and the metal is often less pure than it ought to be. Edinburgh has had since 1681 a proper system of marks to show the year in which a piece was assayed. Silver from other places usually carries only the town mark and the maker's mark, or the maker's mark alone.

The end for the small towns came in 1836 when an Act laid down that all Scottish silver had to be assayed in Edinburgh, Glasgow, or London.

The Scottish silversmiths of the eighteenth century tended to avoid the fripperies of English fashions and were especially good at engraving. But gradually the influence of England predominated, as in so many other fields, and the Glasgow assay office was closed in 1964 for lack of business.

Irish Silver

The silversmiths of Ireland achieved great heights of craftsmanship and design in the eighteenth century. The departure of this glory followed, as is so often the case, political disruption; the part played by England was vital. Dublin, which dominated the craft, was the stronghold of the Protestant ascendancy. The Dublin silversmiths were at times fanatically anti-Roman Catholic. It was the Act of Union of 1800, which united the two kingdoms, that crushed hopes of an Irish cultural revival. Moreover, machine-made silver was imported from England from the end of the eighteenth century onwards.

But in the flowering of the Georgian period the Irish evolved characteristic forms of silverware quite different from anyone else's.

Overseeing the craft then, as now, was the Goldsmiths' Company of Dublin, originally a medieval guild.

The Protestant ruling classes spent lavishly on dinner parties, clothes, and horses. For this they needed silver dishes, vessels, and so on; silver buckles and buttons; even silver items for harness.

Objects made in the earlier years of the century, until about 1740, were mainly in the Queen Anne Style: plain surfaces and elegant proportion were the thing.

Ireland was late in taking up rococo fancies and often translated them into a different language. The Irish makers especially went in for farmyard scenes, birds, and fishes. The scenes with milkmaids, cows, goats, farm houses, and haystacks are often quite out of proportion with one another.

Characteristically Irish are:

Piggins or little pails for serving cream. Little ladles were made to go with them.

Herbal pots, like tiny teapots, less than three inches high. They were probably for infusing medicines such as saffron tea, camomile, or wormwood.

Dish crosses were invented in Ireland about 1730. Putting a hot vessel on the table was likely to mark the wood, so they were placed on a contraption with four arms forming a cross. The arms could usually be extended or contracted: in the middle was a spirit lamp to keep the food or drink warm. This invention was taken up by the English.

Dish rings, of cylindrical form, served the same purpose. Strangely, they are sometimes called potato rings. The story goes that they were put on plates and filled with potatoes. But the records of the Goldsmiths' Company always call them dish rings. Very beautiful decoration was applied by the Irish silversmiths to these pieces.

Freedom boxes. Irish towns and cities were especially fond of presenting their 'freedom' to distinguished people. With the scroll or citation went an ornamental and inscribed box.

Occasional oddities are found. Clontarf Parish Church has a chalice inscribed: 'The Gift of Charles Melville Sen., Esq., April

A gold freedom box, made in Dublin in 1780 by Abraham Tuppy. It is 2½ inches (6.3 cm) across and weighs but 3 ounces. On the top are the arms of Drogheda, which awarded the freedom, and underneath are the arms of the second Earl of Buckingham, the recipient. The Earl was Lord Lieutenant of Ireland from 1776 to 1780

8th 1721.' It later left the church, for also on it, most incongruously, is 'Cheltenham July 18th 1833 won by Exile 5 year old.' The chalice was returned to the parish in about 1900. A salver is inscribed: 'This was purchased with the premium got for the best Hogshead of Mead made in Ireland in the year 1744 by Mrs. Metge of Navan, Aerii Mellis Caelestia Dona.' (The heavenly gifts of air borne honey.)

The Goldsmiths Company of Dublin was supposed to test all silver for the quality of the metal and to hallmark it. But sending articles from far-off towns was inconvenient, slow, and dangerous because of highwaymen and footpads. Other centres went their own way and applied their own marks. Dublin's is a crowned harp, to denote the fineness of the metal, but also the town's mark. Cork's is a ship between two castles, or the word 'Sterling' with various spellings and abbreviations; Limerick's a gateway between two towers, or 'Sterling'; Galway's an anchor or ship.

Duty was imposed on plate in Ireland as it was in Britain, and special hallmarks were brought in to show that the duty had been paid. These are: the figure of a seated woman, Hibernia, who has a harp at her side, from 1730; and the sovereign's head, from 1807.

The dating of Dublin silver can be a complicated task because the usual date letter was in many cases not used. Subtle changes in the form of the harp and of Hibernia give clues.

Hallmarks

One of the oldest forms of consumer protection is the system of testing or assaying the quality of silver and gold and then stamping it with a special mark. But the hallmarks also give a great deal of other information – date and place of assay, standard of purity of the metal, and in many cases the maker's identity and whether duty had been paid (at the times when the law required duty).

As association of goldsmiths (the term goldsmiths includes silversmiths) existed in London by 1180, for records show that in this year the association was fined for not having a licence from the King. And in 1267 a battle took place in the streets of London between 500 of the goldsmiths and 500 of the tailors: many bodies were thrown into the Thames. A statute of 1300 laid down that all articles of silver or gold had to be examined by the leaders of the guild and marked, if of proper quality, with a leopard's head. Gold was also to be tested and at a later date it too was marked at Goldsmiths' Hall. Penalties were imposed, including death, for infringement of the law. Two London goldsmiths were found guilty in 1597 of forging marks on substandard plate. Each man was nailed to

Coffee pot made in Dublin in 1772. The decoration includes a milkmaid and a cow: farmyard scenes and rustic figures are characteristic of Irish rococo silver. This piece is also enhanced by spirited floral chasing round the rococo cartouche

the pillory by his ears, fined 10 marks, and had an ear cut off. The maximum penalty for counterfeiting is now a fine of up to £400 or, for graver offences, imprisonment for up to 10 years.

Where was it made?

The leopard's head mark became the one used for London. Sometimes it has a crown, and the form of the crown varies from time to time. Such differences help to fix the period of the mark. By far the greatest amount of silver had, and has, the London mark. Other places and their symbols found on silver made between 1700 and 1830 are:

Birmingham: An anchor (from 1773)

Chester: The arms of the city, three lions on one side of the shield and wheatsheaves on the other. This was changed in 1779 to three wheatsheaves and a sword.

Dublin: a crowned harp and the seated figure of a woman, Hibernia (the latter from 1730).

Edinburgh: a triple-towered castle.

Exeter: a triple-towered castle.

Glasgow: The arms of the city – a tree, bell, bird and fish.

Newcastle: three towers.

Sheffield: a crown (from 1773).

Norwich and York also had assay offices and marks attributed to other towns are found, although they were not necessarily struck at authorized assay offices. Examples are Gateshead, Carlisle, Plymouth, Montrose, Aberdeen, and so on.

When was it made?

The date is revealed by a letter of the alphabet, which was changed once a year. The London cycle began with the letter A in 1478. When the alphabet has been gone through a new cycle begins again with A. Twenty letters only were used at the London office. Changes are made in the form of the letters or the shield round them, so as to distinguish between the cycles. It is sometimes hard, if the marks are worn, to tell the cycle to which a particular letter belongs but the problem can usually be resolved through the other marks and the style of the article. Assay offices outside London changed the letter at different times in the year and were not in step with the letters they used for particular years. London's letter for 1700 is E, Dublin's N, York's A.

What is the standard?

The lion signifies that the metal is sterling silver. Mostly the lion is in heraldic terms 'passant,' or walking forward, right forepaw raised, and looking ahead; sometimes it is 'passant gardant', or looking sideways. The lion passant was not used at the Scottish assay offices. A thistle was used by Edinburgh after 1759 and a lion rampant, or standing on its hind legs, by Glasgow after 1819.

The higher standard of purity made compulsory in 1697 required another mark; the seated figure of Britannia to be used in place of the lion passant. The leopard's head was at the same time replaced by a lion's head 'erased', or jagged at the neck as if the head had been torn from the body. The old standard was restored and the lion passant and leopard's head reappeared in 1720. The Britannia mark was not abolished and the Britannia mark is still in force for the higher quality of metal when it is used.

Who made it?

The whole system was designed to prevent fraud on the public; the maker of each piece had to be identifiable. It was laid down in 1363 that each master goldsmith in London was to have his own mark, which was registered at Goldsmiths' Hall. Symbols were the first type – perhaps a pun on the craftsman's name (for example a Bell), or perhaps the sign which stood outside his workshop. Initials began to appear about 1550. Records of the makers' names and marks kept at Goldsmiths' Hall in London were lost in a fire at the Assay Office in 1681. The marks were, it is thought, struck on metal plates and the names were recorded alongside on sheets of parchment or vellum. Only one plate has survived.

The Act of Parliament which introduced the Britannia standard also laid down new rules for makers' marks. Fresh ones had to be registered and they took the form of the first two letters of the surname. Restoration of the Sterling standard in 1720 brought yet more changes: the mark was to be the initials of the Christian name and surname.

Records of the London makers are fairly complete from 1697 to the present day.

What are the other marks that are found?

Silversmiths grumbled about the Britannia standard, partly because it was more expensive and partly because conservative members of the craft preferred old ways. A price had to be paid for the return of the old standard: the Government imposed a duty of sixpence an ounce on wrought plate, collected when the hallmarks were put on. Abolition of the tax came in 1758 because it was being extensively dodged but it was restored in 1784. This time an extra mark was put on to show that the tax had been paid: the sovereign's head mark. For the first two years of George III it faced left and after

Silver marks *(opposite page)*
a Leopard's head with crown b Britannia c the lion passant d the leopard's head e the Irish harp f the Glasgow arms g the Sheffield crown h the Birmingham anchor i the date letter for London 1716 j London 1736 k London 1756 l London 1776 m London 1796 n London 1816 o the sovereign's head for 1786 p mark of Hester Bateman, 1771, Bunhill Row q Hester Bateman 1787 r Peter Bateman with Ann and William Bateman, 1800, Bunhill Row s Paul De Lamerie, 1712 t De Lamerie, 1712 t De Lamerie 1732, St James u Philip Rundell, 1819, Dean Street, Soho v John Bridge w Paul Storr, 1817, Dean Street, Soho.

that to the right. George IV and William IV face to the right; Queen Victoria to the left. The duty and the sovereign's head mark were abolished in 1890.

An extremely rare mark, used between December 1, 1784, and July, 1785, is of Britannia standing. It was put on exported plate and showed that the duty had been refunded. If the article was brought back into the country, the duty would have to be paid. But the mark was put on after the article was polished and finished and so was liable to damage the appearance. After its abolition the duty was repaid on production of invoices and other documents.

Special marks are struck for special events: The silver wedding of George V and Queen Mary was commemorated by a Jubilee mark showing their heads in profile and used from 1933 to 1935. The coronation of Elizabeth was commemorated by her profile on all silver made in Britain in 1952 and 1953.

The present rules
A drastic reform of the law came into force on January 1, 1973, under the Hallmarking Act, 1973 – a highly technical measure which in some of its provisions was long overdue. (see page 109)

The process of assaying
Pure silver is too soft for use in objects which are handled, including coins; it has to be mixed with copper. But this gives a chance for the unscrupulous to defraud the public by putting in too much base metal.

Testing the purity was done with a fair degree of accuracy, by a process used for about 500 years but now replaced by more advanced techniques of chemical analysis. Tiny pieces of metal were scraped from different parts of the object to be assayed and were weighed. They were then wrapped in lead and put in a shallow porous cup of bone ash in a furnace. Air was allowed to flow into the furnace; the combination of heat, oxygen, and lead removed base metals from the silver and into the cup of bone ash. What was left was a button of pure silver. This was weighed; the difference between the original and final weights revealed how much base metal was in the original sample. The process is called cupellation, after the cup of ash – the 'cupel'.

The unit of weight
Silver is usually weighed by the troy scale. The troy divisions are:

    1 lb = 12 oz
    1 oz = 20 dwt (pennyweight)
    1 dwt = 24 grains

One troy ounce is equal to 31.1 grammes; and the avoirdupois ounce is slightly heavier than the Troy ounce:

avoirdupois	troy
1 oz	18 dwt $5\frac{1}{2}$ grains
100 oz	91 oz 2 dwt 20 grains

Mostly the weight of a piece is given simply in ounces, but if it is small, in pennyweights too. The troy pound is never used, no matter how heavy the piece may be. The tendency nowadays is to use grams instead of troy ounces.

Pitfalls

Forgeries

Out-and-out forgery is very rare nowadays but, for example, a large amount of spurious plate was discovered in London in 1880. The haul included 643 items of cutlery pretending to be of the Queen Anne period. Old forgeries have by now acquired a genuine appearance of age; and they may have been in the same family for years – a long pedigree adds to their credibility. False punches

This object is made up from a tankard, which forms the upper part. The bulbous lower part and the spout have been added; part of the handle is from the original tankard. The aim was to make the object heavier and more valuable. The hallmarks are for 1729

(the dies for stamping the marks) were sometimes made from copper and not, as the proper ones are, from steel. Copper punches give a blurred appearance to the marks. People who are in the trade and see genuine marks all the time can tell the difference. Another method is to take a genuine article, say a spoon, make a mould from it, and cast more pieces from the mould. But cast silver does not have the flexible feel of hammered silver. And in a set of genuine spoons the marks are not positioned identically because they are struck individually; a set of pieces faked in this way all look exactly alike.

Fakers sometimes make stupid mistakes – for example, to put on a tankard the mark of a maker who specialized in spoons; or to put a maker's mark alongside a date mark for a year in which he was not yet born or already dead. More subtle fakes give themselves away by flaws in the style or patina. Or perhaps the forger, wanting to do the job really well, turns out something that is too good to be true.

Some articles suddenly change their careers late in life. One of the most extraordinary cases of this type is a tea pot with Elizabethan hallmarks. The Elizabethans did not, of course, take tea. The faker had taken a communion cup of the period, turned it upside down, and added a spout and handle. He was not to know that the original cup would now be worth a fortune compared with

Faked apostle spoons. This type of spoon was made in the sixteenth and seventeenth centuries as christening presents for children of wealthy families. At the end of each spoon was a little figure of Christ or an apostle. The ones shown here started life as dessert spoons and have hallmarks for 1778. The shape of the bowls has been altered and the figures have been added

the monstrosity he was turning out. There are other tricks, all to make a piece look rarer. For example, an ordinary spoon may be shortened at the stem and altered at the bowl to become a caddy spoon: or its bowl may be made into prongs to become a fork. An eggcup may be given a perforated cover to become a pepper pot. The bowl of a punch ladle may be given a handle and spout to become a mint sauce boat.

Improvements

Another kind of alteration was done without nefarious intent. The Victorians often found eighteenth century plate not to their liking, so they sent it away for 'improvement.' A plain tankard would be given a spout; a kettle would be given a tap instead of its spout to convert it into an urn; a large plain dish would be given feet and fancy trimmings and become a fruit bowl. This practice reduces the intrinsic merit of the article, at least in the eyes of many people. Moreover, the law in Victorian times said that a piece whose basic use was changed should be hallmarked again. This was often ignored. When it was done, the article has marks of a later date than the original date of manufacture, which makes it of no great antiquarian interest to serious collectors.

The Victorians also had plain pieces embossed or chased in a florid style; they could hardly bear to see a flat surface without decoration. A revulsion against Victorian taste during this century meant attempts were made to restore embossed pieces to their original state. The results can be unsatisfactory, and the surface can never be quite the same again after two drastic alterations.

Duty dodgers

An Act of Parliament in 1720 laid down that a tax of 6d an ounce was to be paid on all new plate, as has been mentioned above. The aim was to reduce the trade in luxury goods as well as to raise revenue. Tax was paid when the hallmarks were put on. Ingenious ways of evading the tax were worked out. Some small object was made and taxed; then it was incorporated in a much larger and heavier article. Someone who looked at the whole article would think that the tax had been properly paid. For example, a dish about three inches across, properly marked, would be used as the base of a coffee pot. Detection is difficult: the article has to be heated and the solder melted – then the inserted piece comes away.

Paul De Lamerie made a ewer in 1736 for Philip Yorke, Baron Hardwicke, later Lord Chancellor. Its hallmarks and De Lamerie's own mark are on a small disc soldered into the piece, between the foot and the body. The ewer, now in the Victoria and Albert

Museum, is a duty dodger. Perhaps De Lamerie was responsible, perhaps one of his assistants. The duty, if it had been properly paid, would have been £2 19s – a sum worth saving.

Transposed marks

Hallmarks can be taken away from one article and fixed into another; they are then called transposed marks. This was done to dodge the duty and for other more unscrupulous reasons, namely to pass off inferior metal as being the right standard; or to make an article appear to be older than it really is, or by a famous maker.

Transposed marks can sometimes be detected if one breathes on the surface. The condensation shows up the patch.

Owners of silver which may be 'wrong' can have it examined by the Antique Plate Committee of the Goldsmiths' Company – a panel of experts who advise the Wardens of the Company on pieces suspected of contravening the law. Scientific tests are often carried out on the articles to assist the Committee.

The Hallmarking Act of 1973 substantially altered the law about dubious pieces. It was an offence, until the Act came into force, knowingly to possess a piece with forged or transposed marks including a duty dodger. Such a piece could not be legally sold unless the old marks were obliterated and fresh ones put on. This was unsatisfactory from the collector's point of view if the forgery or transposition was an old one. The old marks are always of interest; and new marks on an old piece are out of character and period.

Now the old marks do not have to be obliterated, providing they were struck on the article or transposed into it before 1854; they are instead cancelled with a thin line. New marks are not necessary. It is still an offence knowingly to possess a piece of silverware with counterfeit or transposed marks which were struck or transposed after 1854: the object should be taken to an assay office for the marks to be obliterated and replaced.

Much heartbreak has been caused by failure in the past of some silversmiths to have their products marked at an assay office. They simply punched their own mark several times. It is thought that this was done when a client brought along some of his silver which was worn, damaged, or out of fashion and got the silversmith to use the metal in making other articles. The practice of putting on maker's marks only may not have been an infringement of the law because the articles were never actually sold: the deal between craftsman and client was just for remaking.

It was strictly speaking an offence to sell articles which had only makers' marks. Enforcement was impractical because so much silver of this kind is about. The Hallmarking Act 1973 laid down that articles with only makers' marks can be legally sold if manufactured before 1900 and not subsequently altered. The same rule applies to all articles made before 1900 which were not hallmarked. They can now be legally sold as silver if the metal is at least 80 per cent pure and the article has not been altered since 1900. This is especially helpful to owners of Victorian jewellery which was often unmarked.

The Act gave a new name to the old 'maker's mark.' It is now called the 'sponsor's mark.' Specialization in the craft is very ancient. A document of the Goldsmiths' Company, written in 1607, says: "Very few workmen are able to furnish and perfect a piece of plate singularly . . . without the help of many and several hands, which inconvenience is grown by reason that many of the idler sort betake themselves to the sole practice and exercise of one slighte and easy part . . ."

The time has long since passed when each costly article was made to order, after a discussion between the client and the silversmith. The eighteenth century saw, as has been mentioned, a growth in partnerships; some workshops became quite large. Mass production and the springing up of retail shops continued the process. The term 'maker's mark' became a misnomer because it really signified not the hand of one man but the hands of many – designer, engraver, caster, chaser, retailer, and so on. This is why the term 'sponsor's mark' was adopted – to show the identity of the person who is responsible for the whole manufacture and who submits the article for assay.

The Hallmarking Act modernized and codified the whole system and ruthlessly pruned ancient and sometimes curious laws such as the 'Act for encouraging the bringing in wrought plate to be coined' of 1696, the 'Act for continuing the Act made in the eighth year of His late Majesty's reign for better preventing the counterfeiting the current coin of this kingdom' of 1702, certain parts of the Common Informers Act of 1951, and so on.

Wear and repair

Worn marks detract from the value; they ought to be almost perfect if they are in a position where the article will not usually be polished, such as the base of a tankard.

Polishing also wears away the high parts of embossing, where the metal has already been 'stretched' in the making. Holes may even appear in these areas. The bottoms of dishes are liable during use to be scored by the cutlery. These cuts are sometimes removed by heavy polishing; but that makes the metal thin, which is undesirable.

Crests and coats of arms, if well engraved and if done when the piece was made, are attractive features. Yet they have in many cases been erased – again leaving the metal thin, and spoiling the patina. People seem to have been ashamed of owning plate with the arms of someone else.

Such thin areas may have been replaced with a new patch of silver, which detracts from the value. Very many articles were given crests, coats of arms, or initials – not only to show family pride but also as a discouragement to thieves.

Matthew Boulton

Collectors of many kinds of objects – silver, coins and medals, Sheffield plate, buttons, buckles, and other things – owe a debt to one of the geniuses of the industrial revolution, Matthew Boulton. His factory at Birmingham was one of the tourist sights of the country; he pioneered the use of James Watt's steam engines; he was skilled at publicity; he was a friend of leading intellectuals; he helped to bring beautiful objects within the financial means of more and more people. Yet he was rather an inefficient business man, sometimes neglected his family, and was often in imminent risk of bankruptcy.

Boulton was born in 1728; his father, also called Matthew, was a fairly well-to-do maker of buttons and buckles in Birmingham. The young Matthew took over the business when his father died in 1759. The great factory was built at Soho, close to Birmingham, between 1759 and 1766, at a spot where water power was available. The original estimate was £2000 and the final cost £10,000 – a typical state of affairs with Boulton. Letters from his partner John Fothergill tell about their financial straits – he wrote in 1771: "What will become of us I can't be answerable;" and in 1773: "We are entirely out of luck respecting money matters and we have this day ransacked the whole town for cash without effect and our situation becomes every day more critical and serious, for God's sake, do try to procure some money before you leave London . . . I am already at a loss what steps to take in this unhappy situation."

The troubles sprang from several causes. Boulton did not work out the true cost of many of the products he was selling, and so the public was getting them too cheaply. Vast unsold stocks accumulated, locking up capital. Management and supervision were slack.

Capital came from his first wife, Mary Robinson, the daughter of a rich mercer of Lichfield. They were married for eight years but all their children were either stillborn or died in childhood.

Matthew Boulton, by an unknown artist

Mary died in the same year as the elder Matthew Boulton, and the younger Matthew married her sister Anne, in 1760. His second wife brought him a considerable dowry, most of which was probably swallowed up in the building of the Soho factory. They had a boy and a girl, but Anne was found mysteriously drowned in 1783; she was described as 'subject to fits'. Their daughter, also Anne, had a diseased hip all her life and their son, Matthew, seems to have been a slightly disturbed person.

Birmingham at this time was full of able, energetic, and inquiring men. The city was unhampered by trade guilds and welcomed Dissenters. The Lunar Society, which met about the time of the full moon, brought together some of the most remarkable

One of a pair of ewers in blue john and ormolu, 19¼ inches (49 cm) high, supplied by Boulton and Fothergill in 1772 to the Earl of Sefton. The price (for the pair) was 14 guineas

Salt cellar in Sheffield plate, by Matthew Boulton, of about 1780. It is 5½ inches high, has a blue glass liner, and is gilded. Sheffield plate was gilded only rarely (left)

men of the time. Members included Boulton, the scientist Erasmus Darwin, the potter Josiah Wedgwood, the philosopher and man of science Joseph Priestley, the master printer and typographer John Baskerville, and the engineer James Watt.

Among the inventions which Boulton used were rolling mills and stamping mills for the quick, mass production of articles in silver or Sheffield plate. Silver was rolled very thin and then the patterns were stamped out with steel dies. These parts could be assembled into all sorts of silver ware such as candlesticks, salt cellars, and teapots; or used for such simple pieces as spoons and forks.

Sheffield plate was also made by machinery; it is a base of copper with a thin coating of silver. It had, when new, all the appearance of silver at a fraction of the cost – another source of trouble to the London silversmiths. Output of Sheffield plate was enormous.

Soho was still making the bread-and-butter stuff such as buttons, buckles, and snuff boxes; and more luxurious articles such as steel sword hilts and mounts of gilded brass for clocks, furniture, and vases.

Fothergill wrote in 1773: "Having continually many irons in the fire, has been the occasion of our present and perhaps future distress!" Boulton built up a vast organization and needed a huge volume of orders which sometimes fell hopelessly in arrears; he became a master of procrastination, as far as his clients were concerned.

His family life suffered too. He was constantly away from home on some business trip or other. His daughter was sent to doctor after doctor for her affliction. The treatment recommended by the most eminent was sea bathing. His son went to school after school, three of them abroad. Boulton wrote in 1780: "Nothing could be in the least degree palliate this long, this cold, this very distant separation, from my dearest wife and children but the certain knowledge that I am preparing for their ease, happiness and prosperity, and when that is the prise, I know no hardships that I would not encounter with, to obtain it."

Financial stability and indeed wealth came from a partnership he formed with James Watt for the exploitation of Watt's improved steam engine. Watt visited Boulton in 1767 and 1768. It was Watt who perfected the invention and Boulton who was vital in bringing it into general use. As usual, bankruptcy constantly loomed while this was being done.

The steam engines were employed for one of the factory's great projects: the striking of coins, medals, and 'trade tokens,'

Pewter tappit hen: a Scottish measure, of the 18th century. It is 12 inches (31 cm) high. Strictly speaking, a tappit hen holds one Scots pint, equivalent to three Imperial pints. The origin of the curious name is obscure; the term is also applied to this particular shape. Other measures of the same shape are, for example, the mutchkin ($\frac{3}{4}$ imperial pint) and the chopin ($1\frac{1}{2}$ imperial pints). Tappit hens are sought after in Britain, the United States, and Continental countries, partly because of their pleasing shape and partly because of the name

the money issued privately by firms because of the hopeless shortage of small change. Presses for coining were set up in 1788 and in 1797 Boulton undertook the production of a new copper coinage for the whole country. Among the most famous of his coins are the 'cartwheels' which are pennies and twopennies – the twopennies of impressive and satisfying size.

All this does not exhaust the range of Boulton's interests. He was also involved in a special patent lamp; copying machines; mechanical paintings; spinning machines; and the beautiful stone found in Derbyshire, blue john, which he mounted in ormolu as vases and other decorative objects.

He died in 1809, aged 81, and he left £150,000. Young Matthew lived in luxury in Oxfordshire; Anne received a settlement of £5000 and died, unmarried, at the age of 61.

Pewter

A wit has suggested that someone in the future will collect old milk bottles – "the last milk bottles were made in the late 1970s; here is a fine example of a Unigate bottle, made in London in the 1960s". The throwaways of one age are the prizes of the next.

Loving cup of about 1700. It is $5\frac{3}{4}$ inches (14.6 cm) high and $6\frac{1}{2}$ inches (16.4 cm) across the top; the marks suggest hallmarks on silver. The term loving cup is now used to describe any two-handled cup; originally the type was probably for weddings and anniversaries but they were also for communal drinking of toasts

Pewter used to be thought of as a humble thing. Now almost every antique shop has some examples. The best pieces come up at the big salerooms. Learned articles appear in the fine art journals. Yet here is a field where someone can form a collection quite inexpensively. The scope is enormous although vast amounts of pewter have been exported to the United States. There are tankards, flagons, plates and chargers, salt cellars, spoons, measures for ale or spirits, snuff boxes, inkstands, even chalices and patens.

Pewter as an everyday material partly replaced wood, horn, leather, and primitive pottery. It was in turn partly replaced when technology improved and made cheap and elegant glass and ceramics available to all.

What we fashionably call recycling has almost always been the fate of pewter. The metal is soft and is easily dented or scratched. Worn or damaged pieces would be given to the equivalent of the rag-and-bone men and the metal re-used. Candlesticks were especially vulnerable because a candle left to burn to the socket would melt the metal.

British pewter has a character all its own. Derbyshire produced the lead and Cornwall the tin. The Scots were excellent craftsmen. British pewter depends on good material and workmanship: the Continental pewter was more ornate and, some people think, often of poorer quality.

A handsome piece: a monteith of about 1700. It is 8½ inches (21.5 cm) high and 14 inches (35.6 cm) across the top. Such items are rare

The golden age of pewter, if such a term can be used, was from about 1666 to about 1705. Earlier items are rare and costly; but a great deal has survived from the best period and even more from the 18th and 19th centuries. The material had a late flowering when it was used by designers and artists of the Art Nouveau movement.

The trend for collectors is to specialize in, for example, a whole range of plates, or matching measures for ales and spirits.

The patina of old pewter is delightful, with a glow and texture unparalleled in any other kind of object. Another joy in collecting pewter is in the detective work. Countless faked pieces have been made since the 1920s. It is not difficult to take a plaster cast of a genuine piece and mould a forgery. Rather more difficult is making the surface of the new object appear old. Pewter becomes oxidized, flaked and pitted with age; the forger has to reproduce in hours or days what naturally takes place over decades or even hundreds of years. Some forgeries more than 50 years old are now showing signs of age in the usual way. Experience in handling many pieces is the only sure way of being able to detect true from false.

Another danger lies in genuine items which have been given spurious decoration or inscriptions – such as dates – to make them more interesting.

Pewter has in fact often pretended to be something that it is not – silver. So modern forgeries give the story a somewhat ironic twist. The pewter craftsmen borrowed designs from the silversmiths. The products when new and highly burnished were not unlike silver at a distance and at a casual glance. To add to the deception, imitation hallmarks were added. This angered the silversmiths, who tried through the Goldsmiths' Company to have the practice stopped.

The Pewterers' Company governed the craft in London – at least in theory – for hundreds of years; it was first officially recognized in 1348. Other guilds existed outside London, for example in York and Edinburgh. The Pewterers' Company was concerned with the product's quality and the registration of craftsmen. In some respects it was a closed shop for the benefit of its members.

Every pewterer in London who completed his apprenticeship and set up business on his own had to register his special mark or 'touch' on a pewter plaque owned by the Company. The marking with touches of all wares was made compulsory in 1503 – at least in theory. The plaques or touch plates were destroyed in the Fire of London. They were re-started soon afterwards and were kept up until the end of the 18th century, but a remarkable record had been lost. The touch plates for the guild at York have also been lost, but those for Edinburgh of the period 1600 to about 1760 have survived.

Items may carry a variety of stamps in addition to the touches,

Pewter marks
i originally intended as a mark of quality, later used indiscriminately *ii* mark used from 1688 to about the end of the 18th century, indicating standard capacity *iii* mark of John Cuthbertson, Edinburgh 1712.

but none of them signify the exact date of manufacture as is the case with silver and gold. Examples of such marks include the Scottish thistle, the harp or figure of Hibernia used in Ireland, the words 'Made in London', 'English Block Tin', a crowned X, originally to signify high quality but later put on indiscriminately, and so on.

Capacity marks on tankards and measures showed that they complied with the weights and measures regulations. These marks include 'hR', 'WIV', and 'VR', all embellished with a crown. Initials of a tavern keeper or the name of a tavern were intended to ensure that the thing was not stolen. (The slogan "If sold stole" has been found.)

Until recently collectors would look only at pewter – a mixture of tin and either lead or copper. The more lead, the poorer the quality; and lead is also dangerous as a container for food or drink. But now a kindred material is sought after: Britannia metal – tin with some antimony. It was invented in 1769 and became highly popular. Pewter was moulded and cast; Britannia metal was made in sheets and pressed. It could be fashioned with more delicate lines and more decoration. Early Britannia metal can be elegant or charming but the Victorians were inclined to ornament it heavily, with results unpleasing to modern taste. Dating pewter accurately is difficult because makers used their moulds for a long time.

Sheffield Plate

Status seekers in the eighteenth century who could not afford silver might make do with highly polished pewter; but the invention of Sheffield plate about 1743 provided a convincing substitute for the real thing at low cost.

It was the invention of a cutler in Sheffield, Thomas Boulsover (or Bolsover). A piece of copper and a piece of silver were fused by heat in a furnace. The two metals could then be worked as one, the copper always retaining its coating of silver, however thinly it was rolled. This process was the foundation of an important industry, especially in Sheffield and Birmingham.

Factories were also set up in Nottingham, London, Paris, St Petersburg, and elsewhere. The British products were widely exported, for example to North America.

Horace Walpole wrote in 1760: "I passed through Sheffield which is one of the foulest towns in England, in the most charming situation . . . One man there has discovered the art of plating copper with silver. I bought a pair of candlesticks for two guineas that are quite pretty."

Boulsover made small articles such as buttons and snuff-boxes.

A candlestick of about 1775, made in Sheffield. The decoration is in the Adam style with corn husks, scrolls, fluting and beading

His former apprentice Joseph Hancock carried the invention further by using rolling mills, and all kinds of domestic pieces were made, such as cake stands, teapots, candlesticks, dishes, and salt cellars. Another leading maker was Matthew Boulton of Birmingham.

But old Sheffield plate has two disadvantages. The first is that the coating of silver wears away with use, revealing the copper underneath. Countless objects must have been thrown away when this happened. The only thing that can be done is to have the object resilvered by the electro-plating method, a later invention. This reduces its appeal because the original character has been lost.

One other aspect of replating is that it may conceal the characteristic seams which show that the object is old Sheffield plate and not a later product.

The other disadvantage of Sheffield plate is that copper is revealed where the flat sheet is cut or the surface penetrated during manufacture. A teapot, for example, would have many edges where the copper might show. The craftsmen had several ingenious devices for getting round the difficulty.

Silver solder, silver wire, or plated copper wire were used to cover the exposed areas. The edges were also folded over so that only the silver showed.

Results were so convincing that the nobility, landed gentry, and wealthy people bought plated ware. They sometimes wanted their goods to have monograms, coats of arms, or crests. Silver ware could be engraved, but not Sheffield plate because engraving would reveal the copper. So sometimes a section of metal was cut out and replaced with a panel of silver or of very heavily plated copper; or a panel of silver was soldered on; or in later years a thin sheet of silver was heated and pushed into the surface.

Early pieces were sometimes given marks arranged so that at a casual glance they looked like the hallmarks on silver. This enraged the silversmiths, who managed to get the practice forbidden by law in 1774. Plated ware was not to have any marks at all. The rule was relaxed ten years later; around 1820 there was another outbreak of pseudo-hallmarks.

Makers within 100 miles of Sheffield were supposed to register their marks at the Sheffield assay office but marks were not compulsory and indeed not usually put on. Matthew Boulton used a sun and Roberts, Cadman, and Co. a bell. Marks are also found signifying capacity, the maker's stock number, or a particular workman who handled a piece.

Early examples were made by individual craftsmen but mass production became possible through technical advances. Ornament was stamped out in a very thin silver and soldered on to basic, simple shapes. Stamping was carried to extremes in the 1830s and 1840s when designs became highly elaborate.

Entire candlesticks, for example, were of thin metal filled out with solder. The hollow parts were strengthened with an iron spike and the rest of the space was packed with pitch or resin.

The proportion of silver to copper dropped, in general, steadily throughout the main period of production. One part of silver to ten of copper was common in the 1760s; by the turn of the century it was one to fifteen; and in the 1840s was sometimes one to fifty.

The last stage of the history of Sheffield plate began in 1830 when German silver (now called nickel silver) or another form of white alloy was used between the copper and the outer surface. This saved costs and helped to prevent the copper showing through.

The industry collapsed with amazing speed. The Birmingham firm of Elkingtons patented in 1840 the process of electroplating. Objects were made in a cheap alloy and the silver was deposited on them by the newly-exploited process. By 1862 the manufacture of old Sheffield plate was a rarity although the name Sheffield plate was

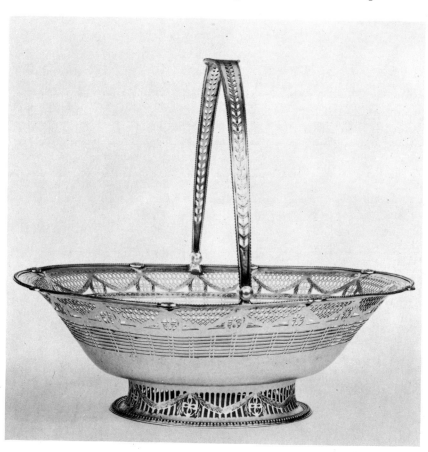

Cake basket made in Sheffield and 11¾ inches (29.8 cm) long. It was made about 1785 and the decoration is typically neoclassical. The handle can fold down

given to some goods made under the new process.

Wine coolers are popular because they are decorative and can also be used for holding plants or flowers. Coasters (trays for holding decanters or bottles at table), salvers, and candlesticks are desirable.

But a badly worn piece can be worth very little. Replating not only adds a modern element but gives a harsher, whiter surface than the original antique. Collectors of Sheffield plate are not as numerous and dedicated as of silver, but fairly strong interest exists in the United States.

Forgeries can be fairly old themselves but are often betrayed by crudity of workmanship. Points to look for in the genuine articles, apart from condition, are neatness of soldering and fine quality in the wire work and mountings.

Double wine coaster, 13 inches (33 cm) long with wooden base; about 1790

The cake basket, from above

Pottery and porcelain

Pottery and porcelain have different natures which notably affect their appearance and the ways in which they can be shaped and decorated. Pottery is simpler, less adaptable; porcelain is finer and more suitable for the greatest expression of the craft. Pottery is fired only until the particles of clay begin to fuse together; porcelain also contains other minerals and is white, non-porous, and translucent (unless it is very thick).

The secret of making porcelain was virtually unknown in Europe until the early eighteenth century. Some articles found their way overland from the Orient during the Middle Ages and it was regarded as an almost magical substance. Its whiteness, translucency, the delicacy with which it could be shaped, the brilliance of its glaze and colour – all were astonishing when compared with the qualities of ordinary pottery. It was kept in royal treasuries and mounted in precious metals. Kings and aristocrats lavished fortunes on it.

The Portuguese explorers were the first Europeans to reach the Far East by sea, in the early 16th century. Porcelain was naturally among the things they brought back and a thriving trade had grown up by about 1600. Yet Sir Thomas Browne wrote in the mid-seventeenth century: "We are not thoroughly resolved concerning Porcellane or China dishes, that according to common belief they are made of Earth." Immense quantities were imported by the East Indies companies of several European countries and had to be paid for in gold; the drain on Europe was considerable. Moreover, tea, coffee, and cocoa were becoming popular towards the end of the seventeenth century and seemed to taste much better when drunk from porcelain.

A European who discovered the secret of how to make this material would be wealthy indeed. Generations of experimenters tried to solve the mystery. The Venetians made an opaque white glass, like porcelain, between 1490 and 1520, but only twelve examples are known to have survived. A kind of porcelain was made in Florence in the sixteenth century but stopped after the death of the factory's patron, Francesco Maria de' Medici, in 1587. John Dwight, a potter of Fulham, London, tried hard but failed in the late seventeenth century.

The breakthrough in reproducing the fine hard porcelain of

China was made by two Germans, Johann Friedrich Böttger and Graf Ehrenfried Walter von Tschirnhaus. They first met in 1702 when Böttger was only twenty-one.

Böttger was an alchemist bemused by the medieval fantasy of discovering the Philosopher's Stone and transmuting base metals into gold. Von Tschirnhaus was a physicist and mathematician of repute. A third name has to be added: Augustus the Strong, King of Poland and Elector of Saxony. (Saxony was then the most powerful of the German States.) He was a stocky, physically powerful man. He could crush a horseshoe with one hand and had approximately 365 official bastards. He was obsessed with porcelain and in 1717 did a deal with Frederick William I of Prussia – 600 of Augustus's soldiers for 117 pieces of Frederick William's Chinese porcelain.

Von Tschirnhaus had been occupied in research for the magic formula as early as 1694. The Saxon domains were ransacked for the essential ingredients of the true hard porcelain – china clay and china stone; and the search was successful. Böttger's efforts to change base metals into gold for Augustus were of course an ignominious failure and Böttger was reduced to faking evidence that he had succeeded. But the collaboration began on a project that promised just as much wealth. The great breakthroughs came in 1708 and 1709, and work continued on perfecting the product. In the meantime the factory, at Meissen near the Saxon capital of Dresden, made exceptionally good red stoneware (a hard pottery which can be polished like a jewel).

Böttger died in 1719, aged 37. His health was affected by drink.

The early Meissen ware is tea caddies, beakers, cups, bowls, sugar basins, and suchlike. Johann Gregorius Herold or Höroldt reorganized the factory and improved the porcelain and colours, and especially the painting. From about 1730, design of figures was dominated by Johann Joachim Kändler, who did birds, dogs, monkeys, and squirrels; elegant ladies and gentlemen; beggar musicians; and characters from the *commedia dell'arte*. He was a genius at sculpture in miniature.

War dealt a severe blow to the Meissen factory. Frederick the Great had for long wanted to add Saxony to his dominions and very nearly did so during the Seven Years' War (1756–63). Saxony was crushed and many of the workmen from the factory at Meissen were removed to one at Berlin.

The secret of manufacture, so valuable to Meissen, escaped as early as 1717, to a small Viennese factory. Arcanists (those who knew the secret) defected from one factory to another for money; imposters or pseudo-arcanists tricked ambitious princes into parting with more money. Joseph Jakob Ringler received 100 ducats in

1759 for the arcanum, from Duke Carl Eugen of Württemberg. The same Ringler spread the word to several other places. Peter Anton Hannong sold secrets to the Sèvres factory in France in 1761 for a lump sum of £6000 and an annuity of £3000.

So rival factories sprang up, especially Sèvres which was heavily subsidized. Meissen ran out of creative ideas by 1760 and never recovered. But every factory in Europe owed a great deal to the pioneering that was done there both in design and technique.

The nature of the material

Porcelain is of two types. 'True' or hard-paste porcelain is from a mixture of china clay (kaolin) and china stone (petuntse). 'Artificial' or soft paste porcelain is from a mixture of white clay and a fusible substance such as ground glass. Soft paste porcelain scratches easily, tends to absorb dirt, and is fairly easily damaged by heat. Almost all British production during the eighteenth century was in soft paste; but at the end of the century a new body was evolved: bone china. It contains the ashes of animals' bones, an ingredient which gives strength and was first used at the Bow factory in the mid-eighteenth century. Bone china is compact and can be thinly moulded or thrown on the wheel.

Glaze, a thin film of glass, has several purposes. It covers the surface with an impenetrable skin – this is necessary if the body underneath is porous: it can be coloured for decoration: and it gives an effect pleasing to the eye and hand.

Colours can also be put on below the glaze or above it; the colours above the glaze are a mixture of glass and metallic oxides and are called enamels. Colours above the glaze have to be fired separately because they are fixed at a lower temperature.

Style

Porcelain began to be made in Britain when the rococo was becoming well established: the material and the style were a perfect match and a marvellous accident of history. Porcelain is totally adaptable to extravagant shapes and writhing scrolls. Cabinet makers had a far less tractable material with which to translate the rococo and indeed it was the carvers who had the best success. Porcelain was, however, not particularly appropriate for the neo-classical style and most of the factories went out of business at this time. The only one to survive to the present day is the factory at Worcester. Pottery was more suited to the neo-classical than porcelain.

Figures

Wealthy people ornamented their dinner tables with little figures of wax or sugar; they appeared at the dessert course. These objects were, in the early eighteenth century, replaced by figures in porcelain, more permanent, more attractive, and more fashionable. Horace Walpole wrote in 1783: "Jellies, biscuits, sugar-plumbs, and creams have long given way to harlequins, gondoliers, Turks, Chinese, and shepherdesses of Saxon China. But these, unconnected, and only seeming to wander among groves of curled papers and silk flowers, were soon discovered to be too insipid and unmeaning. By degrees whole meadows of cattle, of the same brittle materials, spread themselves over the whole table; pigmy Neptunes in cars of cockle-shells triumphed over oceans of looking glass or seas of silver tissue, and at length the whole system of Ovid's metamorphoses succeeded to all the transformations which Chloe and other great professors had introduced into the science of hieroglyphic eating. Confectioners found their trade moulder away, while toymen and china-shops were the only fashionable purveyors of the last stage of polite entertainment. Women of the first quality came home from Chenevix's laden with dolls and babies, not for their children, but their house-keeper. At last even these puerile puppet-shows are sinking into disuse, and more manly ways of concluding our repasts are stab-lished. Gigantic figures succeed to pigmies; and if the present taste continues, Rysbrack, and other neglected statuaries, who might have adorned Grecian salons, though not Grecian desserts, may come into vogue."

Figures for the dessert course tended to go out of fashion during the years 1750–1775; but others were made for the mantelpiece and the display cabinet. The newer figures were not viewed from every angle, only from the front; this influenced the design.

Blue and white

Most of the porcelain imported from China before the eighteenth century was blue and white. Practically every porcelain factory in Britain did at least some imitations of this style, even the potters of humble delftware. The home-produced wares were for everyday use and were inexpensive. Results are a charming mixture of European shapes, such as sauce boats, and decorations in chinoiserie. Much less than half the blue and white was marked, and telling what factory made a particular piece needs much experience. The best was in general made between the early 1750s and about 1770. The decline in quality was partly due to hand-painted decoration being replaced by transfer-printing, a more mechanical method.

Transfer printing

This remarkable technical advance was first devised in Britain. A copper plate was engraved with the design. The plate was inked and the surface wiped; this left some pigment still in the crevices of the design. A sheet of paper was pressed down on to the plate and the design was thus transferred to the paper. Then the paper was placed on the surface of the object to be decorated; the paper was peeled away, and the design remained. Firing in the kiln fixed on the pigment. The inventor was John Brooks, an Irish designer and engraver, who managed the Battersea enamel factory until it went bankrupt in 1756 (see page 234).

A variation on the method is called bat printing. The copper sheet was coated in oil, which was picked up by a flexible sheet (bat) of gelatine or glue and from that the oil was deposited on the surface to be decorated. Colour was dusted on and stuck to the oil; and the piece was fired.

Decorators

A factory which did not have the time or resources to decorate all its output might farm the work out to a contractor, or might sell quantities to a dealer who in turn farmed the work out. This had its drawbacks financially and artistically – others might profit, or the decoration might be so bad that the factory's reputation suffered.

One of the leading decorators in London was James Giles (1718–after 1780) who had premises in Camden Town and Soho. He worked on wares from Chelsea, Longton Hall, Bow, Worcester and Plymouth. This characteristic manner of painting can be detected on porcelain from several different places: cut fruit or exotic birds with dishevelled appearance. His handiwork adds considerably to the desirability of an object in the eyes of collectors.

Pitfalls

A factory in Paris has reproduced, since 1845, all kinds of old pottery and porcelain, sometimes so skilfully that many collectors have at some time or another been deceived. The firm, Edmé Samson et Cie, used marks rather like the ones of the factories whose products were being reproduced, generally also with the letter S. The difficulty is that unscrupulous people can remove the S with acid or by grinding, leaving only the imitation mark. Samson did imitations of the highly prized Chelsea, Bow, Derby, and Worcester wares of the 1760s and 1770s. They are not exact reproductions. The flowers and branches of the originals are too detailed to be copied by taking moulds; and the parts that are moulded from the originals are smaller because porcelain shrinks in the firing.

The Samson versions of British eighteenth century pieces are in hard paste while the originals are soft paste.

Other imitations by Samson include Meissen, Sèvres, and Dutch blue and white delft. Wealthy people in the eighteenth century used to order tableware from China with their coats of arms as decoration. Status seekers can still do the same from Samson.

Other dangerous pieces have been made to deceive, for example in Torquay, Devon; and some factories have plagiarized one another's designs and marks, turned out famous old wares for years and years, or indulged in outright forgery.

Another dishonest technique is to remove a simple decoration from a piece, redecorate it in a more elaborate manner, and refire it. Repairs are not usually done with fraud in mind, but can be dangerous. The merest hairline crack can drastically reduce an item's value; and for a figure to lose its head or an arm is a disaster:

> China, like women, should be kept with care,
> One flaw debases it to common ware.

So the restorer has a powerful motive for perfecting his art. One useful way of tracking down his work is to put a suspect piece under ultra-violet light. This will usually reveal any paint which is covering repairs. The addition of false marks is another pitfall: some especially prized marks are commoner on fakes than on originals. Ingenious people have made false objects and then broken and repaired them to give an air of authenticity.

Yet an old fake or reproduction can itself be worthwhile and collectable, for it shows what interested people at the time it was made. Samson's fakes have in recent years changed hands at higher prices than the originals. Most fakes subconsciously show the taste of the time when they were made. Marks are, then, by no means a reliable guide, even if a piece does have them. Far more important are style, body, glaze, and colour. A mark should be considered only after all these other signs about period and place of manufacture have been taken into account. Collectors should beware of gilding and colour which have been badly rubbed from constant use.

1: Pottery Forerunners of the eighteenth century

John Dwight has been mentioned as one of those who sought the secret of making porcelain but he is also important because he produced some notable types of pottery and a few outstanding pieces of what can be called sculpture in ceramics. His life is mysterious. He was born in Gloucestershire about 1640, took an M.A.

Slipware dish in dark and light brown, with a naive decoration of a plant and two birds. This is very different from the elegance and fashion which were achieved by the craftsmen in porcelain and in the refined forms of pottery

degree at Christ Church, Oxford, and became an ecclesiastical lawyer and 'register and scribe' to the bishop of Chester. How he came to run a pottery in Fulham, then in a village on the outskirts of London, is unknown. He took out a patent in 1672 for "the mystery and invention of making . . . stoneware, vulgarly called *Cologne* ware . . . never before made in England". Stoneware is pottery fired at a high temperature until it becomes extremely hard. The same patent speaks of his invention of "transparent earthenware commonly known by the names of Porcelaine or China and Persian ware". Another patent of 1684 mentions "marbled Porcellane", but it is most doubtful if he ever succeeded in making true porcelain. The ceramic sculptures, exceedingly rare, include small busts of Charles II and James II and a life-size bust of Prince Rupert. Others are statuettes of Jupiter, Neptune, Meleager, and Mars. The most moving of all is a half length figure of his daughter, aged seven, lying on her deathbed and holding a bunch of flowers. It is inscribed 'Lydia Dwight dyed March 3 1673'. Dwight did not model these figures himself but commissioned them; one theory is that the carver Grinling Gibbons did some of the work.

The scientist Robert Hooke wrote in 1673: "Saw Mr Dwight's English China, Dr Willis his head, A little boye with a hawke on his fist, Severall little Jarrs of severall colours all exceedingly hard as flint, very light, of very good shape. The performance is very admirable and outoing any European potters."

Dwight had considerable commercial success with his articles made for use: mugs, small jugs, and Bellarmines (round-bellied jugs with the face of a bearded man at the neck. They are supposed to caricature Bellarmine, a cardinal who was extremely unpopular with the Dutch during the religious wars of the sixteenth century. It is also said they represented the Duke of Alva, a Spanish general who fought the Dutch). Dwight used both coarse and semi-translucent bodies. He was trying to make porcelain by refining stoneware but was on a false trail. Some experimenters, including Dwight, were misled by a Chinese red stoneware which was thought to be a version of porcelain.

Industrial espionage and plagiarism were problems for all makers of pottery and porcelain, as has been mentioned in the case of the arcanum of porcelain. Dwight had the same trouble. He took out an action in 1693 against a group of potters for allegedly enticing away one of Dwight's employees, John Chandler, so that Chandler would betray his master's secrets. Among the potters Dwight complained about were several called Wedgwood and two brothers called Elers. The brothers were to have a crucial part in the development of the craft. Acquiring an authentic piece by Dwight is most

White saltglaze teapot, 4½ inches (11.2 cm) high. It is from Staffordshire and is in the form of a house. The handle and the spout are like snakes

unlikely because most of them are in museums and if any others came on the market they would be extremely expensive. But early stoneware from such places as Nottingham, Lambeth, Mortlake, and Bristol is fairly easy to find.

The Elers brothers

David Elers was born at Amsterdam in 1656 and John Philip Elers at Utrecht in 1664. They may have come to Britain after the accession of William of Orange in 1688. Both were trained as silversmiths, like many potters of the eighteenth century, and they used in their pottery shapes derived from silverware. The Elers brothers worked in Vauxhall, London, and Bradwell Heath, Staffordshire, making teapots, jugs, mugs, beakers, and cups and saucers. Decoration is sprigs of flowers, leaves, and other motifs in relief, delicate and beautifully finished. The material red stoneware, glazed or unglazed. Their teapots were expensive – 10s. to 25s. each.

The importance of the Elers was summed up by Josiah Wedgwood I, who wrote: "The improvement introduc'd by Mr E. was the refining of our common red clay, by sifting and making it into Tea and Coffee Ware in imitation of the Chinese Red Porcelaine by casting it in plaister moulds, and turning it on the outside upon Lathes, and ornamenting it with the Tea branch in relief, in imitation of the Chinese manner of ornamenting this ware. For these improvements, and very great ones they were for the time, we are indebted to the very ingenious Messrs Elers, and I shall gladly contribute all in my power to honour their memories, and transmit to posterity

Staffordshire lustre jugs in silver lustre and yellow. The one on the left shows especially well the use of the resist and the ordinary techniques

the knowledge of the obligations we owe them". But the Elers were declared bankrupt in 1700 and probably left the country soon after that.

They always worked in great secrecy. The story goes that they employed only half-wits so that their methods would not leak out; and that John Astbury and Josiah Twyford pretended to be half-wits, got employment with the Elers, and stole the secrets.

The Staffordshire potteries

Staffordshire provided a strategic centre for pottery manufacture, being well placed for many raw materials. It had adequate water for preparing clay and powering the water mills. It had plenty of coal and ordinary clay. Better kinds of clay were brought by sea from Devon and Cornwall, through Liverpool. Flint, to strengthen the clay in the firing, was brought from east and south-east England through Hull. Water-borne traffic was made easier and cheaper by the construction of the 'Grand Trunk' Canal: the link to Hull was completed in 1772 and to Liverpool in 1777. Cheshire, a neighbouring county, had deposits of salt for use in a special type of glazing.

It was in this district that many of the glories of British potteries were achieved. The wonders of Wedgwood are a long way from the primitive slipwares – pottery decorated with liquid clay, sometimes trailed over the surface from a quill.

Delftware

A Staffordshire cow creamer – a jug for cream, in the form of a cow. The tail is the handle and the mouth is the spout; the cream is put through an opening in the back which has a lid. This example is in black, brown and green and has a milkmaid as well. The same kind of design is found in silver; an example of how ideas are exchanged between different crafts

The poorest people in the early eighteenth century ate and drank from lead glazed earthenware, and the rather better off from pewter and delftware; it was not till later that more sophisticated kinds of pottery became cheap and available to all. Delftware is earthenware with a glaze of lead made opaque by the addition of tin. The word is really a misnomer because this pottery was made in many places – including Britain – long before it was ever made in the Dutch town. Its origins were Moorish Spain and Renaissance Italy, and it was first made in England towards the end of Elizabeth I's reign. The earliest dated piece with an inscription in English is a large dish with a view of a town, the words: "The Rose is Red The Leaves are Grene God Save Elizabeth our Queene" and the date 1600. This was meant for display and not for use. Ornamental plates called blue dash chargers were hung on a wall or put on a dresser. They have 'dashes' or splodges round the rim. Portraits of royalty or notables are favourite themes for chargers and in the eighteenth century the people honoured in this way included the Duke of Marlborough, the Duke of Ormond, Prince Eugene, Queen Anne, and Queen Anne's husband Prince George of Denmark. A few are found with George I and George II. (Many more have William III and other monarchs – perhaps the Georges were considered dull.)

The portraits are hardly portraits at all – indeed the prudent potters made one figure serve for several personages, simply changing the caption as necessary.

Chargers also show Adam and Eve with the tree and serpent, the Return of the Prodigal Son, Abraham about to sacrifice Isaac, Jacob's dream, etc. The type went out of fashion in the early 1700s.

But at this time appeared decorations in the chinoiserie style and the makers were more lavish with colours – bright reds, greens, and yellows. At the same time they still had the blue and white which many people associate with delft. The chinoiserie and the blue and white reminded the customers of costly Oriental porcelain.

Wine bottles, drinking vessels, and punchbowls often have charming inscriptions. Some potters sent a present of a punchbowl to the man in Cornwall who supplied them with tin. It is dated 1731 and inscribed:

John Udy of Luxillion
His tin was so fine
It glidered this punch bowl
And made it to shine
pray fill it with punch
Let the tinners sitt round
they never will budge
till the bottom they found.

Plates in sets of six have each a single line from this verse:
What is a Merry Man?
Let him do what he can
To entertain his guest
With wine and merry jest
But if his wife does frown
All merriment goes down.

Politics came in too. Plates were specially made for candidates in elections. ('Creswell Esq For Ever'.) The rising of '45 brought forth the slogans on delftware: 'No Pretender' and 'God Save the Duke' (the 'butcher' Duke of Cumberland). Jacobite items are rare. The revolt of the American colonists was commemorated by 'Success to the British arms in America,'

Events which caught the public imagination were good material, such as the ascent of Lunardi's balloon in 1783. Horace Walpole recorded the sensation that it caused: "Do not wonder that we do not entirely attend to things of earth: fashion has ascended to a

Delftware plates in several colours, to catch the interest in ballooning

higher element. All our views are directed to the air. Balloons occupy philosophers, ladies, everybody."

Frederick the Great, King of Prussia, was an ally of Britain during the Seven Years' War; Admirals Keppel, Ross, and Rodney were national heroes. They appeared on delftware.

More domestic happenings were remembered. Plates and other objects were made with the initials of an engaged or newly-married couple, and the date. (A date can add a great deal to the interest because it can help scholars to trace the development of a style or a material.) Captains or owners of ships could have bowls made specially to order, with a design showing the ship and a suitable motto such as 'Success to the Monmouth' or 'Success to the Africa Trade.' It seems that foreign vessels which put into British ports were also customers for this kind of bowl, for inscriptions have been found in Dutch or Swedish.

Plates and dishes are by far the most common things in delftware, and are decorated with ships, windmills, spouting whales, or simple floral patterns. But the range of other shapes is wide: everything needed for taking tea; sauceboats; wine labels (see page 244); tureens;

Blue dash charger of early eighteenth century. A naïve and folksy piece

ladles for punchbowls; vases – some with flat backs so that they can hang on walls; mugs and tankards; jars to hold drugs in apothecaries' shops; candlesticks; tiles; and slightly strange objects called bricks, which seem to have been made only in Britain. Bricks are rectangular boxes with holes in the top, either for flowers or for pen and ink.

Delftware does not have the elegance of porcelain but has a simplicity and directness all its own. The colour had to be applied quickly and mistakes could not be altered – the process was rather like painting on blotting paper. This gives spontaneity to the designs. A special form of decoration is called *bianco sopra bianco* – literally, white on white. It is not really white on white at all, but white on a slightly bluish white. It is most attractive when combined with decoration in several other colours.

Factories were established at Lambeth, Bristol, Wincanton, Liverpool, Glasgow, Dublin, and elsewhere. Ascribing pieces to a particular factory is tricky, and the potters very rarely put on their name or mark. The disadvantage of delftware was that it easily became chipped and scratched and it was not very good at resisting heat. Manufacture lasted until about 1800 but delftware could not compete with wares that were invented during the eighteenth century. The new ones were easier to mass-produce and easy to decorate with transfer-printing. Delftware transfer-printing was difficult to execute.

Tea and saltglaze

The custom of drinking tea had even more effect upon the potters than it had upon the silversmiths. Even a vigorous attack in 1757, by Jonas Hanway in his *Essay on Tea*, could not stop the trend: "We have abundance of milk; beer of many kinds; lime which we import from countries in Europe near at hand; infusions of many salutary and well-tasted herbs; preparations of barley and oats; and above all, in most places, exceedingly good water." Tea, he alleged, "when it is genuine . . . hurts many, when adulterated or dyed, it has been found poisonous . . . What a deplorable situation is that poor creature in, who having but three pence or a groat a day, consumes a quarter part or more of her income in the infusion of a drug which is but a remove from poison . . . The young and old, the healthy and infirm, the superlatively rich, down to vagabonds and beggars, drink this enchanting beverage, when they are thirsty and when they are not thirsty." Hanway urged people to 'follow the dictates of their own common sense' and 'disdain such a servility to custom.'

"Tea," he wrote, "which should by no means be exposed to the air, being brought from China in the packing of porcelain to serve the purpose of saw dust, or sold in the streets out of wheel-barrows, you must imagine will make a most delicious liquor!"

Dr Johnson was the greatest tea drinker of all but still said: "I have no desire to appear captious, and shall readily admit, that tea is not proper for the lower classes of the people, as it supplies no strength to labour, or relief to disease, but gratifies the taste without nourishing the body."

The Count de La Rochefoucauld visited Britain in 1784 and wrote: "Throughout the whole of England the drinking of tea is general. You have it twice a day and, though the expense is considerable, the humblest peasant has his tea twice a day just like the rich man: the total consumption is immense. The high cost of sugar or molasses, of which large quantities are required, does not prevent this custom being a universal one . . . it provides the rich with an opportunity to display their magnificence in the matter of tea pots, cups, and so on, which are always of most elegant design based on Etruscan and other models of antiquity."

Drinking tea required proper cups, saucers, pots, and so on. Porcelain was comparatively expensive; the older forms of pottery not very suitable for gracious living. A new ware was made in Staffordshire and elsewhere to meet the need: salt-glazed stone ware, from a mixture of clay and sand. It has a fine white body, does not soak up liquids, and can be given attractive decoration. Stoneware is dense and heavy and is fired at a high temperature. The glaze is achieved by throwing salt into the kiln; the salt combines chemically with the surface of the clay. It is said that when the salt was thrown in,

A teapot in salt-glaze, 4½ inches (11.2 cm) high, with a lady and a gallant in a pastoral landscape. On the other side is a rustic figure walking towards a building. The colours are green, puce, yellow and turquoise, outlined in black – in fact the range used in the common Oriental patterns of the period; but the shape and the views are characteristically English

thick smoke covered the neighbourhood. Salt-glazed wares have a pitted texture rather like the skin of an orange. The type had been known for a long time, but a refined version began to be made in the late 1720s: what had been a peasant craft was being turned into an industry. The great years were from about 1740 to about 1760 when technical advances began to make salt-glazed stoneware obsolete. It is, however, still used in the manufacture of pipes for drainage.

A huge variety of things were made in it: plates, dishes, teapots, mugs, jugs, cups. Ideas for shapes were often borrowed from objects in silver or porcelain.

Popular too were tea caddies, loving cups, souvenirs of betrothals, christenings, and birthdays, harvest flasks, and puzzle jugs – a source of harmless amusement, also made in other kinds of pottery. Puzzle jugs have a hollow handle which leads from the inside of the jug to a tube going round the rim. From the tube come several spouts. A drinker who is not in the know about how it works will get a soaking. The trick is to stop up all the holes except one and to suck the drink up through that. Some of the jugs have jolly inscriptions such as:

Here, gentlemen, come try your skill,
I'll hold a wager if you will
That you can't drink this liquor all
Without you spill and let some fall.

Monstrous and fantastic things were thought up too: jugs and teapots in the shape of camels, Palladian mansions, men-of-war (to celebrate Admiral Vernon's victories in 1739 and 1740).

Decorations took two forms – mouldings and colour – but they are not generally found on the same pieces. The mouldings are often in the form of handles and spouts like gnarled and knotted branches. The coloured wares are mainly in the Oriental style because of the prestige of Chinese and Japanese porcelain.

Another staple product of Staffordshire from the 1740s was a curious ware called agate, after the veined mineral. The craftsmen took clays stained in different colours and mingled them but did not thoroughly mix them. This resulted in a marbled effect. Of agate were made teapots and mugs and animals such as cats. The cats have been widely faked.

Sir Toby and others

Nothing seems to need ornamentation more than the British mantelpiece, and Toby jugs have had an honoured place there for more than 200 years. Their origin was perhaps a song called the Brown Jug, published in 1761. It tells of a great drinker, Toby Fillpot, who died and whose body became clay; a potter took the

A puzzle jug in blue and white delft from Liverpool, 6¾ inches high. How does one drink from it when the neck is pierced with holes?

clay and made it into a brown drinking jug. The song was published with an engraving of a fat toper. This picture may have inspired a real potter to mould a jug in the shape of Toby.

Manufacture of these objects is still a tradition. Sir Toby is the commonest by far, but the eighteenth and early nineteenth century potters also made highly desirable jugs of characters associated with conviviality: Bluff King Hal, the Squire, the Gin Woman, the Sailor, the Hearty Good Fellow, Admiral Howe, and Martha Gunn (she was a bathing attendant at Brighton who liked water – but not for drinking). All these figures are shown holding a mug or jar and sometimes a pipe. Other early Staffordshire figures for mantel-pieces are musicians, horsemen, portrait busts, figures from mythology, and animals such as deer, cows, rams, dogs, cats, horses, and elephants.

A pioneer was John Astbury (1686–1743), who is supposed to have acquired secrets from the Elers brothers by pretending to be a half-wit and getting work from them. He was the first potter to use ground calcined flint and is said to have been the first to bring white clay from Devon to Staffordshire. These ingredients produced a much better body than was previously possible. Astbury's characteristic is red, brown and black earthenware with a silky lead glaze, with applied reliefs in clay of a contrasting colour. The term Astbury is also given to imitations by other makers. Among Astbury's apprentices was Thomas Whieldon (1719–1795) who became one of the finest craftsmen of his time, made a fortune, and was appointed

Ralph Wood toby jug: Admiral Lord Howe, also called Man on the Barrel, 8 inches high

Whieldon teapot. The handle and spout are in the 'crabstock' form; the top of the lid is in the shape of a bird; the body has scrolled vines and is splashed with a mottled manganese (brown) glaze

High Sheriff of Staffordshire in 1786. Josiah Wedgwood I was in partnership with him for a while. Whieldon is noted for figures of drinkers, musicians, horsemen, animals, and gods. The term 'Whieldon' is given to the products of many factories as well as his own; they vary a lot in quality.

Whieldon also made plates, teapots, sugar basins, and suchlike table ware. He used splashy colours – green, yellow, brown, and blue. They have a tortoiseshell effect because his colours tended to 'run' in the kiln. He made agate ware as well.

One of Whieldon's workmen was Aaron Wood (1717–1785), who was a member of a great family of potters: many Woods made their mark, and they had many imitators. Aaron cut the moulds for salt-glazed teapots in the shape of camels, men-of-war, and houses. It is claimed that he also did a special form of ornaments for chimneypieces, called pew groups. They are naive groups of two or more figures sitting on a high-backed bench or pew. Sometimes they hold musical instruments. Their faces and details of their clothes are picked out in dark brown or black. Pew Groups, also made by other potters are, however, rare and beyond the reach of most collectors. Of Aaron Wood it was said that although he never swore, sang, or took snuff he was the merriest man in the country.

Aaron's brother Ralph, called Ralph the Elder (1715–1772), began to make his figures in the 1750s and was one of the first makers of Toby jugs. Among the other figures are Sir Hudibras, the hero of the seventeenth-century comic poem by Samuel Butler; St George; Jupiter, Apollo, Venus, and Neptune; and the Vicar and Moses. The Vicar and Moses group shows the vicar asleep in his pulpit while his clerk reads the lesson for him. Maybe the vicar has had too much to drink. Ralph Wood the Younger (1748–1795) continued to make figures like his father's and introduced new ones – for example, of Milton and Shakespeare. Enoch Wood, the youngest son of Aaron (1759–1840), did busts of Voltaire and the preachers Wesley and Whitfield; the Evangelists; the allegories of Prudence and Fortitude. He was one of the finest modellers.

Not many fakes are found but Toby jugs were reissued in the nineteenth century and these examples could be confused with older ones. The Vicar and Moses and other types have also been made in recent years. Portrait busts of the Tsar Alexander I of Russia by Enoch Wood have also been widely faked for some curious reason.

Prattware

Felix Pratt of Fenton, Staffordshire, has given his name to attractive

Prattware pipe in the form of a woman smoking, 4¾ inches high. The handle is formed of a turquoise dolphin and an eel; the woman wears a mob cap, spotted yellow dress and spotted blue apron; she strokes a marmalade cat on her lap. A folksy ornament for the mantelpiece, not for use.

figures, groups, and decorative wares dating from about 1780 to about 1820, but several other potters produced them too. Quality is variable. The colour is distinctive – bold yellow, orange, brown, blue, and green. The figures are children, heroes of the day, dogs, sheep, lions, horses, and cows formed as cream jugs (the mouth is the spout). Plaques were made in relief, for example of scenes from 'Othello'; stirrup cups: jugs with scenes of Chaunticleer and the Fox and caricatures; money boxes; pipes; watch stands. The themes of much more sophisticated makers were echoed in allegorical personages: Faith, Hope, and Charity and the Seasons.

Wedgwood

The greatest British potter of all, Josiah Wedgwood (1730–1795), was also a leader of taste, a brilliant experimental scientist and Fellow of the Royal Society, a supporter of the American Revolution, a campaigner against slavery, a pioneer of canals, a friend of George Stubbs the artist, and a good publicist and businessman. Yet he was the last of thirteen children and started work when he was eleven years old. He caught smallpox when he was twelve and this left him with an abscess on the knee which often prevented him from pedalling a potter's wheel; the leg had to be amputated in 1768.

He was in the fourth generation of a family of potters in Staffordshire and he was followed by five more generations. Wedgwood served his apprenticeship until he was nineteen and entered a partnership when he was twenty-four with Thomas Whieldon (see

The Wedgwood family in the garden of Etruria Hall, by Stubbs. The children in the miniature carriage are Mary Anne and Sarah; they are being pulled by Kitty. On horseback are, from the left, Tom, Susannah (mother of Charles Darwin), Josiah II, and John. Beside Wedgwood and his wife is a black basalt vase on a tripod table. The painting was done in 1780 and is $47\frac{1}{2}$ inches (120.8 cm) by $59\frac{1}{2}$ inches (151.2 cm)

page 134). Wedgwood was able to carry out experiments to improve the wares: it may have been the ailment in his leg that led his energies in this direction.

Pioneering days

Wedgwood, during the later years of the partnership with Whieldon, was associated with a deep green glaze which was quite new for earthenware. This was applied to tureens and teapots which were in the shape of cabbages, cauliflowers, and other vegetables. The invention was the forerunner of many more.

He set up on his own when he was twenty-nine in his home town, Burslem, and soon began to make a special product: a cream coloured earthenware which was based on a traditional sort but which he much improved and refined. Wedgwood described it as "a species of earthenware for the table quite new in its appearance, covered with a rich and brilliant glaze bearing sudden alterations of heat and cold, manufactured with ease and expedition, and consequently cheap". Creamware, with a hard glaze of lead, was better than delft, with its soft glaze of tin. Creamware could be processed in several ways – turned on a lathe, thrown on a wheel, or moulded. Immense quantities were exported and even the great Continental factories with royal subsidies felt the pinch of competition. A French traveller, Faujas de Saint-Fond, wrote: "In travelling from Paris to St Petersburg, from Amsterdam to the farthest points of Sweden, from Dunkirk to the southern extremity of France, one is served at every inn from English earthenware. The same fine article adorns the tables of Spain, Portugal and Italy; it provides the cargoes of ships to the East Indies, the West Indies and the American Continent."

Portrait medallion of George III

Portrait medallion of Queen Charlotte. Her patronage helped Wedgwood

Two strokes of luck gave the creamware the very best sort of publicity. Queen Charlotte, wife of George III, ordered a tea set of it in 1765. Josiah wrote to his brother in London who was helping in the business: "Pray put on *the best suit of Cloathes you ever had in your life* and take the first opportunity of going to Court". The Queen was shown samples and patterns. The tea set she ordered has, however, disappeared.

She gave Wedgwood permission to call himself 'Potter to Her Majesty', a title with immense cachet and commercial advantages. Wedgwood, like Matthew Boulton, knew well the benefits to be had from such patronage from the higher levels of society and named his creamware 'Queensware'. He once wrote: "Begin at the Head first, and then proceed to the inferior members". He also wrote: "Few ladies . . . dare venture at anything out of the common stile till authoris'd by their betters – by the ladies of superior spirit who set the tone".

The other stroke of luck was a commission from Catherine the Great of Russia for a table and dessert service of new fewer than 952

Trial plate for the Frog service, showing a stately home in Gloucestershire. The frog is lacking, which shows that this was not intended for the actual service pieces. The order came in 1773; the service was for her Palace of La Grenouillère. *Grenouille* means Frog and the service carries the emblem of a frog. (Almost all of it survives in the Soviet Union.)

The basic creamware for it cost only £52, but each piece was decorated with a different English scene: a house, garden, or view. This brought the final bill to 16,406 roubles and 43 kopeks, then about £2700. The Empress paid on the nail, to Wedgwood's relief. It is thought that the profit was small in terms of cash but it was large in terms of prestige. Special shows of the Frog service were put on in London; the visitors included Queen Charlotte and the King and Queen of Sweden. The nobility and gentry followed, especially those whose country seats were depicted on the service.

Bentley and neo–classicism

Wedgwood was on business in Liverpool in 1762 when he was laid up for several weeks by his troublesome leg. It was during this time that he met a man who was to be of crucial importance to the business: Thomas Bentley. Bentley was not only a merchant but also

Bowl with foot in tri-coloured jasper ware, 8 inches high, of about 1790. The colours are blue, yellow, and white

a man of refined taste, had travelled widely in Europe, had an excellent classical education which Wedgwood lacked, and was sensitive to the latest fashions in design. They worked together from 1767 and made a formal partnership in 1769. (Wedgwood had in the meantime married a distant cousin, Sarah Wedgwood: the couple were to have four daughters and three sons.)

The next invention after creamware was a dense black pottery with a smooth surface which in time took on a patina. This Wedgwood called basalt because he thought it resembled the mineral. Basalt wares were made in the neo-classical style; for example, reproductions of the classical vases found in tombs in Etruria, central Italy. They were then called Etruscan vases, although we now know that they were mostly made by Greek craftsmen. Sir William Hamilton, the British Vice-Consul in Naples, published illustrated books of his fine collection of vases; Wedgwood drew on the illustrations for his reproductions.

Portrait busts were made of basalt to adorn the libraries and public rooms of large houses. These pieces depict ancient and modern notables such as Homer, Demosthenes, Virgil, and Horace; Shakespeare, Milton, and Pope; Palladio and Inigo Jones; Voltaire and Rousseau. Basalt was also used for plaques and medallions.

The obsession with neo-classicism was shown by the name chosen for a factory which the firm built in the Potteries district of Staffordshire: Etruria. The ceremonial opening was on June 13, 1769, when Wedgwood and Bentley together made six copies of a black Etruscan vase. Wedgwood threw the clay and Bentley turned the wheel. The vases bore the inscription *Artes Etruriae Renascuntur* (the arts of Etruria are reborn).

Soon Bentley went to London to look after the sales end of the business; decoration of some wares was also done in London. The business acumen of the partnership is shown in a letter of Wedgwood's: "Deliver cards at the houses of the Nobility and Gentry and in the City . . . have an Auction . . . at the same time mention our rooms in Newport Street and have another Auction in the full season at Bath of such things as we have now in hand just *sprinkled over* with a few new articles to give them an air of novelty . . . and a few modest puffs in the Papers from some of our friends".

Again, he wrote: "Every Gentle and Decent push should be made to have our things seen and sold at Foreign Markets. If we drop or do not hit of such opportunities ourselves we cannot expect other People to be so attentive to them and our trade will decline and wither, or flourish and expand itself, in proportions as these little turns or opportunitys are neglected or made the most of." Bentley, in his turn, gave advice on taste and the market.

Leading artists were employed to design the ornament. John Flaxman, a brilliant young sculptor, was among them. He was, however, told that he must avoid nudity for his figures. Covering nudity with leaves was not enough – draperies had to do the trick "for none either male or female, of the present generation, will take [the products] if the figures are naked." Wedgwood may, however, have been prudish himself. He commissioned a painting from Joseph Wright of Derby in 1784 but soon wrote to him: "I could not speak to you when I was with the ladies at your home about the particular sort of drapery of the Corinthian Maid which I liked the least, but finding afterwards that some of the ladies had seen that part in the same light as myself . . . I begged Dr Darwin to mention it to you. The objections were to the division of the posteriors appearing too plainly through the drapery, and its sticking too close . . . giving that part a heavy hanging-like appearance . . . It is unfortunate in my opinion that the maid shows too much of her back."

Jasper

Most people associate the factory with the blue and white pottery with a matt finish, called jasper ware. It was inspired by one of Robert Adam's favourite decorations: plasterwork in low relief, on a coloured ground and usually with figures. Experiments to devise this ware took up a lot of Wedgwood's energies in the early 1770s. Success came in 1775, after maddening difficulties. Jasper has a pure

Queen's ware; the decoration is of convolvulus, about 1775

white body with a very fine grain and does not need glazing; it is impervious to water; it can be stained blue, lilac, black, sage green, or yellow by means of metallic oxides; when very thin it is almost translucent. Wedgwood said this ware was 'of exquisite beauty and delicacy'. Other factories paid him the ultimate compliment of imitating it widely and blatantly.

He used the coloured variety as a background for white figures in low relief. They fitted in very well with neo-classical taste, reminding people of classical marble statues. The figures were made separately in moulds and stuck on before firing. Articles made of jasper were small portrait medallions, cameos, bas reliefs, teapots, jugs, bowls, vases, cups and saucers, and plaques for chimney pieces. (Many plaques were removed from chimney pieces in Victorian times). Small ornaments of jasper were mounted on belt buckles, rings, lockets, necklaces, and bracelets, or used as buttons. Larger ones were set in furniture.

The masterpieces of his career were copies in jasper of the Portland vase. This famous work is Roman, of the first century BC, and is a dark blue, almost black, glass with figures of white glass in relief. It was found in a tomb near Rome in 1644, and eventually found its way into Sir William Hamilton's collection. He sold it to the Duke of Portland, who lent it to Wedgwood. The factory took orders for fifty copies of it in jasper imitating the original colours

Custard set in jasper ware of about 1790

and a few more with light blue instead of dark. Perhaps twenty-five or fifty were made and between sixteen and twenty are thought to have survived. These examples do not have any mark except a pencilled number inside the neck. Other versions were made in the nineteenth century with the Wedgwood mark but they are not of such good quality.

Medallions

Jasper and basalt were the materials for a large series of portrait medallions which were aimed at the collectors of the day, just as silver and bronze medals are now made for all kinds of anniversaries, notable events, and commemorations. Wedgwood had series of Caesars, emperors, all the Popes down to his own times, and what he called Illustrious Moderns.

The Illustrious Moderns were a greater commercial success than the Popes, who did not go down well in Protestant Britain; nor did Roman Catholic countries buy the Popes as eagerly as Wedgwood hoped. The Caesars, emperors, and some of the Popes were imaginary likenesses but the Moderns were done from drawings, portraits, engravings, sculptures, or commemorative medals, or from the life. They include a gallery of the great statesmen, explorers, scientists, musicians, writers, and artists; royalty and aristocracy; generals and admirals. Most tend to idealize or flatter the subject, especially if he or she is a public figure. More truthful are the portraits done on special commission from the sitter's family or friends. One of the most powerful depictions is of Edward Bourne, a brickworker at Etruria. Of this portrait Wedgwood wrote: "Old Bourne's is the man himself with every wrinkle, crink, and cranny in the whole visage". But William V of the Netherlands is shown with frankness: large nose, weak chin, flabby cheeks, and air of self-importance. A physiognomist would say it is easy to tell he weakened his country by getting involved in wars and that revolution forced him to flee to Britain. No more flattering is one of George III.

Some of the illustrations were more illustrious than others. Among the obscure are some French literary figures of the seventeenth century and British doctors of medicine. Even the famous do not include General Wolfe, Lord Clive, Gainsborough, or Hogarth. But they all do have one thing in common: none of the moderns is notorious or ill-famed (this could hardly be avoided with some of the Caesars and emperors). Perhaps Wedgwood's prudishness was the reason.

The artists who made the master models included Flaxman, William Hackwood, and Eley George Mountstephen, an Irishman.

Wedgwood by Wedgwood – a portrait medallion of Josiah I

Opposite page
Wedgwood vases in jasper ware. The taller one is 12 inches (30.5 cm) high, and is decorated with Venus in her chariot. The other vase is 10½ inches (26.7 cm) high, and depicts a sacrifice to Ceres. Both were made in 1790. These are from a set of three made as ornaments for a mantelpiece. (Wedgwood Museum, Barlaston)

Copy of the Portland vase by Wedgwood. It is 9½ inches high. Slight variations occurred in the firing and some copies may be larger or smaller than others

But Wedgwood discouraged them from signing their work and so few pieces can be said with certainty to be by a particular artist.

Prices varied from a shilling to five guineas or more. Sizes varied from less than an inch high to 17 inches by 14 for one of Peter the Great. The smaller ones were for mounting on rings, scent bottles, and the like; most were for keeping in cabinets or putting on the wall. Late productions and forgeries are sometimes traps. The main and most important series came to an end in the early 1800s with a change in public taste.

The British in the last quarter of the eighteenth century had a passion which has scarcely been paralleled for portraits of all kinds. Moreover, the cult of neo-classicism encouraged the collection of classical gems – hardstones such as chalcedony and agate carved with figures. The portrait medallion was akin to the classical gem.

Style and fashion

The pioneering work on new forms of pottery was important; but just as important was his understanding of the public demand for things in the neo-classical style. Creamware was very suitable for the newly-fashionable shapes – and indeed Wedgwood ware was one of the mediums for spreading this style to homes throughout the land.

Another key to his success was his understanding of the economics of taste. Other potters had access to canals and turnpike roads for cheap transport and fuel, or could, like him, organize his workers on a production-line system. But Wedgwood also knew how important it was to maintain quality and to keep in favour with trend-setters. The potters of Staffordshire in the first half of the eighteenth century tried to make a living by cutting costs and reducing quality. Wedgwood believed that this was harmful to the trade in general. He aimed for the best; his reputation was high; and he was able to charge much more than his competitors. He wrote, perhaps a little cynically: "Fashion is infinitely superior to merit in many respects; and it is plain from a 1000 instances that if you have a favourite child you wish the public to fondle and take notice of, you have only to make a choice of proper sponsors. If you are lucky in them no matter what the brat is, black, brown, or fair, its fortune is made!".

His other interests

Wedgwood's enormous energy took him into many enterprises only indirectly linked to his profession, or not at all. He was a leading sponsor of improved roads in his home district and helped to get legislation for them through Parliament. Roads were however not

Opposite page
Canary, $5\frac{1}{2}$ inches (14 cm) high, made at the 'Girl-on-a-Swing' factory in the mid-eighteenth century. The factory, about which little is known, was in London; its name is from one of the figures it made. (Sotheby's)

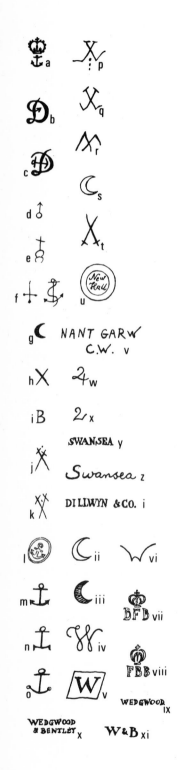

as useful to the industry as canals, which were better than pack horses for carrying heavy loads of clay and fragile loads of finished pottery. He was active in promoting the Grand Trunk Canal which linked the factories in Staffordshire with the ports of Hull and Liverpool. The campaign went on during the 1760s and the canal, 100 miles long, was completed in 1777. It cost £300,000. It passed Etruria and cut the expense of transport from 10d a ton a mile to $1\frac{1}{2}$d.

Wedgwood's election to the Royal Academy was partly to mark his invention of a pyrometer, which is a thermometer able to measure very high temperatures such as are reached in a kiln. He was also a member of the Lunar Society, the club for people interested in science (see page 111).

He was a supporter of the American colonies in their fight for independence, writing: "Somebody should be made to say distinctly what has been the object of the present most wicked and preposterous war with our brethren and best friends . . . I am glad that America is free and rejoice most sincerely that it is so, and the pleasing idea of a refuge being provided for those who choose rather to flee from than to submit to the iron hand of tyranny raises much hilarity in my mind". His attitude to the French Revolution was similar, at the beginning: "I know you will rejoice with me in the glorious revolution which has taken place in France. The politicians tell me that as a manufacturer I shall be ruined if France has her liberty, but I am willing to take a chance in that respect, nor do I yet see that the happiness of one nation includes in it the misery of its next neighbour".

He was a member of the committee of the Society for the Suppression of the Slave Trade, and his factory produced a special medallion as part of the propaganda. It was designed by the chief modeller at Etruria and shows a Negro, kneeling and holding up his chains; the motto round the figure is: "Am I not a man and a brother?". Hundreds of them were made, and wearing them became a fashion for a while.

A curious episode was the attempt, with the great George Stubbs, to produce paintings fired upon large ceramic slabs. Great technical difficulties were met and the success was limited. Stubbs also made, of basalt, some plaques in relief. They include one of Stubbs's favourite themes, a lion frightening a horse. The expense to the factory was considerable and was partly offset by a painting Stubbs did of Josiah Wedgwood and his family in the garden of their home, Etruria Hall (see illustration, page 136).

The four eldest children are on horses or ponies; Wedgwood and his wife are seated – he rather awkwardly because of his missing leg; beside Wedgwood is one of his basalt vases. The portrait is in the Wedgwood Museum in Barlaston.

His achievements, death, and the factory's decline

The Potteries district of Staffordshire was, when Wedgwood started his career, isolated and relatively unimportant. It was by the end of the eighteenth century a flourishing place, trading through Liverpool and Hull with North America and the Continent and in the early 1800s Etruria was probably the largest factory of its kind in the world. Wedgwood played a large part in the transformation. Gladstone said he was "the greatest man who ever, in any age or country, applied himself to the important work of uniting art with industry . . ."

Wedgwood gradually gave up business from 1790, when he was sixty. He was succeeded in the business by his nephew, Tom Byerley, and his sons Josiah II and Tom; the eldest son, John, had gone through an academic education and was not interested in the day-to-day routine at Etruria. Wedgwood died in 1795, very well-off.

His daughter, Susannah, later married Robert Darwin, son of his friend Dr Erasmus Darwin, a leading doctor and writer. Robert and Susannah were the parents of Charles Darwin.

The firm's greatest age was in the eighteenth century. Quality declined after the old man's death. Josiah II began the manufacture of bone china in 1812 but ended it in 1822. Trade was bad in 1828; the showrooms in London were abandoned and the stock-in-hand, moulds, and models were sold for £16,000 – a pity, because they were of great historical interest. Josiah II was an austere man of whom the wit Sidney Smith said: "It is a pity he hates his friends". The firm went through more vicissitudes but now is one of the biggest manufacturers of pottery in the world.

A treasure house of pieces is the Wedgwood Museum at the factory in Barlaston, including a copy of the Portland vase which was bought by Thomas Hope, the wealthy connoisseur who had such influence upon taste in the Regency period.

Marks

The factory was among the first to mark its wares consistently but marks were not put on all the early wares. The most sought-after marks are of the Wedgwood and Bentley partnership, although many of the products after the death of Bentley were of surpassingly fine quality. Competing firms used marks intended to deceive at first glance: the Wedgwood name but with one letter different, such as Wedgewood.

Porcelain marks (*opposite page*) *a* and *b* Chelsea – Derby marks, in gold *c* Chelsea–Derby, in gold, and rarely in red *d* and *e* Bow, early incised marks *f* Bow, painted dagger mark, about 1760–76 *g* Bow, underglaze blue marks, about 1760–76 *h* to *k* Bristol marks, about 1770–81 *l* Chelsea raised anchor, about 1749–52, sometimes in red *m* small red anchor, about 1752–56 *n* and *o* gold anchor mark, about 1756–59, sometimes on Derby pieces painted at Chelsea, about 1769–75 *p* to *r* Longton Hall, pieces are rarely marked, but these marks are occasionally found on early pieces *s* and *t* Lowestoft marks, copies of Worcester and Meissen marks, about 1775–90 *u* New Hall bone china mark, about 1812–35 *v* Nantgarw, impressed mark, 1813–22 *w* and *x* Plymouth painted 'tin symbol' about 1768–70 *y* Swansea, impressed or printed 1814–22 *z* Swansea, painted 1814–22 *i* Swansea, impressed, about 1814–17 *ii* and *iii* Worcester crescents about 1755–90, underglaze blue *iv* to *vi* Worcester, painted or printed, about 1755–70 *vii* Worcester, Flight and Barr, about 1807–13, impressed *viii* Flight and Bar, about 1813–40, impressed *ix* Wedgwood, impressed mark, about 1759 onwards *x* Wedgwood, impressed on ornamental pieces, about 1768–80 *xi* Wedgwood, impressed on small cameos and plaques, about 1768–80

Creamware

The refined form of creamware which was achieved by Wedgwood was taken up by many other potteries, and supreme among them was the one at Leeds. The ware is light and strong and can be worked into pieces of great delicacy. Among the finest are elaborate epergnes, sometimes more than two feet high, with urns and removable baskets, dishes, and jars. More ordinary but still most attractive are the jugs, teapots, coffee pots, plates, bowls, mugs, snuffboxes, sweetmeat dishes, and 'kettles' to hold punch.

Figures were naturally made too: foxes, hens, Ophelia, Hamlet, allegories of the Virtues, Air and Water, musicians, lovers, Andromache mourning at the tomb of her husband Hector. Decoration was of various sorts: mouldings with flowers and scrolls, coloured glazes, enamel colours, and transfer printing. The enamel colours were for flowers, landscapes, birds, and inscriptions such as 'God Speed the Plough', 'Success to Sir Charles Holte Esq' (a candidate for Parliament in 1774), 'Wilkes and Liberty', or simply, on drinking vessels, 'Ale'. Masonic themes are found too. Printed ornament includes portraits of Wesley; the Virtues; as well as flowers and landscapes.

An enormous trade was carried on with the continent – so great indeed, that continental potteries were obliged by economic necessity to make creamware of their own. The export trade had a curious effect which has indirectly been of benefit. Duty was charged by some countries on these imports and was calculated according to the weight. The British manufacturers cleverly reduced the weight by doing pierced openwork decoration, which required much skill. Catalogues were issued for wholesalers and retailers – not only in English but also in French, Dutch and Spanish. Some of the ware was exported in the plain state and decorated by continental factories. Turnover of the Leeds factory in 1791 was more than £51,500.

Some miniature pieces were made. These were not, as has been claimed, samples for salesmen but were described in the catalogues as 'toys'. They were for children or for adults who enjoyed building and fitting out elaborate and costly dolls' houses. Salesmen did carry samples but they were the full-sized specimens, kept in velvet-lined boxes to avoid breakages.

Donald Towner, collector and scholar, has written that in the eighteenth century the craft of pottery reached its climax in creamware "with its fine form, thin body, clean and brilliant glaze which formed a perfect background for the ingenious, harmonious, and free painting of the earthenware enamellers . . . it was the

A Leeds creamware teapot, 6 inches (15.2 cm) high, painted in red with an exotic bird among shrubs

prototype of the lead glazed earthenware that is manufactured today, though standardization and mass production have largely destroyed its charm, individuality, and beauty of potting and design. At its best it did not seek to imitate porcelain either in colour, form, or decoration, but remained essentially true to its English earthenware tradition. Even when the creamware potters sought inspiration from the work of the silversmith, the metal forms were freely adapted to form a more plastic idiom suitable to the clay medium."

The magic ingredients were quite different from the coarse clay of the primitive pottery – they were local clay, helped out by china stone and calcined flint.

A variation on creamware is pearlware, which has a greyish tint. Wedgwood invented the name although pearlware was a traditional Staffordshire product. He developed the line in the late 1770s because he wanted to feed the market's demand for novelty, but it was never as popular as creamware. Every collector in this field wants to own one of the 'Leeds horses', which are 15 or 16 inches high. They are technical triumphs: they stand unsupported and their legs are thin and delicate. It is thought that they were made as advertising displays for the shop windows of harness makers and other tradesmen who supplied the needs of horsemen. Perhaps other factories as well as Leeds made them.

Attributing creamware to one or other of the many factories is difficult. Leeds rarely used a mark but when it did the mark was LEEDS * POTTERY. Reproductions are common and have discouraged some people from going in for creamware. A firm in Leeds early in this century used old pattern books and old moulds to imitate the original and genuine article. Sometimes examples of the French version of creamware turn up but are yellow and coarse compared with the British. In general creamware is inexpensive compared with other kinds of old pottery.

Lustre ware

This is characteristically British and many of the pieces with lustre decoration are of great social interest: they reflect the humour, interests, aspirations, and fears of the ordinary people in a way that is ignored by conventional history books.

The metallic sheen was developed in Staffordshire by about 1790 and production was in full swing by about 1800. The effect was achieved through applying a thin film of dissolved gold or platinum. Gold results in different hues according to the colour of the pottery underneath: on brown or black, a coppery shade; on white or cream, various reddish shades from pale rose through pink to deep purple. The commonest is pink.

Platinum results in a silvery colour. This process was used to make substitutes for silver plate and Sheffield plate – and the pottery has the advantage of not needing to be polished. Massive objects were entirely covered in silver lustre. They are not very attractive to present-day collectors. Deposits of platinum were found by the Spanish conquerors in South America. It was always expensive, but the potters were able to dilute it greatly.

Much more attractive is 'resist lustre'. Parts of the surface were covered in a waxy or greasy substance before the metallic wash was applied. The substance 'resisted' the wash and the parts underneath were left plain. Another way of achieving roughly the same effect was to apply colour to a lustred surface by means of a paper stencil.

Almost every object made in pottery was decorated with lustre, although tea and table ware are the most common. The Wedgwood factory specialized in a pink all-over lustre with a peculiar mottled effect called moonlight lustre. One might dare to say it is rather garish – but Wedgwood has a devoted band of collectors who will leap to defend their specialism. Moonlight lustre was mostly made between 1810 and 1815.

One of the main centres of production was Sunderland, County Durham, and many jugs commemorate the famous iron bridge over the river Wear in Sunderland. This prodigy of engineering had a span of 236 feet. It was built in 1796 and rebuilt in 1859 and 1929. At least 28 kinds of jug with a view of the bridge have been recorded.

Part of a coffee service in copper lustre: all the dark parts are in lustre. About 1810

Some other pieces have a nautical flavour (Newcastle and Swansea were among the centres of manufacture and they may have had a souvenir trade with seamen.) One jug is inscribed:

From rocks and sands
And barren lands
Kind fortune keep me free
And from great guns and women's tongues
Good Lord deliver me.

Chamber pots are fairly common and are found with inscriptions such as this on a double-handled specimen:

Dear lovely wife pray rise and p-ss,
Take you that handle and I this.
This present which to us is sent,
To make some mirth it seems was meant.
So let it be as they have said,
We'll laugh and p-ss and then to bed.

Other inscriptions give the flavour of this folk art:

Success to the Fleece
To the Plough and the Sail.
May our Taxes grow Less
And our Commerce ne'er Fail.

The 'Negro's Complaint,' dating from the anti-slavery campaign, reads:

Fleecy locks and black complexion,
Cannot forfeit nature's claim:
Skin may differ but affection,
Dwells in white and black the same.
Slaves of gold whose sordid dealings
Tarnish all your bloated powers:
Prove that you have human feelings
Ere you boldly question ours.

The more fanciful lustre ware objects include watch holders (stands on which to hang the watch at night); chimney ornaments such as animals and figures of Napoleon, the Duke of Wellington, Nelson, and Wesley; and joke mugs (as you drink and as the level of the contents falls, a hideous frog is revealed).

It is generally hard to ascribe unmarked pieces to a factory and a period. Lustre was made in the Victorian era as well as the Regency and reproductions of modern date are about, so caution is important. Much of the ware is crude. The most valuable and interesting dates from the early 1800s. Something to look out for is silver resist with a canary yellow background, rare and popular with collectors.

Commemorative ware

The tradition of issuing specially made pieces to commemorate newsworthy events has been established for nearly two centuries. But the antique ones seem far more robust and down-to-earth than the modern. Our ancestors loved to record victories, disasters, social reforms and other political matters, and the lives and deaths of royalty and statesmen.

The jugs, plates, mugs, and so on began to appear in large numbers around 1780: technical advances and mass production had brought down prices. Hardly a single example exists which does not have rich associations, and the collector can get a lot of pleasure from research into the background. For example, articles were made in the 1780s which have the head of George III and the rhyme: "Britons Rejoice, Cheer up and Sing and drink this Health, God Save the King". Such items were for the Tories worried about the King's bout of madness and fearful that they would lose their ally.

Staffordshire jug to commemorate the boxing matches between Tom Cribb and Tom Molineaux. It is 5⅝ inches high with lustre decoration and a black transfer-printed scene. Cribb (1781–1829) was the English champion when he twice defeated Molineaux, in 1810 and 1811. Molineaux was formerly a slave in the United States

Royalty is a recurrent theme, although a lot depended on whether the sovereign was popular or not at a particular time. The bitter estrangement between the Prince Regent (later George IV) and his wife Caroline resulted in the extraordinary escapade when she tried to enter Westminster Abbey for his coronation and was turned away. A piece dating from shortly after her death has

> T'is true out Gracious Queen has di'd
> No Peace for her on Earth was giv'n
> And they on Earth a Crown deny'd.
> We hope she'll wear a crown in Heaven.

Naval and military victories gripped people's imaginations. A seaman, Jack Crawford, achieved imperishable fame at the battle of Camperdown:

> At Camperdown we fought
> And when at worst the fray
> Our mizzen near the top, boys,
> Was fairly shot away.
> The foe thought we had struck,
> But Jack cried out 'Avast'
> And the colours of old England
> He nailed up to the mast.

Nelson and Wellington were hero-worshipped. Nelson was shown surrounded by laurel wreaths, symbols of war, and:

> Show me my country's foes
> The Hero cry'd
> He saw – He fought – He conquer'd
> And he died.

Propaganda was not ignored. A delightful mug of about 1800 has a picture of a fat man with a bottle of wine, a foaming mug of beer, and carving a joint of meat. The inscription says: "BRITISH SLAVERY. Ah! this cursed Ministry, they'll ruin us all with their damn'd Taxes! Why zounds, they're making slaves of us all and starving us to Death."

Transfer printing was very common and sometimes the copper plates were reworked so that they could be used for a new hero or a new event. The real heyday was in Victorian times and some of these later pieces are reproductions of old ones. The surrender of Cornwallis to Washington at Yorktown in 1781 is an example: the vanquished is handing over his sword to the victor. This theme was used throughout the nineteenth century on pieces for export to the United States. Style and type of pottery give a clue to the real date of doubtful items.

The people's humour: This mug is decorated with a story which also appears in the form of grouped figures. It concerns a greedy parson and a poor woman who tries to hand him her child instead of her pig as a tithe:

"In Country Village lives a Vicar
Fond – as all are – of Tythes and Liquor
To Mirth his Ears are seldom Shut
He'll Crack a Joke and laugh at Smut
But when his Tythes he gathers in,
True Parson then – no Coin no Grin
On Fish, on Flesh, on Bird, on Beast
Alike lays hold the Churlish Priest.
Hob's wife and son as Gossips tell
Both at a time in pieces fell.
The Parson comes, the Pig he claims,
And the good Wife with taunts inflames.
But she quite Arch bow'd low and smiled
Kept back the Pig and held the Child.
The Priest looked Gruff, the wife looked Big
L . . . ds Sir! quoth she, no Child, no Pig"

2: Porcelain

Chelsea

Of all the porcelain made in Britain, Chelsea is the most famous and the finest, and the factory was almost certainly the first to be set up. It was for a long time the only one in Britain to concentrate on the carriage trade. Yet it lacked the huge subsidies received by the great factories on the Continent: the stolid Havoverian kings of the mid-eighteenth century had no ambitions to venture into that kind of costly status-seeking.

The origins and history are obscure because much important information has been lost. The founders seem to have been two Huguenots, Nicholas Sprimont (1716–1771), a silversmith from Liège, and Charles Gouyn, a jeweller who had acquired some knowledge at the St Cloud factory in France and who probably put up capital. They recruited craftsmen from Staffordshire and output seems to have started about 1743. Sprimont prudently kept up his work as a silversmith until at least 1747.

Chelsea's products are traditionally divided into four categories, according to its four types of marks, but the division is rather artificial because a change in mark did not necessarily come at the same time as a change in style or materials. The marks and their approximate dates are:

Incised triangle (1743–1750): a triangular outline was cut into the porcelain. Pieces of this period show great imagination and brilliant use of material, but they are rare and found mainly in museums and rich private collections. Designs were borrowed from silverware – for example, a little cream jug which incorporates a goat and a bee. Sprimont's own designs would naturally reflect his background as a silversmith. Oriental porcelain was copied; so too was Meissen. Sir Everard Fawkener, secretary to the Duke of Cumberland, went to Dresden in 1749, brought back Meissen figures, and lent them to the factory. Moulds were taken direct from them. Sprimont borrowed a Meissen service in 1751.

Gouyn seems to have given up his partnership by 1750; Fawkener may have helped the factory to expand at this point.

Raised anchor (1750–1752): the motif was on a small oval pad or medallion. This is some of the loveliest porcelain of all. Figures of birds were made; the source for them was George Edward's *Natural History of Uncommon Birds,* published in two parts in 1743 and 1747. But Meissen was becoming more and more the great influence on Chelsea – for example, in the figures from the Italian comedy

Chelsea vase and cover, 12½ inches (31.5 cm) high. An elaborate and florid piece. The handles are enriched with gilding; the scene, of excellent quality, is La Leçon de Flute and is derived from a painting by Boucher; more gilding is on the body of the vase; the ground colour is mazarine blue. Gold anchor mark

(Harlequin, Columbine, Pierrot, Punchinello, and so on) and of ordinary but picturesque characters such as a hurdy-gurdy player. More original are plates excellently decorated with illustrations of the fables of Aesop, perhaps done by Jefferyes Hamett O'Neale, who later worked at Worcester.

Another notable line was a series of plates, decorated with flowers, which are called after Sir Hans Sloane (1660–1753), a physician, scientist, philanthropist, and collector. They have, however, almost nothing to do with him. He founded a botanical garden in Chelsea; the head of the garden, Philip Miller, published a book on plants; the illustrations were by G. D. Ehret; and the factory copied these illustrations with imagination and creativity. The name of Sloane still is given to the plates. Pieces from this period are almost as rare and costly as from the previous one.

Red anchor (1752–1760): the mark is painted on. Figures from this period are among the most beautiful of all examples of British porcelain. The most famous is perhaps one called The Nurse, a miniature sculpture of a woman and child, full of sweetness, charm, and repose. It is from a French original and was also made in the raised anchor period. Others are a nun, ladies and gallants, the Senses and the Seasons with appropriate symbols, still more characters from the Italian comedy, classical figures, animals, and birds.

A Chelsea dish of the Hans Sloane type, $10\frac{7}{8}$ inches (27.5 cm) long. It has yellow-green leaves and two exotic fruits, a butterfly and two ladybirds. Red anchor mark

Chelsea figures of a Chinese gentleman and lady with urns for holding flowers, each 7¾ inches (19.6 cm) high. They both have green robes and she has a puce and yellow skirt. The scrolled bases are picked out with flowers and gilding. Gold anchor mark. Some collectors specialize, for example, only in gold anchor pieces, or only in gold anchor figures, or in the work of one particular modeller

A new development was of tureens in forms which sometimes verge on the bizarre. They include a hen with chicks (one of them perched on its back); bundles of asparagus; rabbits ('BIG AS LIFE', as a sale catalogue of 1755 says); lemons and melons, ducks and swans; carp and plaice; coiled eels. Many of the tureens which survive are 'marriages' between the top of one and the bottom of another. Originally the top and bottom were each given an identical number, and a look at these telltale marks will reveal if a 'marriage' has taken place.

Purists might say that these extraordinary tureens are merely trivial flights of fancy. Yet they are typical of rococo high spirits

and must have brought an element of surprise to the meal.

Much admired on the Continent as well as in Britain were the 'toys' – trifles such as snuffboxes, seals, scent bottles, *bonbonnières* and what are called nowadays bodkin cases, but which may originally have been for toothpicks. A sale of them was held in 1754 and the announcement said: "Snuff-boxes, Smelling-bottles, Etwees [i.e. étuis, small cases for needles and toilet articles] and Trinkets for Watches (mounted in Gold and unmounted) in various beautiful Shapes, of an elegant Design and curiously painted . . . A large parcel of Porcelain Hafts for table and Dessert knives and Forks". Sometimes they have sentimental inscriptions in badly spelt French such as: 'Je vous charmeiay' for 'Je vous charmerai'. These 'toys' were first made in the raised anchor period and were continued until the factory closed. They were, as might be expected, an invention of Meissen.

Gold anchor (1760–1769): a notable change in taste. Lushness and elaboration came in. Gilding was used much more lavishly. The bases of figures, which had been flat, were now given rococo scrolls. Figures were also given backgrounds of flowers and leaves, called *bocages* – a British invention. The whole impression is of magnificence verging on vulgarity and the Victorians loved it. (In 1868 Lord Dudley paid 3000 guineas for a vase, 24 inches high, of the gold anchor period; and 2000 guineas for another. The two were sold at Christie's in 1963 for only £1500.) Not all the gold anchor Chelsea is inferior, however. Coloured grounds were applied boldly – they were described in 1759 as 'found at very large expence, incredible Labour, and close Application'. The vases were often in the most extreme form of rococo and have been described as the perfect embodiment in porcelain of the 'Chippendale' style. Horace Walpole, always with a sharp pen and a good eye for style, said of some other productions of this period: "The forms are neither new, beautiful nor various".

Sir Everard Fawkener died in 1758 and Sprimont apparently became sole owner in 1759. By 1763 he was said to have made a fortune out of the business. Perhaps this was due to a change in the formula for the porcelain – the introduction of the ashes from burned bones. This ingredient reduced the losses during firing.

Chelsea – Derby

Sprimont, whose health had been poor, sold his business in 1769 and after a short interval it was taken over by William Duesbury of the Derby porcelain factory. Duesbury ran it until 1784, when he closed it down. This phase really comes under the Derby factory and is recounted on page 168.

A Chelsea figure of a parakeet, 5 inches (12.5 cm) high. From the *Natural History of Uncommon Birds*. The plumage is mainly white; the tail is blue; wing-feathers purple; beak pale pink; crest red; eyebrows yellow and puce. Raised red anchor mark

Chelsea's products are uneven in quality and often depend on continental and oriental ideas. But the masterpieces stand comparison with the best of any country. Even the imperfections – cracks, warping, faulty glaze – have an appeal of their own. The technical perfection of nineteenth-century porcelain has something cold and unattractive about it.

Above
A set of four Derby-Chelsea figures emblematic of the Continents, about 7 inches (18 cm) high. Europe is a crowned nymph holding a globe; Asia, a nymph with a camel; America, a Red Indian with an alligator; Africa, a black nymph with a lion. About 1785–1790

Below
Pair of Derby figures with candlesticks, 11 inches (28 cm) high, of about 1790. The man's cloak is pink and green; his jacket and breeches are painted with flowers in colours and gold. The woman's bodice is pink and her dress decorated with flowers. Not in the most exquisite of taste. These are called Ranelagh dancers: the woman has a sash from which hangs a ticket of admission to the Ranelagh pleasure gardens

Girl-on-a-swing

A curious offshoot of Chelsea was a mysterious factory which has been nicknamed the 'Girl-on-a-Swing' factory. It takes its name from one of the figures it made and seems to have been in production from about 1749 to about 1754. It introduced to Britain the making of miniature scent-bottles, seals, and suchlike 'toys'. Perhaps Gouyn, after leaving the management of Chelsea, gave his backing to a group of Staffordshire workmen who seceded from Chelsea.

Sprimont put advertisements in the newspapers in 1749 and 1751, dissociating himself from a 'Chelsea China Warehouse' in St James's. The owner of the warehouse retorted: "My China Warehouse is not supply'd by any other person except Mr *Charles Gouyn* late Proprietor and Chief Manager of the Chelsea-House". Girl-on-a-swing items are rare and are the most costly in all the field of British porcelain.

Pitfalls and marks

Red anchor marks are found on other porcelains and can deceive the non-expert. Chelsea's red anchors are usually small and hard to find; large ones in a prominent position are suspect. A blue anchor is sometimes found from about 1752–1758 on Chelsea's blue and white ware, which is very beautiful and very rare. Gold anchors are often found on German nineteenth-century porcelain. The Girl-on-a-swing factory used no marks.

Bow

The next great name in porcelain is linked with a factory on the other side of London from Chelsea: the one at Bow. The geography is in a way symbolic. Ware from Chelsea, in the west, is fashionable and sophisticated; Bow, in the east, is more down-to-earth, cheaper, and more durable. The aim was to seize some of the profitable trade in porcelain carried on by the East India Company, and the factory succeeded in doing so.

The founders were two men of strangely differing backgrounds. Thomas Frye was born near Dublin in 1710; he was an accomplished artist. Edward Heylyn was a merchant, born in Westminster in 1695. Capital came from a shrewd linen-draper, Alderman George Arnold. Production began on a commercial scale in 1746 to 1747 and an edition of Daniel Defoe's *Tour through the Whole Island of Great Britain,* published in 1748, said: "They have already made large quantities of *Tea-cups, saucers, etc.* which by some skilful persons are said to be little inferior to those brought from China. If they can work this so as to undersell the Foreign Porcelaine, it may become a very profitable business to the Undertakers, and save great sums to the Public, which are annually sent abroad for this Commodity". (This was not written by Defoe, who died in 1731, but by a later editor of the book).

The bread-and-butter business was in blue and white wares for ordinary use: dishes, plates, sauceboats, jugs, and so on. The decorations are fanciful pagodas in landscapes, flowering plants on terraces, and similar 'Chinese' themes. Shapes were copies from silver ware of a slightly earlier date. The figures, plain or coloured, include birds, pug dogs, lions and lionesses, street criers, musicians, cooks, and the ones that were usual for so many of the eighteenth-century factories: Harlequin, Columbine, Pierrot, and the other characters from the Italian Comedy; and allegorical personages to symbolize the Seasons, the Elements, and similar subjects. Among the most interesting are an actor and an actress: Kitty Clive and Henry

Opposite page
Porcelain jug of the Worcester factory, made in the early years (the 'Dr Wall' period, after the principal founder). It is 10¾ inches (27 cm) high. The panels have Oriental figures fishing, in a landscape. (Christie's)

A rare Bow plate, transfer printed in sepia with each print picked out in colour, 8¾ inches (22.2 cm) across. One figure is selling the other the wares that are displayed on the table. Anchor and dagger mark

Woodward. They are depicted in the parts of the Fine Lady and the Fine Gentleman in Garrick's farce *Lethe*. (The factory was cashing in on its London connections). Both of the designs were based on engravings, which were also the source for figures of statesmen and generals who were the heroes of the hour. General Wolfe and the Marquis of Granby are among the best of these; they were done after the victories of Quebec and Minden in 1759. The figures may not have been as brilliant and accomplished as Chelsea's but they are often original and unique to the factory.

The best period was the early one, from about 1752 to about 1760. Another edition of the *Tour of Great Britain* said in 1761 that Bow china "though not so fine as some made at *Chelsea*, or as that from *Dresden,* is much stronger than either and therefore better for common Use; and, being much cheaper than any other China, there is a greater Demand for it. The Proprietors of this Manufactory have also procured some very good Artists in Painting, who are employed in painting some of their finest Sort of Porcelain, and it is so well performed, as to equal most of that from Dresden in this Respect".

But a decline had set in by the early 1770s. The modelling and colours became crude, almost ghastly. Heavy gilding was used and over-elaboration crept in, just as it did in Chelsea. The rococo was going out of fashion but Bow did not change with the times and was bound to go under. Frye had retired in 1759 because of ill-health and he died three years later. The business was carried on by others until it was bought in 1776 by William Duesbury, owner of the porcelain factory at Derby. He closed down Bow and the buildings became a turpentine factory 'and small Tenements'. A curious anomaly is that they were not really in Bow at all, but in an adjacent district, Stratford.

Some technical advances are to the credit of Bow. It was the first to use transfer printing on porcelain – see page 123. And it was the first to mix the burned bones of animals with the clay. The calcined bones made the product harder and stronger and reduced the amount lost in the kiln by distortion or collapse. The idea was further developed by potters in Staffordshire around 1800 and modern British bone china is now famous all over the world.

Bow was unique in another way – its supplies of clay were, according to some scholars, brought from North America. A poverty-stricken potter from Savannah, Georgia, named Andrew Duché, arrived in London in 1743 with samples of clay he had discovered in the hinterland of the Cherokee territory. It proved to be suitable and Alderman Arnold financed Duché in buying the land from the Cherokee nation. It seems that a contract was

Opposite page
Harlequin and Columbine – group made in about 1760 at the Chelsea factory. About 8 inches (20.3 cm) high. Characters such as these, from the Italian comedy, were popular. (Antique Porcelain Co.)

Above
Pair of Bow figures symbolizing Liberty and Matrimony,
$7\frac{1}{2}$ inches (19 cm) high. The
man, Liberty, has a bird's nest
at his feet and holds an egg. His
jacket is pink and his breeches
have sprays of flowers. The
woman, Matrimony, carries a
bird cage. Her bodice is yellow
and her dress painted with
flowers. Very charming and
well modelled

Below
Pair of Bow white figures. 10
inches (25.5 cm) high. They
depict Henry Woodward as
the Fine Gentleman and Kitty
Clive as the Fine Lady in the
farce *Lethe*. The Fine Lady has
a King Charles spaniel under
one arm

agreed upon between Duché and the owners of the factory for a regular supply, and this source gave Bow an economic advantage over its rivals. Duché settled in Philadelphia and when he died in 1778 was very rich indeed.

Marks and forgeries

The marks are confusing and irregular: an anchor and a dagger in red; an arrow with a ring at one end; a crescent; the letters A or I; pseudo-Chinese scribbles which may have been intended to deceive buyers into thinking that the wares were Oriental. Sometimes the red dagger has been ground away and the anchor left, presumably in the hope that the piece may be mistaken for red anchor Chelsea.

Reproductions were made by the Samson factory and fakes have been made in recent times at a pottery in Torquay, Devon. One disadvantage of Bow is that the white areas tend to go brown with age.

Lowestoft

A bizarre story was invented in the nineteenth century about the porcelain factory that was in production at Lowestoft from 1757 to about 1799. The story is even now not quite dead. It says that the huge quantities of porcelain made in China during the eighteenth and nineteenth centuries for export to Europe and North America were from Lowestoft.

The idea is, in fact, preposterous. Chinese porcelain is quite different from almost all porcelain made in this country – hard paste rather than soft paste. The Lowestoft factory perhaps employed no more than 70 people at the most, and probably far fewer on average. Its wares were simple, even naive, and were mainly for local people. The proprietors were even described in 1795 as 'China manufacturers and Herring curers' – the factory was not their only business. A lot has been discovered about the factory since the myth was first started, yet even now the Chinese export porcelain is occasionally called 'Lowestoft', 'Chinese Lowestoft', or 'Oriental Lowestoft'.

Demand for porcelain was high in the 1750s – it was costly to import, and the British makers were trying to rival the products of China and of Meissen. A likely-looking clay was found at Gunton, near Lowestoft. Tradition says that samples of it were sent off to a factory in London to test if it was suitable. And tradition also says that workmen brought to the town to carry out trial runs were bribed to spoil their own efforts.

The enterprise was, however, launched by four partners of whom Robert Browne, a chemist, and Philip Walker, a tile manufacturer; seem to have had most to do with the day-to-day running. Lowestoft was a resort in the eighteenth century and a diarist, Dr Silas Neville, recorded in 1772: "Went to Lowestoft . . . consists of one pretty street . . . Dined at the Crown. After dinner visited the china manufactory carried on here. Most of it is rather ordinary. The Painting branch is done by women."

Ordinary indeed it is in comparison with the glittering achievements of Meissen, Chelsea, and other places; but it has great charm and devoted admirers. Most of the output was for the table – plates, tea and coffee services, jugs, bowls, mugs, and so on. Much of it was in blue and white and the rest was coloured. Most interesting for the collector are:

'*Trifles*'. These are souvenirs made for the visitors and are generally inscribed 'A trifle from Lowestoft'. Also found are the names of places in the district: Bungay, Lynn, Hingham, Holt, and Wangford. The 'trifles' are perhaps the direct ancestors of the

A coloured birth tablet, 3 inches across

Back of the tablet

Another coloured birth tablet, 3 inches across

Back of the tablet

souvenir pottery that was mass produced in later years for practically every holiday spot in the country – and perhaps even an ancestor of seaside rock with the name all the way through. Most of the Lowestoft trifles are mugs but some are teapots, ink pots, or pounce pots (for scattering 'sand' on writing paper to stop the ink from running).

Birth Tablets: Small circular plaques made specially to commemorate a birth. They are unique to Lowestoft, rare, and several are for the children of workers in the factory. Each has the child's name, the date, some decoration, and one or two holes for suspension.

Animals: Swans, cats, sheep, dogs. They are quite small, on average just over two inches high. It is known that deer were also made but none is known to have survived. A newly-discovered deer would be very valuable.

Human figures including standing musicians, one playing a flute and the other a mandolin. Birth tablets, animals, and human figures are all rare.

Marks are a problem. Lowestoft had no special mark of its own, and it sometimes copied the marks of other factories. Identification is possible, however. The site of the factory was later occupied by a brewery. Work to extend the brewery in 1902 revealed quantities of broken, spoiled, and discarded porcelain and a large number of the original plaster moulds. More finds were made in 1967. (On the spot now stands a block of flats). These discoveries provide evidence about what was made.

Teapot, 5½ inches (14 cm) high; probably made for a wedding or anniversary. Dated pieces help to trace a factory's development

Robert Browne was succeeded by his son, also named Robert, in 1771. The younger man introduced the coloured wares. The factory probably closed down in 1799. The owners were wealthy but getting too old to carry on. Competition from Staffordshire and other parts of the country was intense. Lowestoft did not keep up with fashion and novelty. Some of the more skilled workers went to Worcester in 1799.

Longton Hall

Staffordshire in the 1740s had plenty of experienced potters and plenty of natural advantages for the craft. Yet only one short-lived factory for the making of porcelain was set up there during the time when porcelain factories were being set up in many other parts of the country. Perhaps the Staffordshire people were too conservative – they even ignored the chance of making delftware – or perhaps they were not willing to take the risk of embarking on a tricky and expensive sort of venture. The one factory that was established

Longton Hall 'strawberry dish' – so called because of the pattern round the rim which is characteristic of the factory

early on, Longton Hall, went through grave financial difficulties. The lesson may have stuck in the minds of everyone, for it was not until 1781 that another venture of the kind was made in Staffordshire.

Longton Hall did, however, produce a great deal and its types are very varied. The original proprietor was a William Jenkinson, of whom little is known, and the site was at the town of Longton near Newcastle-under-Lyme. Production began in 1749 but Jenkinson sold out in 1753: he seems to have been the only person involved in the venture who gained any financial benefit. An injection of capital came in 1755 from the Rev Robert Charlesworth of Bakewell, Derbyshire, who advanced £1200.

Difficulties of production were great, for a high proportion of the pieces was spoiled during the firing. The factory was not using either of the two materials that help to reduce wastage, soapstone and bone ash.

Much better known than Jenkinson is William Littler who was named as one of the people originally involved. He may have worked at a factory in Limehouse, London, which operated from about 1745 to 1748. He may have been the person who brought to Longton Hall the porcelain-making skill. His name is now given to a very strong blue – Littler's blue. William Duesbury, formerly a decorator of porcelain in London and later to achieve much higher things, spent two years at Longton Hall, again as a decorator. He improved the quality of the output.

The factory still lost money and Charlesworth put up another £300 in 1756 to prevent immediate closure and a year later another £300. Littler soldiered on but the end came in 1760. Charlesworth published a notice in the *Birmingham Gazette* announcing the dissolution of the partnership and seized most of the stock. He sent more than 90,000 pieces, and perhaps moulds and equipment too, for auction in Salisbury.

Littler refused to give up. He took some of the stock and moved to West Pans, near Musselburgh, where he decorated it and may have made more porcelain.

Longton Hall's output has several unusual features. It copied figures from sculptures – for example a figure of Cupid riding a horse is taken from an Italian Renaissance bronze. One painter of considerable talent worked at Longton Hall and has been nicknamed the 'castle painter;' he did classical ruins and romantic continental scenes. His name was probably John Hayfield. Many pieces show a strange mixture of influences from China, Meissen, and Chelsea – and the local potteries which were making salt-glazed stoneware. Some figures unique to Longton Hall have been called 'snowmen'

A Longton Hall mug painted in colours with yellow and red cranes among Oriental flowers. 3¾ inches (9.5 cm) high. The handle is typical of this factory

because they are white and thickly covered with a glaze that obscures much of the detail.

More in the run of ordinary themes of the time are blue and white wares, teapots, sauce boats after silver originals, birds and animals, mugs, figures of the seasons, and characters from mythology.

Marks

These include crossed Ls or a J crossed with an L, perhaps for 'Jenkinson-Littler' or 'Jenkinson-Longton;' a reversed swastika; a simple cross; various individual letters.

Derby

Origins of the porcelain factory at Derby have been almost completely obscured by time, yet it was to reach pinnacles of excellence. It was also to last for nearly a hundred years – a remarkable record. The credit rests with two men, William Duesbury and his son William Duesbury the second. Each contributed in different ways. The elder, a hard-headed businessman, provided financial stability during difficult times; the younger gathered round him a team of brilliant artists.

Production began, it is thought, in 1750 or shortly before then. A partnership seems to have been in existence between John Heath, a financier, and Andrew Planché, a silversmith and one of the Huguenots who brought such talent to their host country. Nobody

A pair of Longston Hall figures of a boy and girl symbolizing autumn and summer, $4\frac{3}{4}$ inches (12 cm) high

now knows the identity of the person who had the skill to make porcelain. Planché dropped out at an early stage and his place was filled by Duesbury, who had been working in London as a decorator of other people's wares. An agreement was drawn up between Heath, Planché, and Duesbury in 1756 – at about the time when the factory at Meissen near Dresden was overrun by Prussian troops. This gave Duesbury an opportunity. He borrowed Meissen specimens, copied them, and boldly called his factory 'the second Dresden.' Output shot up and it was claimed that the goods were cheaper than those from elsewhere. Duesbury bought the Chelsea factory in 1770, running it and Derby together. Chelsea's workers had a lot of skill and experience and the name was highly esteemed.

During the Derby/Chelsea era the northern factory dominated the London one. The great days were over and few workers seem to have been employed at Chelsea. Figures from Chelsea are dull and repetitive; vases show the influence of the neo-classical style.

Duesbury closed the Chelsea end of the business in 1784, perhaps because he was in poor health or perhaps because it was more economic to concentrate on one centre.

Derby did not make much ordinary ware for everyday use: the porcelain did not stand up well to heat. The factory specialized instead in figures and in the costlier sort of table ware. Planché's figures – up to 50 different types are known – are spontaneous, vigorous, and superbly modelled. Some are imitations of Meissen but others are original. The change of ownership brought a change in style. Figures had less charm and vivacity but were immensely popular. Many hundreds of different kinds were made and were the usual types – celebrities (Shakespeare, Milton, Rodney, Howe) gods and goddesses (Juno, Jupiter, Minerva), royalty, allegories, shepherds and shepherdesses, musicians, animals, and birds. Among the most beautiful are those in biscuit; an ivory-coloured unglazed porcelain with a flawless surface like satin. They date from the late eighteenth and early nineteenth century. Flaws in many figures could be disguised by colours, gilding, or glaze but not in these.

Some models were in production for decades, Dating them has to be done by examining the glaze and the body, which varied from time to time. Designers often were told to rough out their figures in the nude and add the clothes afterwards; this achieved naturalism and anatomical accuracy. But even the best friends of Derby admit that quality was very variable and some figures, especially the larger sort, are unattractive, for the colours are crude and gaudy, the subjects sentimental, and the body flawed.

The years from about 1775 to about 1800 were distinguished for painting of brilliant quality: landscapes, seascapes, flowers, and birds. Landscapes were similar in style to British water colours of the period and were mostly 'borrowed' from engravings and illustrated topographical books. Many of the Derby artists are known. 'Jockey' Hill (so called because he went to work on a horse) specialized in landscapes. James Banford, when he was sober, combined classical scenes and landscapes. William Billingsley, who was later to work in Wales and elsewhere, did flowers, especially roses. Billingsley was succeeded by William 'Quaker' Pegg, who throughout his life was afflicted by religious mania but who was perhaps one of the finest artists. His flowers are boldly done and large. Pegg's career as a china painter ended in 1820: he believed that the occupation was sinful.

Derby ice pail, 8½ inches (21.5 cm) high, of about 1815. Richly gilt and with a pretty landscape. The top part lifts off and an inner vessel also of porcelain, is removable. Ice was packed round the liner and in the top part to keep the fruit inside the liner cool

The modellers are known, too. Pierre Stephan, a Huguenot, worked from 1770 to 1795 and Jean Jacques Spengler, son of the director of the Zurich porcelain factory, from 1790.

William Duesbury the elder died in 1786. His son was not such a good businessman but had better artistic taste. He took into partnership in 1795 an Irish miniature painter, Michael Kean. Duesbury the younger died in 1797, aged only 34. Kean took over, and married his former partner's widow in 1798 but the workers did not like him and many left. Times were hard during the wars with France because the export trade was hit. Kean leased the factory and sold the stock in 1814 to Robert Bloor, an employee who had to borrow capital for the deal. He recouped the money by a policy which was full of danger. In the warehouses were several tons of faulty porcelain – 'seconds' – including many figures. Bloor had them gaudily decorated, in the taste of the time, in an attempt to conceal the flaws and sold them off. Money came in but the reputation of the factory suffered. Pieces treated in this way often are a strange mixture of late eighteenth century form and Regency decoration.

Bloor became mentally ill in 1828 and was unable to carry on any of the day-to-day work. The rest of the factory's history is outside the scope of this book; but it did continue until 1848 when the whole business was closed down, the buildings demolished, and the materials sold. Many of the old patterns and moulds continued in use. The present Royal Crown Derby Porcelain Co. Ltd. is not a direct successor of the one founded in the mid-eighteenth century, although a myth persists that it is. Modern Derby is associated especially with richly coloured brocade-like 'Japan' patterns derived from the Japanese porcelain called Imari. It is in black, red, gold, and blue and was first made in Britain during the Chelsea–Derby period.

Collecting Derby has a strange history. Most of the early pieces were at one time thought to be from Chelsea and were thus highly prized. Their real origin was discovered in the 1930s and prices of them fell.

Worcester

The great British porcelain factories of the eighteenth century one by one went bankrupt or were amalgamated with others – except for Worcester, which still produces fine work.

Few classes of antiques are more collected and written about. One of the golden ages of Worcester was roughly from its foundation in 1751 to 1776, when pressure of competition brought in a decline.

Pair of Derby figures of Milton and Shakespeare, after an original model by Scheemakers; 9¾ inches (25 cm) high. About 1815, earlier ones are from 1760–1765

Worcester maintained its high standards for longer than its rivals at Chelsea or Bow, but knowledge of the early history of the factory was incomplete until its original site near the cathedral by the banks of the Severn was excavated in 1968.

This revealed that many objects previously thought to have come from another factory – Caughley in Shropshire, farther up the Severn – were in fact from Worcester (see page 175).

The real founder was Dr John Wall, a successful physician, a good amateur artist, the discoverer of the benefits of Malvern water, and writer on the danger of drinking cider from vessels glazed with lead (the drinker could be poisoned).

He practised as a doctor in Worcester from 1740 to 1774. He is also thought to have painted some porcelain himself – for example a mug which commemorates a parliamentary election at Worcester in 1747 and shows scenes of Conquest and Gratitude.

Dr Wall and his 14 partners transferred workmen and materials from the short-lived factory at Bristol, Miller and Lund's Glass House. The new enterprise was set up in an old mansion, Warmstry House, which was probably of Tudor origin.

Worcester owed a lot of its early success to the useful ingredient soapstone or steatite, which was quarried near the Lizard in Corn-

Tureen of the Dr Wall period in the form of a partridge sitting on her nest. It was probably meant for holding eggs. The colours are green and brown. About 1770

wall; the Bristol factory also used it. Soapstone meant that the china resisted boiling water and did not 'craze'. Crazing is a pattern of tiny cracks in the surface.

The special properties of the porcelain led the factory to concentrate on useful rather than ornamental wares – cups and saucers, tea and coffee pots, plates, and such like. A few decorative figures were made but they are rare.

At first the shapes were derived from silver sauceboats, cream jugs, and teapots, and indeed moulds were probably taken directly from them; but soon shapes were devised which were more suitable to the porcelain material and of finer proportions.

Blue and white ware was the staple and Worcester blue and white of the early years is among the finest made in Europe. The factory was the first to use transfer printing for ceramics – a method at first highly thought of although it was later responsible in part for mass production and a general decline in quality. The process seems to have been brought to Worcester in 1755 by Robert Hancock, who probably learned the skill at the Battersea enamel factory where it was invented.

Apart from blue and white and transfer printed ware for ordinary use, the factory made a vast range of other types with costly and lavish colouring in turquoise, yellow (very desirable), pea green, claret and a specially dramatic blue unlike the ordinary type. Gilding, from honey mixed with gold, was soft and mellow. Borrowing of ideas went on, and influences are clear from Meissen, China, Japan, and London. Some of the best painters from Chelsea were hired in 1768, and some of the coloured decoration was done by James Giles in his London workshop.

The different periods of Worcester are divided according to the styles and the owners; the course of the firms' history changed with time and circumstance.

1751–1756: the first or Dr Wall period, the most highly esteemed of all. The rococo was in full flower.

1756–1793: The Flight/Davis or middle period, rather undistinguished. Output was concentrated on cheaper, more competitive products. William Davis, an apothecary and one of the original partners, was in charge at first and in 1783 William Flight, the firm's London agent, bought the business for £3000. George III visited the factory in 1788 and gave it his patronage and the royal patent. William Flight's son John was manager until John died in 1791 when another son, Joseph, took over. Martin Barr became a partner in 1793.

1793–1840: Flight and Barr period. Martin Barr junior was a partner from 1807 and another son, George, from 1813. The Flight

Dr Wall, a founder of the Worcester factory

and Barr period up to 1807 shows a steady improvement of quality. The 1810s and 1820s saw the production of pieces lavishly gilded and painted in the current mode. The factory ran into competition on its own doorstep. Robert Chamberlain, a former employee, started a rival concern in the 1780s. He first decorated porcelain he bought in, mostly from Caughley, and then made his own. His product reached a high quality, although the Flight concern also had such high standards that it, too, was prosperous. Then in 1801 Thomas Grainger, a former employee of Chamberlain's and his son-in-law, started up a decorating concern; Grainger made porcelain from 1815 to 1820, when he turned to bone china. All three manufacturers had at one time their own shops and showrooms in the High Street of Worcester.

The Chamberlain and Flight firms amalgamated in 1840: it was said to be a marriage of convenience rather than love. The Grainger firm was taken over in 1889 and the direct successor of Dr Wall's foundation is now called the Worcester Royal Porcelain Co. The modern factory is on the site of Chamberlain's and a technical college stands on the original site.

Many fakes and copies were produced in the late nineteenth and early twentieth centuries. Fairly plain objects have been given extra coloured decoration, usually red or green. Some nineteenth century and genuine objects are masquerading as Dr Wall period: the tell-tale nineteenth century marks have been removed by acid or by grinding. The body sometimes gives a clue, for bone china and hard paste porcelain were not made at Worcester during the eighteenth century.

Large tureen of the Dr Wall period. The shape derived from examples of silver but the decoration, in blue, is in the *chinoiserie* manner. The handle is in the form of a dolphin. About 1758

Marks are confusing. They include a scratched cross, painters' special marks or initials, a crescent, a man in the moon, numerals disguised as squiggly pseudo-Chinese characters, the letter W, the letters BFB or FBB for the Flight and Bar period, or the word Flight. The other factories in the city used 'Chamberlains Worcester' and 'Grainger Lee and Co.' with variations.

The best collection in the world is open to the public in Worcester. It was set up in 1879, originally to inspire the workers by letting them see the masterpieces of their predecessors. This collection was later bought by the late C. W. Dyson Perrins, of the Lee and Perrins Worcester sauce family. He added his own outstanding collection and set up in 1951 the Dyson Perrins Museum Trust. The Worcester Royal Porcelain Company gives to the museum from time to time specimens of its production.

Caughley

Collectors of old porcelain had to rearrange their treasures and labels during the late 1960s. What they had thought was from the Caughley factory in Shropshire was, it turned out, not from there at all but from Worcester. Experts had followed the mistakes of nineteenth century writers. The mistake was understandable – the products are rather alike. But open cast mining for clay on the site of the Caughley factory (pronounced Carfly, with emphasis on the first syllable) revealed large numbers of wasters (fragments and spoiled pieces). Comparison of these with complete objects revealed the truth.

Above
Jug of the Flight and Barr period. The view shows the Severn, the porcelain factory, and the Cathedral and is all in sepia

Below
A Chamberlain's Worcester inkstand, $11\frac{3}{4}$ inches (30 cm) wide, of about 1820. It has flowers, foliage, and gilding. On the left and right are an inkwell and cover and a bowl and cover; in the centre is a taperstick

What was not discovered was just as interesting. Many blue and white pieces with fancy numeral marks in a Chinese style had been thought of as Caughley; yet none of the wasters matched up with them. These pieces were thus from Worcester – and excavations at Worcester have confirmed that.

The founder of Caughley was Thomas Turner, who was apprenticed at Worcester in the mid-1760s and set up independently, with one partner, in the early 1770s. Production was in full swing by 1775. The site had its own coal mine only 220 yards away and was not far from the river Severn, which the factory used for transporting its wares. (Writers used to allege that the site was on the banks of the river; in fact the river cannot be seen from it).

Caughley concentrated on blue and white printed decoration. Many impressions from the copper plates have been preserved and are a help in identification. Tea services were probably the biggest line in blue and white and they cost £2 a set. Dessert and dinner services, sauceboats, and jugs were made too, and in many cases shipped in the plain white form to Worcester, 30 miles down the Severn, where they were decorated. Caughley did its own attractive decoration too – fine enamelling and gilding. No figures were made.

Output went on for nearly 25 years but in 1799 Turner sold all the working material and the leases of the factory and the coal mine to the owners of the factory at Coalport. He kept for himself the finished stock-in-trade and this was auctioned at Shrewsbury. An advertisement for the auction said: "China Ware. Being the

Worcester inkwell of the Flight, Barr and Barr period. The basic colour is lime green; the piece also has gilding and naturalistic flowers and insects

valuable stock of the Royal Salopian porcelain manufactory . . . .
the property of Thomas Turner, Esq., (who from his indifferent
state of health declines continuing the said manufactory . . .) The
stock consists of a great number of beautiful tea and coffee equipages
of various much approved patterns . . . richly executed in enamel
and burnished gold together with a great variety of new and
elegant blue and white tea and coffee sets, table, dinner, and dessert
services, muffin plates, butter tubs, etc., mugs, jugs, egg cups and
drainers, butter cups, custard cups of different sorts and sizes,
pickle shells, eye baths, asparagus servers, toy table and tea sets, and
candlesticks . . . with a great variety of other articles".

The 'toy table and tea sets' are miniature objects in blue and
white of great charm; they seem to have been a speciality of
Caughley.

The new proprietors carried on business at the site until 1814
when they concentrated production at Coalport.

Coalport

The factory, in Shropshire near Caughley, began in a comparatively
small and undistinguished way, but was to produce some classic
examples of the more dubious taste of the Regency and Victorian
eras. The founders were John Rose, a former apprentice at Caughley,
his nephew W. F. Rose, and William Pugh. Coalport was established
about 1796 and took a firm step forward with the buying out of the
Caughley establishment. Products of Caughley and early Coalport

Coalport vase and pair of cache-
pots and stands, of about 1805.
The vase is 10 inches (25.5 cm)
high. The grounds are in stripes
of orange and gold

are hard to distinguish from each other. Coalport in the early years made blue and white ware and undecorated ware for the wholesale market. Great advances were, however, made during the years 1800 to 1830 in producing new and more striking colours. The factory achieved high standards during the Victorian era, when it also reproduced – even faked – products of Sèvres and Chelsea.

Another notable step was the acquisition of moulds from the Nantgarw factory (see page 182) and the employment of its remarkable founder, William Billingsley. The rococo taste was revived from about 1820 – an ominous symptom of what was to come in the Victorian era when almost every previous style under the sun was revived and translated into Victorian terms. Coalport was at this time capable of producing very fine porcelain and received an award in 1820 from the Society of Arts for the invention of a leadless glaze. The award was not so much for the quality of the glaze as for the benefits which might be brought to the workers. A Dr Richard Warner wrote in 1801, after visiting the factory at Worcester: "The *trimmer* . . . smooths the surface of the article, and rubs off any little inequalities of the glaze; the most unwholesome part of the process, as he frequently inspires particles of the white lead, etc to the great detriment of his stomach and lungs; which, indeed, he is obliged to relieve by frequent emetics."

The revived rococo inspired many vases and ornamental pieces, sometimes with raised flowers. Chelsea vases were the originals but were much elaborated. Table wares tended to follow the example of Swansea and Nantgarw.

Marks
'Coalport' in script, used until about 1829.

Liverpool

Several porcelain factories were set up in the city in the mid-eighteenth century. The port gave an advantage in bringing in the raw materials and sending out the finished goods, especially to North America. Skilled workmen were recruited to teach the techniques, from Worcester, Staffordshire, and London. But a great deal of what was made is rather ordinary blue and white ware and telling which factory made what is difficult. The most interesting is in several colours and in the chinoiserie style or with birds and flowers. Richard Chaffers and Co (about 1754–1765) is the best-known manufacturer and in its first advertisement said that its ware was 'proved with boiling water before it is exposed to sale.' This was something that not all factories of the time could claim.

Plymouth and Bristol

The products of these two factories are of extraordinary interest to collectors because they were the first to be made in this country of the true hard paste porcelain and because of the remarkable scientific achievement this represents. The story hinges upon the careers of two men, both Quakers but of different backgrounds and personalities.

Meissen's discovery of the secret of making the true porcelain had taken immense sums and immense efforts; yet it was done by William Cookworthy (1705–1780) with very few resources and very little information to go on. He was an apothecary with cultured tastes, could converse fluently in French and Latin, and was a dedicated Quaker preacher. His business was in Plymouth but his preaching took him to many other places. From the 1740s he was searching for the all-important china stone and china clay. The only guide he had to the making of porcelain was an inadequate account of how the Chinese did it. This was written by a Jesuit who lived in China, Père d'Entrecolles, and was translated into English in 1738.

Cookworthy found the china clay in Cornwall before 1758 and perhaps as early as 1745; but not the china stone, also in Cornwall, until much later (both are decayed forms of granite). Experiments to make porcelain lasted years but at last in 1768 he took out a patent for the process and at once began production in Plymouth. The firm, a partnership of Cookworthy and 12 others, was called the New Invented Porcelain Manufactory. His output shows that technical flaws and wastage in the kilns was high. Decoration – if it was put on at all – was in simple colours under the glaze.

All was not well and the enterprise was transferred in 1770 to Bristol – a much bigger place, a thriving port, and already a centre for kindred skills in glass and delftware. A Bristol shipowner and merchant, Richard Champion, and a potter of delftware, Thomas Frank, were among the original partners.

Cookworthy stayed in control until 1774 when he gave up to concentrate on preaching. He was in any case nearly 70. His successor was Champion (1743–1791), a Whig with many friends among politicians and the wealthy classes of Bristol. He at this point seemed set on a distinguished career; but he had no scientific background and no experience of making porcelain.

Champion set about improving the product with fresh techniques and more skilful decorators. All that cost money. The partners had an expensive contract with the owner of the land where the china clay and china stone were obtained – Thomas Pitt, later Lord

A rare Bristol figure of a boy holding a dog, $7\frac{1}{2}$ inches (19 cm) high. The jacket is lined in pink and painted with flowers in red and gold; the breeches are green

Camelford. Few of the partners profited financially from their investments.

Cookworthy's patent, which he handed over to Champion when he retired, had to be renewed by Parliament in 1775. Champion sought a 14-year extension. The proceedings went through the Commons without trouble, but Lord Gower raised objections in the Lords: behind this move were Staffordshire potters including Josiah Wedgwood. The Staffordshire potters wanted the rights to use the material and to make the porcelain. Champion ran into enormous expense in fighting his cause, which dragged on for three months. The outcome was that Parliament gave Champion the exclusive right to use the Cornish clay and stone for making translucent porcelain but gave potters free use of them for 'opaque' pottery. It was a grave blow for the Bristol enterprise.

Other troubles were pressing hard. Disputes broke out among the partners. The American war hit shipping and exports. Porcelain from Derby and Worcester was cheaper, and from Meissen and Sèvres was more esteemed. Connoisseurs tended to think that the oriental was really the best after all. In a sense Cookworthy and Champion had arrived too late.

The factory closed in 1781, after only a brief life. Champion tried to save something. Wedgwood wrote in 1780: "Amongst other things Mr Champion of Bristol has taken me up nearly two days. He is come amongst us to dispose of his secret – His patent etc. and, who could have believed it? has chosen me for his friend and confidante. I shall not deceive him for I really feel much for his situation. A wife and eight children (to say nothing of himself) to provide for, and out of what I fear will not be thought of much value here – The secret of China making. He tells me he has sunk fifteen thousand pounds in this gulf, and his idea is now to sell the whole art, mystery, and patent for six, and he is now trying a list of names I have given him of the most substantial and enterprising potters amongst us, and will acquaint me with the event.

"I gave him reasons why I could not be concerned in such a partnership which I believe were satisfactory even to himself."

In the end Champion did sell the patent to a consortium of Staffordshire potters who established New Hall (see next page). Champion became joint deputy Paymaster General of the Forces, a post which took him to London and America. He settled as a farmer at Camden, South Carolina, and died there.

The products of Plymouth and Bristol are varied, from flawed ware to some of the very finest figures made in Britain during the eighteenth century (two series of Seasons and Elements.) Especially interesting are examples made for Champion's partners, perhaps to mollify their disappointment over the financial stringencies. These pieces have the recipient's coats of arms or initials. Champion's wife gave an outstanding tea service to Edmund Burke's wife: Burke, the MP for Bristol, was a staunch ally of Champion's.

Unique to Bristol are some biscuit plaques – rare because they are very fragile – with arms, initials, or portraits such as Benjamin Franklin and George Washington. But the greatest part of the business was in tea and dessert services in the Sèvres style. Champion had, on taking over, introduced neo-classical designs.

Marks

Plymouth: the alchemical sign for both Jupiter and tin – an allusion to Cornwall, the source of both tin and Plymouth's ingredients. *Bristol*: a St Andrew's cross, perhaps from the coat of arms of Plymouth. Two swords, crossed, and a cross, rather like Meissen's. A St Andrew's cross and the letter B, meaning perhaps Bristol. Numerals are also found but their meaning is not clear.

New Hall

A Cinderella among the porcelain factories is the one that started at New Hall, Shelton, Staffordshire, in 1782. It made useful table wares, primarily tea and coffee sets, and almost certainly did not do any figures, busts, or vases. But its body is very similar to the one

Above and left: New Hall porcelain of about 1795–1800. The teapot is $5\frac{3}{4}$ inches high. The shapes and decoration are typical

used at Bristol which was so unusual in Britain (see page 179). The Bristol patent with 15 years to run was in fact acquired by an association of Staffordshire potters who then started New Hall. Some dispute does, however, still go on about the New Hall body – was it really hard-paste or not? The glaze does not combine with the body as it should if it were, in fact, hard-paste. It seems that the Staffordshire ways of firing were used, which made the difference.

New Hall pieces have painting, gilding, or transfer-printing; and *chinoiserie* was a favourite theme. By about 1810 the paste had become a glassy-looking hybrid porcelain and about this time the only recognizable and consistent mark appeared: the words New Hall in script and in a circle. Closure came in 1825; the business lacked a driving personality to keep it going, unlike Derby, Wedgwood, and other firms. Much porcelain rather like New Hall was made elsewhere and has been called 'rustic porcelain'.

Nantgarw and Swansea

Some of the most beautiful porcelain made in this country came from two factories whose story is of hardship and heartbreak. They were at Swansea and at Nantgarw (pronounced Nantgaroo), six miles north of Cardiff. The wares have always been highly thought of and are much collected in Wales, but production lasted a tragically brief time – from 1813 to 1819. The link between the two factories is William Billingsley, whose life was a succession of bold endeavours and bitter disappointments, surpassing skills and personal tragedies.

Nantgarw porcelain is translucent, with a pure whiteness and a rich glaze. The best type of Swansea is slightly cloudy, greenish, and more serviceable.

Billingsley (1758–1828) started as an apprentice in the noted factory at Derby; he was an accomplished painter of flowers on porcelain as well as the inventor of the wares that are his memorial. He left Derby to work in turn at Pinxton (Derbyshire), Mansfield (Nottinghamshire), Torksey (Lincolnshire), and Worcester; at one point he changed his name to Beeley, perhaps to avoid imprisonment for debt. He arrived at Nantgarw in 1813 with Samuel Walker, his daughter Sarah (who was married to Walker), his daughter Lavinia, and £250 in capital. The spot was remote; but the rent was low and Nantgarw was on the banks of the newly-opened Glamorgan Canal. The canal offered easy transport for the porcelain to Cardiff and the Bristol Channel; and easy transport for coal from the Welsh pits to the kilns. The number of workmen was small – perhaps a total of twenty.

Within six months the £250 was gone and the enterprise was in a desperate way. The reason was that a very high proportion of the ware was spoiled in the kiln during the firing. Controlling the temperature was difficult, the formula did not leave much margin for error, and at that time potters worked by rule of thumb rather than on a scientific basis.

Help came from William Weston Young, a surveyor and entrepreneur. Young was also an artist, antiquarian, writer, and architect. He is said to have lifted an anvil weighing seven hundred-weight. He was a staunch friend to Billingsley's enterprise but himself was constantly in financial trouble. He advanced nearly £600 at the start. Billingsley, Walker, and Young asked the Government in 1814 for a subsidy of £500. French porcelain was then fashionable in London and elsewhere in Britain; Nantgarw was of such high quality that, the three partners hoped, it could wrest this profitable trade from foreign hands and give employment to a home industry. The plea was turned down.

But Lewis Weston Dillwyn, manager of the Cambrian Pottery, Swansea, was told about what was going on and became enthusiastic about the Nantgarw venture. Making pottery is, however, a quite different thing from making porcelain; and this was later the source of trouble. Billingsley and Walker gave up the work at Nantgarw in 1814 and went to Swansea. Billingsley was in charge of

A fine Swansea sauce tureen, cover and stand, 7½ inches (19 cm) wide. The handles and rims are gilt

decorating the ware and Walker experimented on ways to improve the formula.

More disappointments were in store. Dillwyn withdrew from the Cambrian Pottery and handed it over to others who had little success with the porcelain. Billingsley, Walker, and Young scraped together some more money and went back to Nantgarw. Help came from ten wealthy people of the district – probably iron masters and colliery owners – who each put up £100. Most Nantgarw porcelain was made in 1818 and 1819, and much of it was sent to London dealers in the plain white form. The London dealers had it decorated there. This was another disadvantage to the enterprise at Nantgarw for the London dealers took the profits while the factory struggled.

Billingsley's two daughters had died by the time the factory closed. Money ran out in 1819 and Billingsley and Walker left secretly in 1820. They found employment at the factory in Coalport, Shropshire. The story was not quite over, however. Stocks from both Swansea and Nantgarw continued for some years to be decorated and sold; moulds from Nantgarw are said to have been taken to Coalport; and Billingsley worked on until he died in 1828.

Most of the output from the Welsh factories was tableware, as it was easier to manufacture than more complicated shapes. But some candlesticks, small vases, cups and saucers, and similar pieces were also made, especially at Swansea. Apart from the duck-egg green porcelain, Swansea also made less attractive types – one with a brownish tinge and another which has a glassy appearance.

Forms owe a lot to classical taste – for example, the use of handles in the form of ram's heads; dolphins; and lions' paw feet.

The decoration at Swansea is noted for its attractive flowers done in a sentimental and romantic way. Scholars spend a lot of time in trying to sort out which artists did certain types of work. The London decorators tended to lavishness in the current French style. Nantgarw tends to be cold, impersonal, and severe. Indeed the perfection and classical severity of the Welsh porcelains do not appeal to everyone.

Marks

Nantgarw's is straightforward: NANT GARW or NANT-GARW in capital letters, usually above the letters C.W. for china works and pressed into the body. Sometimes it was painted. Not all the genuine products have a mark.

Swansea used 'Dillwyn & Co', a trident or two tridents, or 'Swansea'. They are either pressed into the body or written in colour.

Fakes and other problems

Most painted Nantgarw marks seem to be false. The word Swansea and the tridents, when painted, are suspect. It is also difficult sometimes to distinguish between the products of Nantgarw, Swansea, and Coalport.

Spode and Minton

Josiah Spode (1733–1797) was apprenticed to Thomas Whieldon and later went into business on his own account in Stoke. By about 1813 he had taken into partnership his London representative William Copeland. Spode's firm developed bone china and 'stone china,' which is opaque and somewhere between earthenware and porcelain. Spode's output is extraordinarily varied, from the simplest to the most complex.

Thomas Minton (1765–1836) had an output almost as large as Spode's and the porcelain was of good quality, but the decorative aspects were variable. The Mason family of Lane Delph, Staffordshire, made porcelain and, from 1813, ironstone china – which is particularly durable.

Set of Spode spill vases with fruit and flowers in natural colours on a burnished gold ground

Miscellaneous

Drinking glasses

Eighteenth-century glasses were splendid aids to gracious drinking. But collectors nowadays would have to be rich or brave to use them in the ordinary way.

The excellence in some of the craftsmanship and design was achieved in spite of crippling taxes imposed on the industry to help to pay for wars. And other political events affected drinking habits and the glass-making industry.

For example, an Act was passed in 1703 "for incouraging of the Consumption of Malted Corn and for the better preventing the running of French and Foreign Brandy." Also in 1703, the Methuen Treaty between Britain and Portugal resulted in French wines paying a tax of £55 a tun and Portuguese wines only £7 a tun. Port became popular.

The Gin Act of 1736, much opposed and derided, tried to stop the sale of gin and other strong liquors; drunkenness was worrying the Government. The Act failed and spirits were even hawked in the streets – but under such odd disguises as Cholic and Gripe Water and Cuckold's Comfort. An Excise Act of 1746 taxed quite heavily the raw materials used in glassmaking. This Act was enforced rigorously and was followed by similar ones. Glassware therefore became lighter to reduce the tax. It also was more fragile and the extra breakages may have helped the industry by creating extra demand.

A drinking glass does not seem at first glance to offer much scope for artistry; but in fact the craftsmen did devise many means of decoration. Bowls sometimes have engraved symbols – hops and barley for ale, apples for cider, and vines and grapes for wine. Gilding and enamelling – skilled and difficult jobs – are highly prized.

Another form of decoration is in the form of twisted strands of air trapped in the stem and giving a most attractive appearance. This was a British invention. Bubbles of air were put into a blob of molten glass; this blob was stretched and twisted until the air had taken the form of long and intertwining spirals. Some of the work was done by children.

The technique of air twists was partly replaced about 1760 by a similar one using opaque white or in rare cases coloured glass. Some stems have both air and coloured twists – marvels of beauty and ingenuity. Blobs of opaque or coloured glass were put in a mould and clear molten glass was poured round them. The whole mass was then reheated, stretched and twisted. As many as 36 strands have been counted in one stem. A curious aspect is that the origin of air twists was a fault in manufacture: air sometimes got into the plain glass by error, and some unknown genius discovered how it could be used to advantage.

Specialist collectors delight in the extraordinary variety in the shapes of bowls, feet, and stems. Bowls are technically called trumpet, thistle and funnel shaped; conical, ovoid, ogee, bell, and so on. Feet are conical, domed, beehive, terraced . . . .

Knops are ornamental swellings on the stem, and the forms include the flattened, annular, mushroom, dumb-bell, and bladed. The permutations of design are innumerable.

The rarest colour is yellow, then in order green, red, and blue. Desirability of air twist glasses varies, depending among other things on how rare is the shape of the bowl.

Forgeries and reproductions exist but are not dangerous to the experienced. Examples made during the nineteenth century 'in the old manner' are too good to be true. Some fakes made between the wars are more convincing. The real danger is a specimen made in the eighteenth century but engraved later to boost its value. But genuine English engraving of the period was poor, and fakers are often temped to do a job that is better.

One curious aspect of wine glasses is that the diameter of the foot is greater than the diameter of the bowl. Some people believe the reason is that the custom of the time was to hold the glass by the foot and not by the stem.

A group of glasses showing variation in shape, decoration and purpose. From left: a, bowl of the 'double ogee' shape; the stem has a multi-spiral air twist with swelling knop b, bowl of round funnel shape and engraved with Jacobite symbols; the stem with multi-spiral air twist; the foot domed c, Newcastle wine glass; the bowl engraved with symbols and mottoes of friendship. The stem is one of the most common and most satisfactory types d, glass for ratafia (a kind of liqueur). The stem has opaque twists and the bowl is engraved with leaves, flowers and buds e, ale glass. The bowl is engraved with hops and ears of barley and the stem has air twists f, cordial glass with air twist stem g, another cordial glass. The bowl is engraved with flowers and the stem has air twists. All these glasses date from about 1750 to about 1760

Jacobite glasses

The romantic and tragic story of the Jacobite cause grips the imagination, whatever historians may have to say about the rights and wrongs of it all. Clubs exist to keep fresh the memory of the Old Pretender, James Francis Edward Stuart, and the Young Pretender, Charles Edward Stuart. The collector can acquire all kinds of relics of those times, perhaps of dubious authenticity. Some of the safest of these items are the drinking glasses made in the eighteenth century for sympathizers with the cause. The glasses are engraved with Jacobite symbols, portraits, or mottoes.

It was somewhat risky in Hanoverian Britain to be a Jacobite, so meetings were held by clubs whose nominal purposes were dining and drinking. The glasses they used were similarly 'secret', and were supposed to be understood only by initiates. Among the emblems on the glasses are: *Oak leaves*. The future Charles II escaped from the Battle of Worcester by hiding in the Boscobel oak and, on his triumphant entry to London when he was restored to the throne, he wore oak leaves. Some glasses have a stricken oak to represent the unhappy House of Stuart. The stricken oak may have one or two saplings, or two sprouting leaves, to signify the Old Pretender or the Old Pretender and his son.

Roses are the most common symbols of all. They were once thought to signify James Francis Edward and his sons, Charles Edward and Henry. The present theory is that a large rose stands for the Crown of England and smaller roses or rosebuds beside it for the Old and Young Pretenders. The Old Pretender died in 1766 and glasses made after that carry only one smaller rose.

The *thistle* signifies the Crown of Scotland; the *trefoil* plant, revenge; a *star*, the guiding principle of Jacobitism; the *forget-me-not* and *daffodil* are thought to signify mourning for the Old Pretender. A *jay* was for James or Jacobite and a *blackbird* for the Old Pretender (his family called him Blackbird because of his dark complexion and eyes). A *carnation* is for the Crown because it has indented petals and has a fancied resemblance to a crown. Leaves of the plant *monkshood* were for General Monk who helped Charles II recover the throne. *Grubs* or *caterpillars* appear on the plants; they are obscure in meaning. Some authorities say they signify intrigues or the misfortunes of the cause. Others say they mean the way in which the soul of a dead Scotsman returns to his native land by the low road – underground.

Mottoes on these glasses are in Latin: *fiat* (may it happen), *revirescit* (he grows strong again), *redi, redite*, or *redeat* (may he return), *audentior ibo* (I shall go more boldly – a hint about the next

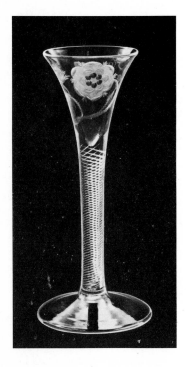

A Jacobite glass of about 1760, engraved with a six-petal rose and two rosebuds, an oak leaf, and 'Fiat'. It is 7 inches (17.8 cm) high

rebellion), *ab obice major* (the great often fall), *reddas incolumen* (may you return safely), *hic vir hic est* (this, this is the man).

Portraits are mostly of the Young Pretender and made after the rebellion of '45. Very rare examples show Flora Macdonald who helped Charles Edward to escape from the Hanoverian forces after the Battle of Culloden. Rare also are the examples called Amen glasses. These are inscribed with the Jacobite version of 'God Save the King' and end with the word Amen. Perhaps just over two dozen of them exist.

The glasses are poorer in quality the later they were made. Forgeries, of course, are a danger. Some are completely new; others are old, genuine, and plain glasses which have been engraved in recent times with the appropriate designs or inscriptions. One clue about genuineness is the amount of wear on the engraved parts of the glasses.

Genuine ones do turn up from time to time; a cache was found fairly recently in an Irish castle, hidden away and gathering dust in a cupboard.

Williamite Glass

The collector who is not inclined to favour the Jacobite cause can always go to the other side and search out Williamite glasses, which were used for drinking loyal toasts to the Protestant reigning House. These glasses show William III, usually on horseback but sometimes only in head and shoulders. Inscriptions sometimes refer to the Battle of the Boyne on July 12, 1690, when William's troops defeated those of James II. Williamite glasses were made from the 1740s to the end of the century; most, if not all of them, may have been made in Ireland. One inscription reads: "To the glorious pious and immortal memory of the great and good King William who freed us from Pope and Popery, knavery and slavery, brass money and wooden shoes. And he who refuses this toast may be damned, crammed and rammed down the great gun of Athlone."

Decorated glass

Some of the finest decorated glass ever made in this country was by the Beilby family, who worked in Newcastle upon Tyne from about 1760 to about 1778. But they had to struggle against hardship and illness and in the end they gave up their craft entirely. Not much is known about them. Their memorial is a handful of masterpieces and a comparatively small number of other objects.

Newcastle had for many years been a great centre for glassmakers; the Beilby family did only the decoration, and did not

A very rare Jacobite 'Amen' glass, $6\frac{3}{4}$ inches (17.1 cm). It is etched in diamond point with a crown and letters JR and the figure 8, signifying the Old Pretender or James VIII. It also has two verses of national anthem. The second verse – the Jacobite variation – says:
God Bless the PRINCE of Wales
The True born Prince of Wales
Sent us by Thee:
Grant us one favour more
The King for to restore
As Thou hast done before
THE FAMILIE

make the glasses. William Beilby was the son of a silversmith who failed in business. His father managed to send him to Birmingham when he was only 11 to learn enamelling on metal and drawing. William returned to the north in 1760 and went to work with his brother Ralph in Newcastle. Ralph was an engraver and seal cutter, and a lover of music.

William experimented with the firing of metals on glass and made remarkable technical discoveries. He first fused pigments into the surface of glass; this was achieved through adding a metallic flux. He also devised important modifications to furnaces to make them more efficient.

Technical difficulties were considerable. If the temperature was too low the enamels would later rub off; if it was too high the whole object would melt. The craftsmen who decorated and fired glass had to work by experience and rule of thumb.

Ralph helped William in the work; and so did their sister Mary, a tragic figure. She was born in 1749 and was about 13 when she began to learn the craft. Her speciality was in flowers, scrolls, vines, barley, and hops and simple pastoral scenes. The vines, barley and hops were symbolic of the drinks. But she never attained the

The Couper goblet by Beilby; an extremely rare enamelled glass with the arms of Couper with Gray. It is $7\frac{3}{4}$ inches (21.5 cm) high and was made about 1765. The colours are pale green, buff, red and white and the rim has traces of gilding. Round the coat of arms is an elaborate rococo border and scroll. On the reverse of the goblet is the Couper crest between two delicate white butterflies. The stem has opaque twists left

Wine glass by Beilby decorated with white enamel with scenes of a garden and a ruin. It is $5\frac{1}{8}$ inches (13 cm) high and made about 1760. The stem has incised twists

skill of William, and when she was 25 she had a stroke which left her disfigured and crippled.

Ralph's apprentice Thomas Bewick fell in love with her. He was to become a brilliant artist in woodcut views of the countryside. Ruskin wrote of him: "I know of no drawing as subtle as Bewick's since the fifteenth century, excepting Holbein's and Turner's." And Wordsworth wrote: "O now that the genius of Bewick were mine, and the skill that he learnt on the banks of the Tyne."

Much of what we know of the Beilbys comes from Bewick's *Memoirs,* where he says: "From the length of time I had known and noticed Miss Beilby, I had formed a strong attachment to her, but I could not make this known to her or to anyone else. I could have married her before I was done with my apprenticeship without any fears on my part, but I felt for her, and pined and fretted at so many bars being in the way of our union. One of the greatest was the supposed contempt in which I was held by the rest of the family, who, I thought, treated me with great hauteur . . ."

William, soon after the technical breakthroughs, produced one of the great achievements, and the one that brought fame and commissions. This was a set of goblets executed in 1762 and engraved with the arms of George III. It is not known how many were originally done; four have survived but one of them is damaged. They seem to commemorate the birth of the Prince of Wales in 1762.

The glasses which have come down to us include many pieces with coats of arms, masonic emblems, or political inscriptions. Some of them are:

A bowl, almost ten inches across, with two unidentified coats of arms, rococo scrolls, and naval emblems. It is in the Victoria and Albert Museum. Some people think that it is William Beilby's finest achievement.

A companion bowl made for the launching of a ship, called *The Margaret and Winneford,* at Newcastle in 1765. The bowl was sold at Sotheby's in 1970 and is now in the Laing Art Gallery, Newcastle. The decoration consists of a coat of arms, a ship in full sail, and a lace-like pattern.

A famous glass called the Standard of Hesleyside. This is eleven inches high and holds as much as an old-fashioned bottle of claret. It was made for Edward Charlton of Hesleyside, a remote manor house in the north Tyne valley, and carries his name and coat of arms. The custom of the family was to challenge its guests to drink its contents at one go without stopping. A Victorian lady of the family wrote: "I always dreaded this calling for the Standard, for some boasters immediately succumbed to the gluttonous operation before they could reach their rooms, and such an exhibition before

A scent bottle of opaque white Bristol glass, 3 inches high and with a gold top. The decoration, done in London, shows an exotic bird perched among flowering plants, with butterflies and a festoon of flowers above. The bottle's original case has survived; it is of shagreen lined with silk and plush velvet

ladies was not quite in keeping . . . . many times I suggested that the convivial vessel should be put under a glass case and kept in the drawing room; but I was always voted down, and in due course it suffered damage by the handling of a drunken butler."

The date at which the Beilbys gave up decorating glass is hard to establish. It seems that some time after 1778 William took his sister to London and that he ran a school in Battersea. It is also thought that they lived for a time in Fife, or elsewhere in Scotland. Mary died in 1797 and William lived for years in Hull where he died in 1819 aged 81. He does not seem to have made any more of the marvellous pieces after leaving Newcastle.

Nailsea
and Bristol glass

Glass has been used to make rather unlikely objects such as walking sticks, shepherds' crooks, rolling pins, bells, tobacco pipes, trumpets, and hats. Others are more obviously ornamental – models of sailing ships, foxhunts, and birds perching in trees. They are all given the name 'Nailsea,' after a place near Bristol where a glass factory operated from 1788 to 1873. Workers in glass factories used their spare time to make little pieces, called 'friggers', for amusement or decoration.

The idea caught on commercially and many pieces were made in the first quarter of the nineteenth century. But they are hard to date and they are still being made as 'antiques.' Nailsea glass often has coloured loops, stripes, streaks, or spots.

All sorts of fanciful stories are told about the rolling pins: that they were for storing salt or tea or for smuggling rum. They may have been mainly just ornaments; but some do have romantic symbols and mottoes and may have been love tokens.

Hollow walking sticks are found, sometimes filled with sweets. 'Witchballs' are globes of coloured or mirrored glass in various sizes. Some people say that they were designed to rest on the tops of jugs to keep out flies and dirt; but if they were they could hardly stop flies getting in at the spout.

Tobacconists may have used the pipes to make their window displays more attractive. 'Yards of ale,' which can be seen in many pubs, are drinking glasses like a long cone with a sphere at the end opposite the rim. The drinker is liable to get a soaking as he drains the last of the beer.

Among the Nailsea products are pairs of bottles joined like Siamese twins and called 'gimmel' flasks. Lovers are supposed to have plighted their troths by drinking simultaneously from the two necks.

These unsophisticated novelties, although they are called Nailsea, were probably made all over the country and sold at fairs and markets. More rare, refined, and costly is Bristol glass – but this is a misnomer too because it was not made only in Bristol. Most of it is a deep blue, but some is found in the green, amethyst, or – rarely – ruby. The most valuable was made in the second half of the eighteenth century.

It was sometimes cut into facets or gilded. Of it were made decanters, finger bowls, and bottles for sauces or scents. It was also used to line silver salt cellars because salt corrodes silver. The decanters often have the name of the drink in gilt letters: rum, brandy, hollands (gin), or shrub (a mixture of orange or lemon juice, sugar, and a spirit).

The blue was achieved by the addition of zaffre, an impure oxide of cobalt, which was imported through Bristol. The name of the place seems to have become attached first to the colour and then to the whole range of articles in blue glass wherever they were made.

The name Bristol has also been applied to another form of glass – an opaque white which sometimes has pretty floral decoration. Much of it may have been made in South Staffordshire. This was a case of economics influencing taste. An Excise Act of 1745 clapped a tax on most kinds of glass and many of the factories and workers fell on hard times. The opaque white glass was not subject to the tax and thus became popular. Moreover, it resembled porcelain, which was then a costly status symbol. Makers of opaque white glass also imitated the shapes and decoration of porcelain. But the material cannot withstand hot water and so was not used for tea cups, saucers, or teapots.

Some of the decoration was not permanent because the articles were not fired again after the decoration was applied. Many pieces which are now plain may at one time have had flowers, foliage, or

Left: Bottle of dark green glass, 5 inches (12.7 cm) high. The seal has the inscription ARK Oxon, a crown, and the date 1706. *Centre:* Bottle of clear green glass, 6 inches (15.2 cm) high. The seal has an abbreviated name. T Bsson and the date 1708. *Right:* Bottle of dark green glass, 5 inches (12.7 cm) high. The seal has the initials REW, a crowned head, and the date 1699. (Ornamented bottles, p.194)

inscriptions. Moreover, this type of glass is unusually thin and fragile and much has probably been lost. The loophole in the law was closed by another Excise Act in 1777.

Nailsea glass of the ordinary sort can be picked up for comparatively small sums. Some Bristol pieces are by decorators such as Lazarus Jacobs and his son Isaac, who had a factory in Bristol from 1771 to 1806, and James Giles of London (1718–1780). Their work is prized. But much of so-called 'Bristol' has been made in Czechoslovakia.

Ornamented bottles

Treasures sometimes turn up in cellars as well as attics; old ornamented wine bottles, made from about 1650 into the nineteenth century. They are eagerly sought after by collectors and people who like them simply as decorations.

These bottles have a 'seal' or button of glass on the side, with a coat of arms, the name or initials of the owner, a tavern sign, a date, or the name of a college, or place.

They were used to bring the wine from cask to table, and stood on the table instead of decanters; and a rich person would have his own bottles filled for him by his wine merchant. This is why they are even now being found in cellars of old houses, where they have perhaps been lying in an obscure corner for 200 years. They vary in colour from green through brown to almost black.

Pepys records in his diary that on October 23, 1663, he "went to Mr Rawlinson's and saw some of my new bottles, made with my crest upon them, filled with wine, about five or six dozen."

Many of the ones with the tavern signs are from Oxford, and the colleges also appear – for example, 'Ch Ch' for Christ Church,

Some examples of bottle seals

and 'BNC' for Brasenose College. But different qualities of wine were served to the dons and to the undergraduates, and to make certain that the undergraduates did not get the better sort some of the bottles have the initials 'CR' to signify that they were for the common room.

A President of Trinity College, Oxford, who had strong views about strong drink, once ordered many sealed bottles in the college's cellars to be emptied, smashed, and the fragments to be placed on the top of certain walls round the buildings to discourage wrongful entries or exits. The fragments can still be seen there, although one collector recently removed a fine specimen while standing on the shoulders of a friend.

Sealed bottles with dates have helped to establish the evolution of the shapes of bottles. The earliest, of the middle of the seventeenth century, are spherical with long necks. Gradually the neck grew shorter, and at the end of the seventeenth and the beginning of the eighteenth century bottles look rather like huge onions, with wide squat bodies and very short necks.

Gradually the 'onion' grew taller and the neck longer, and this form was the commonest from about 1715 to 1750. Then the modern cylindrical shape was evolved; and it has remained because it makes the storing of bottles easier than was the case with the bulbous varieties. People who collect the sealed kind sometimes try to have a whole range spanning the years of evolution.

But there are other ways in which to specialize in sealed bottles – for instance in the heraldic ones only, or ones from a special area of the country. Examples are found from dozens of counties, as far apart as Inverness-shire and Cornwall.

One of the encouraging things about this field is that the prices are not high and therefore the forger has not found it worth his while to produce sealed glass bottles. The few fakes that do exist can be detected easily because the glass is too light in colour and contains many bubbles. One might expect the forger to take an ordinary bottle of the period and add a new seal, but the matching of the colour would be very difficult, and the bottle might crack when the hot seal is added.

Fire plaques

Sometimes an old house has, high on a wall facing the street, a metal plaque with the emblem or name of an insurance company – usually a company which went out of business or was amalgamated with another years ago. The original aim of these plaques during the eighteenth and early nineteenth centuries was to show that the property was insured against fire; now the plaques, called fire marks, are collected and studied.

The emblems are a phoenix, a sun, clasped hands, a coat of arms, an Irish harp, an allegorical figure, and so on. Early examples have the insurance policy's number stamped on them. Late examples, which are less valuable, do not and are called by the purists fire plates.

Fire fighting during this period was done partly by the parish authorities and partly by private enterprise: the insurance companies had their own engines, ladders, hooks, buckets, and men. The story goes that when a building was alight the private brigades turned out and immediately looked for the fire mark. If the building did not have one, or if it had one belonging to another company, the brigade went home or just watched the blaze. The story is often repeated,

Mark of the Dundee Fire Office (1782–1826). It is 8¼ inches by 6¾ inches (21 cm by 17.2 cm). The pot of lilies is a symbol of Dundee and is also found as a hallmark on silver made there

picturesque, and untrue. Documents and pictures of the period show that the private brigades did co-operate.

Fire marks had several purposes. They were an advertisement to passers-by – they were brightly coloured, although nowadays they may have become covered in whitewash or paint or stripped of colour by the weather.

They were also a means of identification. Numbering of houses was not properly organized until the introduction of the penny post in 1840 vastly increased the volume of mail and made the present system essential. For example, some of Milton's poems were printed in 1673 "for Tho. Dring at the Blew Anchor next *Mitre Court* over against *Fetter Lane* in *Fleet Street*." Vague descriptions such as this made it hard to decide exactly which building was insured under a

Mark issued by the Worcester Fire Office, established in 1790

particular policy, so a fire mark was fixed up – high on the wall to be fairly safe from pilfering.

One risk was that a person whose house was burned down or damaged might afterwards take out a policy and claim. So the rule was that the policy was not in force until a fire mark was fixed to the building. A fee of a few shillings was charged for this.

It was the Great Fire of London that gave the impetus for the founding of the modern system. A pioneer was Dr Nicholas Barbon, a son of Praise-God Barebones who gave his name to the Cromwellian Parliament. Nicholas Barbon started with the name Unless-Christ-had-died-for-thee-thou-hadst-been-damned Barebones, but went on to a successful career in property as well as in several other businesses.

He started underwriting in 1667 and set up the Fire Office in 1680; it was also called the Insurance Office for Houses and its address, in the style of the time, was 'on the Backside of the Royal Exchange.' The office that first issued marks was the Friendly Society of London, founded in 1683, but none of its marks is known to have survived. The oldest known marks are by the Hand-in-Hand Office, also called the Amicable Contributionship, founded in 1686.

Many companies collapsed in 1720 because of the economic depression which followed the South Sea Bubble; no new ones were formed until 1767. The latter part of the 18th century and the beginning of the 19th saw an expansion of trade and an improvement of communications by road and rail.

Fire marks were first made of lead, which cannot have been entirely satisfactory because it melts at a comparatively low temperature; but it was cheap and durable. Copper was used in the early 1800s and iron and tin from about 1820. Rare materials are zinc, porcelain, and stoneware (a kind of pottery), and extremely rare are terracotta and carvings in stone set into the building. The last two were issued by the Phoenix and were a sign that the building was a replacement, at the company's expense, of one lost by fire.

From 1825 onwards the insurance companies in London began to pool their fire-fighting equipment. Gradually the whole responsibility was taken over, throughout the country, by the local authorities.

At least 100 companies were founded before 1830. Some of them changed the design of their marks from time to time, the Sun having as many as 26 variants, the Norwich Union 21, and the London Assurance 16. A complete collection, virtually impossible to form nowadays, would total at least 500.

Fire marks are fairly hard to come by. People who have them on their houses are reluctant to part with them, but cases of theft have been known. Forgeries are about: taking a mould of a genuine item and making a casting from it in lead is easy. Old forgeries have acquired an antique appearance.

Repainting or otherwise improving a fire mark should not be done because the original condition, however decayed, is preferred by collectors.

Duelling pistols

The scene is a field or public park at first light. Two groups of men approach each other and talk in quiet tones. They are a surgeon, two men determined to settle a quarrel, and their seconds. A polished wooden case is opened, and the duelling pistols are revealed. This romantic setting was a fairly common one in the late eighteenth and early nineteenth centuries, and it still grips the imagination of historical novelists.

The pistols which were used are not only tangible reminders of those times. They are also of technical brilliance, superb craftsmanship, and admirably fitted for the job they had to do. They are 14 inches or more long, sometimes mounted in silver; the barrels are always octagonal and muzzle-loading.

The pistol-cases, which were made in oak or mahogany, had all sorts of accessories: powder flask, mould for making bullets, cleaning rod, mallet, oil bottle, loading rod, powder measure, and the like. The maker's label was pasted on the inside of the lid and the case had a hinged handle. Accessories, however, are now often missing.

These pistols came into fashion because swords went out of fashion in the eighteenth century. Social custom still demanded some

Mark of the Protector Fire Office, London (1825–35). It is of copper, 9 inches (22.8 cm) by 9¼ inches (by 24.1 cm), has some of the original colouring, and shows a fireman directing water at a flaming house; in the background the scene is a bridge

way in which a real or imagined wrong could be 'satisfied'. Swords gave an advantage to the man who was skilled in fencing, while pistols put all parties on a more even footing. And when a man's life depended on the excellence of his weapon, the gunsmiths had every reason to bring their products to the peak of perfection.

The old inaccurate flintlock pistol was therefore refined and given better balance and a better bore in the barrel. Deliberate aim was banned under the code of duelling. The whole design was to make the pistol a natural extension of the body so that when the arm was brought up to shoulder level the pistol would automatically be on target. Pistols were made to measure, just as expensive shotguns are today.

Some of the great makers in London were Durs Egg (this curious name is Swiss), Henry Nock, H. W. Mortimer, the brothers John and Joe Manton, Robert Wogdon, W. Parker and James Purdey. Fine weapons were made by James Innes in Edinburgh, Westley Richards in Birmingham, John Rigby in Dublin (the Irish were great duellers), and Jeremiah and Ann Patrick in Liverpool.

Joe Manton improved the lock (the mechanism between the trigger and the gunpowder) and made ignition faster. But he was also guilty of sharp practice. Duelling pistols were supposed to have barrels smooth on the inside. Some military ones had rifling: spiral grooves to make the ball fly straighter and with more penetration. What Manton did was to rifle some of his barrels half-way down from the end where the charge and the ball are situated before firing. This secret rifling was hard to detect.

Robert Wogdon, who had a workshop in the Haymarket, London, became almost legendary. He devised a refinement to make pistols more accurate: the axis of the barrel was made at an angle to the line of sight to compensate for a slight optical error in taking aim. Lawyers devised the term 'Wogdon's case' for a dispute which could not be settled in court. James Purdey's firm still flourishes in

One of a pair of percussion pistols of about 1825. The stocks are of walnut inlaid with silver wire scrolls, flowers, and foliage and set with gilt brass mounts. Each pistol has an ivory tipped ram-rod. The pistols still have their fitted case covered with leather and lined with red velvet. 17¼ inches (39 cm) long

Mayfair, making sporting guns which cost a cool £2000 upwards. The original James Purdey charged £31 10s. for a pair of pistols in 1829.

Pistols were made on the flintlock principle until about 1820. When the trigger was pulled, a flint struck down on a pivoted piece of steel, making a spark which set off the gunpowder. But this was superseded by the percussion system: when the trigger was pulled a kind of hammer struck a special chemical, which exploded and set off the powder. This was the invention of an unlikely figure: the craggy-faced Rev Dr Alexander Forsyth, minister of the Church of Scotland in Belhevie, Aberdeenshire. A tradition in his family says he was fond of shooting duck with a flintlock sporting gun; but the flash from the mechanism warned the birds that he was shooting, and they often took evasive action before the shot could reach them. Moreover, damp got into the firing mechanism and spoiled its efficiency. So Dr Forsyth experimented with volatile chemicals, and devised a way of using potassium chlorate. He took his invention to London and after a long struggle proved its worth, but he benefited very little from his invention. Many flintlock pistols were converted to the percussion type. Converted pistols are less valuable now than unconverted and in general percussion ones less than flintlock. The older type seems to have a special charm for collectors.

One should beware of the pistols originally flintlock, then converted to percussion, but re-converted to flintlock in recent times to put up the value. Examples with mounts of silver are more prized than those with mounts of steel. Original accessories are of course desirable. The interest and value will be increased if the pistol has an unusual mechanism or a special refinement. The dedicated amateur in this field has limitless scope for research into the technicalities.

Yet always in the background, for duelling pistols at least, are the stories of pistols for two and coffee for one. It is said that the practice was confined in most cases to young bloods and to ruffians

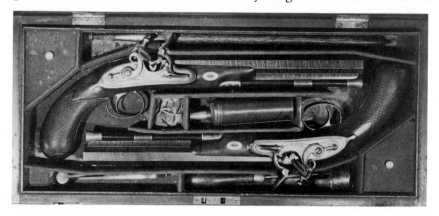

A pair of flintlock duelling pistols made by John Manton in 1828. The stocks are of walnut and are carved with a chequered pattern to give a good grip; the ramrods are tipped with brass; the case, in mahogany, is original and has accessories including a flask covered with leather; the lid has the maker's trade label. The pistols are 15 inches (38 cm) long

with pretensions to gentility; and many of the pistols were used only for the pastime of target shooting. But the élite took part as well, and a few duels have gone down in history.

The Duke of Wellington and the Earl of Winchilsea fought in 1829. The Duke was then aged 61 and was Prime Minister. He favoured Catholic emancipation; the Earl of Winchilsea spoke of the "insidious designs for the encroachment of our liberties" and of "the introduction of Popery into every Department of State". The Duke called out the Earl. Reports of what happened are somewhat conflicting, but it seems that neither shot to kill and both were unharmed.

Colonel Aaron Burr, Vice-President of the United States, killed General Alexander Hamilton, First Secretary to the Treasury, at Weehawken, New Jersey, in 1804. They had been political rivals for 15 years. Hamilton had written of Burr: "Determined to climb to the highest honours of the State and as much higher as circumstances may permit, he cares nothing about the means of effecting his purpose. If we have an embryo Caesar in the United States 'tis Burr."

George Canning, Foreign Secretary, and Lord Castlereagh, War Minister, fought in 1809: the quarrel was political. Canning was hit in the leg. Castlereagh was also hit but a button on his coat deflected the bullet.

The custom could not last forever, and certainly could not survive the Victorian revolution in social manners. A Society for the Suppression of Duelling was set up in 1843. The Articles of War were amended in 1844 so that an officer who took part in a duel was liable to be cashiered.

Fans

Fans gave a chance for a woman to show her taste, display her wealth, and keep up with fashion. They were also useful for flirtation and for concealing love letters.

Some had extras such as a small stiletto, or a thermometer, or a spyglass. Some had panels of transparent material: a woman at the theatre who was embarrassed by a risqué part of the play could cover her face but still see what was going on.

Examples from the seventeenth century or before are rare and costly and beyond the reach of most collectors. The best are of the eighteenth century, and the most elaborate are generally from France.

There are basically two types: *brisé* and ordinary. *Brisé* fans are composed entirely of the blades or spokes (technically called 'sticks') and the blades sometimes numbered as many as 30. Ordinary fans had, on the sticks, a folding mount of paper, silk, lace, or specially

Topographical fan, 10 inches (25.5 cm) wide, showing Cliveden House, Taplow, Buckinghamshire; mid eighteenth century *(top)*

Brisé fan in ivory, 10 inches (25.5 cm) wide with two mythological scenes, probably by Angelica Kauffmann RA (1741–1807), the Swiss painter who worked in London from 1766 to 1781 and was a friend of Sir Joshua Reynolds *(bottom)*

prepared and supple vellum or kid called, misleadingly, chicken-skin. Mounts of paper or silk are the most likely to survive in good condition.

The sticks are of ivory, tortoiseshell, sandalwood, laburnum wood, cut steel, mother-of-pearl, or bone. They are sometimes ornamented with jewels, medallions, miniatures, sequins, spangles, straw, or feathers.

The painted designs on both types of fan are of an enormous range and generally follow the taste of the time – rococo, neo-classical, and so on. Style is usually the only way of dating a particular specimen. Favourite subjects are landscapes; figures from mythology such as Venus and Cupid; flowers; and shepherds and shepherd-esses in the manner of Watteau, Fragonard, and Boucher. (Signatures of famous artists on mounts are, however, almost invariably false.)

Amusing but less usual are gimmicky designs with, for example, instructions for the latest dance steps; the plan of a theatre showing who rented which boxes; the hackney carriage fares for certain journeys in London.

Especially prized are marriage fans, which were given by the bridegroom to the bride and which were fashionable between 1720 and 1800. These have cupids, true-lovers' knots, statues of Hymen, doves, and suchlike symbols. Sometimes they had miniature portraits of the couple. Less costly fans were also given to the maids of honour and the guests. In contrast, fans were also made for mourning and had weeping willows and funereal urns. Types suitable for use in church had the Creed or Psalms.

Sizes varied according to fashion: large in the reign of Queen Anne and large again in the 1740s. The *London Magazine* said in 1744 that fans were "wonderfully increased in size from three quarters of a foot to a foot and three quarters or two feet."

Mounts were printed by means of engraved copper plates and then painted by hand. This made production quicker and easier, and a new and topical mount could be put on old sticks. Special mounts were done for such events as the huge success of *Gulliver's Travels* and the sensation of the early flights by balloons.

The original cases have sometimes survived. They are tubular or hexagonal, made of card, lined with velvet, and covered with paper, leather, or shagreen (sharkskin). They might, too, be mounted in silver. Some cases have the original label of the maker or the retailer.

Collecting fans was popular from about 1880 to about 1910 and again in the years between the wars. Victorian and Edwardian collectors sometimes put their treasures into specially made individual cases, shaped like an open fan and with glass fronts. But these do not always provide ideal conditions. Sunlight fades the watercolours or gouache paints; and the cases allow fluctuations of humidity which are harmful.

The influx of the Huguenots during the last part of the seventeenth century, after the Revocation of the Edict of Nantes, gave a boost to this craft as it did to many others. The makers specialized in certain parts of the trade: there were gilders, carvers, painters, and so on, as well as unskilled workers. The influx of foreigners was probably the reason for the establishment in 1709 of the Worshipful Company of Fan Makers in the City of London.

Barometers

"When two Englishmen meet, their first talk is of the weather," wrote Doctor Johnson. Newspapers, radio, and television give the Meteorological Office forecasts as absolute essentials. Hundreds of thousands of barometers must be tapped every day, and indeed they are probably more common than any other scientific instruments except perhaps thermometers.

Barometers have also achieved an elegance – even beauty – of craftsmanship and design. Their golden age was roughly the eighteenth century and the first half of the nineteenth: since then they generally suffered a decline in quality, as production-line methods of manufacture came in more and more and as the makers strove to produce inexpensive pieces.

The decline went along with a change in the mechanism used. The first barometers worked by a column of mercury in a glass tube; the mercury rises and falls according to changes in atmospheric pressure. Aneroid barometers, the kind made nowadays, work by a metal box from which the air has been pumped out; it expands and contracts as the pressure changes.

The best products of the eighteenth century are in walnut, mahogany, ebony, or other choice woods. These were adorned with gilt metal or brass mounts and with silvered plates or dials, and were sold by leading clockmakers, opticians, and scientific instrument makers. For example, Thomas Tompion (1638–1713), one of the greatest of English clockmakers, made several pieces of exquisite workmanship. Three of them are owned by the Queen.

The type made in the eighteenth century did not usually have the dial and pointer which are commonly seen. Instead they were basically straight glass tubes 31 or so inches long and mounted in a long narrow case of wood. The top of the tube, where the movement of the mercury is seen, has a scale to show the pressure in inches of mercury and the predictions – storms, changeable, fair, and so on. The appearance is rather like a grandfather clock, and these are called 'stick' barometers.

Barometers were, in the early 1700s, used in 'most houses of figure and distinction.' By the early 1800s they were in many middle class homes. The nineteenth century also saw the popularization of models with a large dial and pointer called wheel barometers. They offer much more scope for pleasing decoration and elegant proportion – the dial might be engraved, for instance, with beautiful lettering.

Above
A wheel barometer of the Regency period by J. Russell of Falkirk. It is in mahogany

Below
A marine chronometer made in London in 1831 by Johann Gottlieb Ulrich. Use of the chronometer gave British vessels an advantage at sea at a crucial phase in her history. Some examples were in service for the Admiralty for 100 years

Optional extras could be incorporated more easily; a thermometer, a concave mirror, a level, or a hygrometer. A hygrometer is a device for telling how dry or how damp the air is, but the type used is generally amazingly inefficient. It consists of the beard of a wild oat, which when dry is in a spiral shape and which when damp unwinds. This, in theory, works a pointer; but the oatbeard often disintegrates after a few months.

Wheel barometers are in general less accurate than the stick variety. The tube containing the mercury is U-shaped and one end of it is open. A weight, usually of glass, rests on the mercury in the open end; as the mercury moves up or down the weight, suspended from a pulley, activates the pointer.

Clocks and watches

The art of watchmaking involves establishing the time with scientific accuracy, satisfying the mind with mechanical ingenuity, and pleasing the eye with beauty. Clocks are in two main categories: long case (or 'grandfather' – but that term is an American invention and is disapproved of by the purists); and bracket, to put on a table, mantelpiece or shelf. Long case clocks are driven by weights and bracket clocks by springs. Watches can be categorized by the movement (or mechanism, but again the purists disapprove of that): verge, cylinder, lever, and others. (These technical terms are explained, as far as possible in a non-specialist way, in the glossary.) The chief enemies of accuracy are friction and the difficulty of letting power escape from the spring evenly and regularly – the escapement, in fact.

British makers of clocks and watches were the best in the world during the early part of the period dealt with by this book, and they exported their products to the Continent, Russia, the Middle East, and China.

Styles in clocks
The long case sometimes was very long indeed – up to eight feet six inches high. Fashions varied from time to time in the shape of the hood (the part over the top), details of the size of the dial and other ornaments, and other decoration. Its large area of wood gave scope for veneering, marquetry, and japanning. From about 1750 the traditional design was rarely made in London but was still popular elsewhere, especially in Lancashire and Yorkshire. The long case clock, a British invention, was never popular on the Continent.

Bracket clocks kept to a traditional form for a long time too.

Many were made with cases of ebony or pearwood which has been 'ebonized' or stained black. In about 1760 the balloon clock appeared and was in fashion until about 1810. Different styles such as the Gothic were reflected in the Regency period.

Tavern clocks are another category entirely. William Pitt began in 1797 to levy an annual tax on all clocks and watches, varying from 2s. 6d. to 10s. – a detested measure. Innkeepers started to put up large clocks in their premises to help their customers – Act of Parliament clocks. The name stuck, although the tax was repealed in a year. Most so-called Act of Parliament clocks were in fact made between 1750 and 1830. They have a large painted wooden dial, usually in black with gold numerals, and are about two feet six inches in diameter.

Timepieces for the Middle and Far East tend to be exotic, for the makers studied their market. Turkish buyers liked cases of tortoiseshell and mounts of elaborate gilt metal. Numerals are in the Turkish style. Some of the clocks, as well as striking, play a jig, minuet, or gavotte every three hours or so.

The Chinese had complex clocks of their own but mandarins, scholars, courtiers, and the Emperor were not interested in them. They preferred Western clocks which incorporated mechanical toys: a waterfall, imitated by a piece of twisted glass which revolves; figures which beat time to mechanical music; boats which move on a river. Pieces for the Chinese market usually have imitation jewels. James Cox of London, who was working from 1760 to 1790, was the principal maker of these fantasies. The East India Company gave clocks by him to rulers and officials and much of his work went to Peking. The ones there were looted in 1900 during the Boxer Rebellion and many found their way back to the West.

Regulators: a stately home or large house would have a lot of clocks and watches of different degrees of accuracy in various rooms and in various pockets. The household might lapse into confusion if they all told different times. The answer was a specially accurate long case clock with which everyone could check – a 'regulator' clock. Regulators were also used by astronomers and by retailers of clocks and watches. The regulators are plain, even severe, in design and fit well into a modern decor.

Style in watches

The typical watch of the early eighteenth century was large, robust and thick – the larger it was, the more accurate it could be made. Dials were in silver or gilded metal raised up in a pattern or design. The white enamelled dials were the rage from about 1725.

The casing offered huge scope for artistry. The metal was sometimes given repoussé ornament – the metal is hammered from the back into a raised design. Flowers, foliage, and mythological scenes were favourites. Fashion swung again and this style went out; instead the cases were sometimes given coverings of tortoiseshell, silver, or gilt brass. Even areas normally hidden from sight were decorated. The cases were set with pearls, gems, imitation gems, and semi-precious stones such as agates and cornelians.

Towards the end of the century, too, the seals which were worn with watches reached their full flowering, even to a ridiculous extent. The watch was kept in a small pocket of the breeches, on the right. To it was attached a ribbon or fob chain (also called chatelaine)

Opposite
An extraordinary long case clock made by Peter Garon of London in about 1720. The case is japanned in gold and black with chinoiserie decoration; the dial is surrounded by elaborate silver work with a military theme

The dial of the clock made by Garon

Clock made for the Turkish market by Henry Borrell in 1770; 12 inches high (32 cm). The materials of the case are tortoiseshell and ormolu and the dial is enamelled. The left hand small dial is to let the chiming movement work or stay silent; the right hand small dial is to select a tune for the musical mechanism. The 'Turkish' market extended far beyond the area of modern Turkey to the Balkans, North Africa, and even Zanzibar

which hung from the pocket so that the watch could be pulled out. Seals were attached to the fob chain – sometimes great clusters of them, at least in the case of the very dandified men. One craze was for carrying two watches with two sets of seals, although one of the watches was frequently a sham. Women wore their watches on a larger chatelaine, a complicated panel of chains which hung from the waist. Keys and other useful articles were also kept on women's chatelaines.

All sorts of refinements were devised in the mechanism and are of a highly technical sort: giving the date, striking the hours, or working an alarm bell.

One maker complained in 1724 about frauds by a number of continental watchmakers who "knowing the high value set on an English watch, make no scruple of applying the names of the most skilful English masters to their own vile productions." But later in the eighteenth century the dominance was slipping away and the French makers were gaining the upper hand. People of fashion were demanding smaller and thinner watches but the British makers refused to conform. Continental craftsmen were using machinery to make parts and women to assemble them. Illegal imports of Continental watches added to the troubles.

The makers in Clerkenwell, London – then as now a centre of the industry – were in great financial distress in 1816 and 1817. The House of Commons set up a commission of inquiry, which asked a witness the reason. He replied: "I think it is owing to the number of watches that have been made so exceeding bad that they will hardly look at them in the foreign markets. All with a handsome outside show, and the works hardly fit for anything".

He was asked if he believed many were like this and answered: "No, only a number made up by some low manufacturers. I remember a falloff of the East India work, owing to there being a number of handsome-looking watches sent out, for instance, with hands on, and figures as if they showed seconds. The hands merely went round . . . We had not any East India work for a long time afterwards." The craft in this country did, however, have a late flowering between about 1875 and 1910.

Organization of the trade

Demand for British clocks led to a division of labour among the craftsmen – one specialist for the metal ornaments, one for the engraving, one for the dial, and so on. Assembly and final adjustment were done by the master of the workshop, who often signed his name on the final article. Shopkeepers sometimes put their own names on other people's clocks.

Watch by Thomas Tompion, 2¼ inches (56 mm) across. The dial is of champlevé gold and the case is gold, hallmarked for 1709. This example has a repeating mechanism. (See p.213)

Bracket clock made by Robert Bumstead of London in about 1730. The case is veneered in burr walnut – an expensive material. The small dial is for making the clock go faster or slower. This is typical of a first-class clock by a lesser-known London maker

The trade in London was regulated for generations by the Clockmakers' Company. A charter of Charles I, given in 1631, established the 'Master, Wardens, and Fellowship of the Arts or Mystery of Clockmaking of the City of London', which had wide powers. Someone entering the craft had to spend five years as an apprentice. After two years as a journeyman he could submit a 'masterpiece', a work entirely by himself. If it was satisfactory he was allowed to become a work master. Women were entitled, from 1715, to become apprentices, but very few took advantage of this.

Some great makers

The outstanding English genius was Thomas Tompion (1639–1713). He was not only a designer of genius and taste but an impresario of talent; he ran a large workshop of apprentices and journeymen and commissioned work from craftsmen outside.

His fame was so great among his contemporaries that he was mentioned in plays, his work was given the ultimate compliment of being faked in his lifetime, and William III commissioned him to make costly gifts for foreign potentates. The court painter Sir Godfrey Kneller did his portrait. Many of his pieces have turned up in the Netherlands, Russia, Italy, France, and Spain.

Tompion was the grandson and son of blacksmiths – not an incongruous background, because blacksmiths were among the pioneers of clockmaking, especially for churches. He was born in Ickfield Green, Northill, Bedfordshire, and his early history is lost. His career was fostered by Robert Hooke, a mainstay of the Royal Society, professor of geometry, and experimental physicist.

Hooke had some of his scientific instruments made by Tompion and the connection probably gave Tompion introductions to other scientists, the nobility, and the King. Hooke's diary for 1675 says: 'To Garaways [a coffee house]. I was very brisk. Smoked 4 pipes. Drank 2 chocolate. Discoursed with Tompion . . . about bellows new invented and about ovall watch.' The diary also says: 'Fel out with Tompion'. 'Tompion a Slug'. 'A clownish churlish Dog'. 'A Rascall'. In fact Hooke was what we would call a neurotic.

Hooke's patronage would, however, have been of no importance if Tompion was not a genius and a man for his era. Tompion's powers were at their peak during the reign of William III. His clocks and watches were the status symbols of the time. His most ordinary clocks cost £10 in 1694 – if one could get hold of them – while other makers charged £6 or £7. He charged £11 for a watch in a silver case, £23 for one in gold, and £70 for one in gold with a repeater mechanism. (A repeater has a special device: you operate a string and bells strike the hour and the last quarter of the hour. This was useful in the night and saved the owner getting out his flint and tinder to see the time.) A special clock made in 1695 cost no less than £600.

The most elaborate clocks had other refinements – they ran for a year, or told the difference between mean time and the time accord-

Bracket or table clock made by Tompion and his son-in-law about 1703. It is 14½ inches high and is veneered in ebony. The shape is typical of later bracket clocks by Tompion, being slightly elongated. The left hand dial is to regulate the pendulum and make the clock go faster or slower; the right hand small dial is to let the chiming mechanism work or keep it silent. The dome on top helps to house the bell

ing to the sun, or struck the hours in a special way.

The cases for his instruments were done not in his workshop (at the sign of the Dial and Three Crowns at the corner of Fleet Street and what is now Whitefriars Street, London). They were by other specialists but Tompion must have closely supervised the design and

Back of the Tompion bracket clock of about 1703. The elaborate workmanship is instantly recognizable as being characteristic of Tompion. Almost all the parts shown here are in brass but some are in blued steel

execution. Favourite materials were ebony, mulberry wood, pear wood stained black in imitation of ebony, tortoiseshell, and veneering in walnut and marquetry. The dials and mounts tend towards simplicity. Mostly the mounts are gilded brass but some are silver.

Tompion started in about 1685 to number his clocks, presumably to make record-keeping easier. By the time he died the numbering had reached 550. He had a similar system for watches, and it seems these totalled about 6000. But none of the numbers is known to belong to a particular year and his only dated clock has no number. The system was carried on after his death by his partner and former apprentice, George Graham, another of the great British makers. They are both buried at the same spot in Westminster Abbey. Tompion never married.

His reputation, now so high, faded a little during the nineteenth century. But Benjamin Lewis Vulliamy, a nineteenth-century maker, who was sent a Tompion clock by the Duke of Grafton for repair, claimed that the mechanism was worn out and put in one of his own. He kept Tompion's for himself, knowing its worth, and bequeathed it to the Institution of Civil Engineers.

Much sought after of Tompion's pieces are the examples of unusual size, or early ones, or the more inventive and original ones. Long case clocks are more variable in price and usually cheaper than bracket clocks.

George Graham (about 1673–1751) was not only Tompion's apprentice and then partner but married Tompion's niece Elizabeth and carried on the business after his death. He perfected the dead-beat escapement, modified Tompion's early form of cylinder escapement, and introduced the mercury compensating pendulum (see glossary). He made more than 170 clocks, almost 3000 watches, and some scientific instruments. He became a Fellow of the Royal Society in 1721 and Master of the Clockmakers' Company in 1722.

Graham also was a most attractive personality, lived a simple life, shared his knowledge with other experimenters, and helped struggling people such as the young Harrison (see page 218). He earned in his own day the nickname Honest George, but his work has been widely faked.

Daniel Quare (1647–1724) had a large output which varies from outright masterpieces to pieces of indifferent workmanship. Much of the manufacture was probably done by apprentices and other less skilled employees. He invented the repeating watch in about 1680 and made long case and bracket clocks, and watches with unusual features. He at first refused the office of Clockmaker to George I because of his Quaker principles which, he thought, were incompatible with the oath of allegiance. But the difficulty was overcome, and he was allowed to enter the palace freely by the back doors. "The Yeoman of the Guard" he wrote, "lets me frequently go up without anybody for leave, as otherwise he would tho' persons of quality".

Christopher Pinchbeck was an inventor of 'astronomico-musical clocks'. An advertisement published by him in 1721 said: "He maketh and selleth Watches of all sorts and Clocks, as well for the exact Indication of Time only, as Astronomical, for showing the various Motions and Phenomena of planets and fixed stars, solving at sight several astronomical problems, beside all this a variety of Musical performances, and that to the greatest Nicety of Time and with the usual graces; together with a wonderful imitation of several songs and Voices of an Aviary of Birds so natural that any who saw not the Instrument would be persuaded that it were in Reality what it only represents. He makes Musical Automata or instruments of themselves to play exceedingly well on the Flute, Flagellet or Organ, Setts of Country dances, Minuets, Jiggs, and the Opera Tunes, or the most perfect imitation of the Aviary of Birds above mentioned, fit for the Diversion of those in places where a musician is not at hand. He also makes Organs performing of themselves Psalm Tunes with two, three or more Voluntaries, very convenient for Churches in remote Country Places where Organists cannot be had, or have sufficient Encouragement. And finally he mends Watches and Clocks in such sort that they will perform to an Exactness which possibly thro' a defect in finishing or other Accidents they formerly could not."

This does not end the list of his accomplishments. He also invented the alloy pinchbeck, named after him, which resembles gold and was much used for snuffboxes, étuis, watch cases, seals, and other small objects during the eighteenth century, and for jewellery during the nineteenth. He jealously guarded the formula for the alloy and at one point only his son shared the secret. Christopher Pinchbeck died in 1732, aged 62.

John Ellicott (1706–1772) was one of a family in the business. He was a pioneer of the cylinder escapement and compensation pendulum. He became a Fellow of the Royal Society in 1738 and clockmaker to George III.

John Harrison and the search for the elusive longitude

Navigation was at one time a very hit-and-miss affair. A vessel on a voyage from this country to, for example, the West Indies might arrive scores or even hundreds of miles from its destination. The man who solved the problem was a British eccentric and genius who started his career as a carpenter in a remote part of Lincolnshire. He

John Harrison, after a medallion by James Tassie

was John Harrison, the inventor of the marine chronometer, but a victim of injustice and broken promises. Marine chronometers are elegant, functional, and accurate to an extraordinary degree. They are bought nowadays by yachtsmen, specialists in horology, and by people who want a beautiful timepiece about the house.

A mariner can easily determine his latitude, the distance from the equator, by taking observations from the stars. He can determine his longitude, the distance east or west of Greenwich, by comparing local time with Greenwich mean time: four minutes of difference equals one degree of longitude. But for this he needs an accurate timekeeper, and such an instrument did not exist in the early 18th century – at least none existed which could stand up to the rolling and pitching of a ship and extremes of hot and cold.

Parliament in 1714 offered a prize of £20,000 to anyone who could invent a timekeeper of high accuracy; it would be tested on a voyage to the West Indies. This was an immense sum, but the difficulties were immense too. The Commissioners of the Board of Longitude, set up by the Act of Parliament, had nothing to record in their minutes for the first 22 years of their existence.

John and James Harrison, brothers and carpenters by trade in Barrow-on-Humber, Lincolnshire, were adept at mending clocks and watches. John, born in 1693, was highly skilled by the time he was 20. The brothers had by 1726 produced two long case clocks of revolutionary design, unaffected by variations in temperature and with friction reduced to a minimum: and about 1730 they invented a quite new form which had no pendulum. John set off for London to get help in making his name and fortune. Help came from the East India Company, which had a big stake in 'discovering the longitude', and from 'Honest' George Graham.

The brothers, still carrying on their trade as carpenters, spent the years 1731–1735 making a 'sea clock' which was tested on a voyage to Lisbon and proved a success. The navigators on the vessel, the Centurion, were 60 miles out in their reckoning on the return voyage: Harrison's reckoning was correct.

He asked the Board of Longitude for help in 1737, and they gave him £500 to develop a new machine. John and James moved to London, where skilled metal workers could be found. James returned to Lincolnshire in 1739 to work as a miller and bellfounder.

The Board gave another £500 in 1741 for the machine, to be ready in three years. It was completed 19 years later; Harrison got £3000 in all from the Board, in nine separate subsidies.

His masterpiece was ready in 1760: the longitude watch, the most famous watch ever made – 5¼ inches across, cased in silver, with jewelled bearings, made with the most superb craftsmanship. It is in

Harrison's masterpiece, the longitude watch. It is 5¾ inches (13.3 cm) across

the National Maritime Museum, Greenwich. It was tested on a voyage to Jamaica on H.M.S. Deptford. On the way out the clock, in the charge of John Harrison's son William, proved its worth. The ship unerringly reached Madeira, a victualling point. All the beer on board had been used up and the crew reduced to drinking foul water. Under the old system of steering by intelligent guesswork, the ship might have spent weeks searching for its landfall.

The test at Jamaica was rather bungled, and another test was ordered. A bitter dispute broke out between the Board of Longitude and the Harrisons, father and son, over the prize money. John Harrison seems to have been afflicted by some nervous disease as early as 1730. He often could not express himself on paper with any clarity. His speech was affected too. Never a patient or sympathetic person, he suffered from the early 1760s from an obsession that the Board was a pack of scoundrels determined to rob him of his reward. William was his public relations man, conducting a campaign by pamphlet, agitation in Parliament, and petitions. George III was reported to have said: "By God, Harrison, I will see you righted" and "These people have been cruelly treated"

John Harrison was obliged to make another prototype, his fifth, which was completed when he was aged 79 and after $4\frac{1}{2}$ years of labour. He was then in failing health and his eyesight was poor.

The award should have been made in 1764 but not until 1773

An early nineteenth-century model, in bone, of an 86-gun man-of-war; 20 inches (51 cm) long. It has a figurehead, highly carved details in the poop, 3 boats, a capstan, barrels, a rum keg, a bell and retracting cannon

was justice done, by an Act of Parliament. Harrison was given £8750 – he had already received large sums from the Board. His mechanical devices such as the remontoire, gridiron compensation, and 'grasshopper' escapement, are explained in the glossary.

His ideas were taken up and developed by John Arnold, Thomas Mudge, and Thomas Earnshaw. The classic standard marine chronometer, made from 1830, is in a brass-bound box, usually mahogany but sometimes walnut, satinwood, rosewood, or calamander wood. A lid at the top swings open for the time to be read through a pane of glass. The mechanism, however, cannot be reached unless a second lid is opened with a key. The mechanism swings on two sets of pivots, called gimbals, so that it is always level however much the ship pitches or rolls. Marine chronometers ought to be wound at the same time of day: they like a regular life.

Marine chronometers gave British seafarers an advantage over their competitors at a time when Britain was expanding her overseas trade and possessions.

Byron wrote about a woman in *Don Juan*:

Oh! she was perfect, past all parallel –
Of any modern female saint's comparison;
So far above the cunning powers of hell,
Her guardian angel had given up his garrison;
Even her minutest motions went as well
As those of the best timepieces made by Harrison.

Thomas Mudge (1647–1724), who was apprenticed to Graham, invented the lever escapement, the one that is used on all modern watches. He first put it in a watch which he made for George III and which is still in the royal collection. This watch was also the first to have a device for countering changes in temperature and the effects these changes could have on timekeeping. Ferdinand VI of Spain, who loved mechanical things, commissioned him to produce any horological curiosity he liked at his own price. Mudge came up with a clock which showed apparent and true time, struck the hours, and repeated the hours, quarters, and minutes.

John Arnold (1736–1799). Refined the marine chronometer. He presented to George III in 1764 a quarter-repeating watch set in a ring. The movement was just over one-third of an inch across: a marvel of skill. The King gave him 500 guineas in recognition. It is said that the Empress of Russia offered him 1000 guineas for a duplicate but that he refused, wishing the King's to be unique.

Thomas Earnshaw (1749–1829). Developed the marine chronometer, as Arnold did also; but the two men were at loggerheads over alleged plagiarism. Marine chronometers by him are rare but many of his pocket chronometers (precision watches) exist.

Fakes, forgeries, and restorations

What appears to be a costly and beautiful piece may in fact be mechanically poor. Something which appears to be made in this country may in fact originate from the Continent. A genuine eighteenth century case may contain a later movement; the original having been worn out, broken, or not thought accurate enough. High prices tempt the faker. A later movement may itself be taken away and in its place put one which pretends to be original but is in fact cannibalized – made up of bits and pieces from several movements.

Another problem is over-cleaning of metal parts. Cleaning may wear down fine engraving or a matt finish. A high gloss looks pretty but is perhaps not what the maker intended. Polishing has another purpose. Part of the mechanism may be modern and look quite different from the rest because it has not the patina of age. So everything in the movement gets polished to disguise this.

Decoration in lacquer adds to the value and has often been applied to a plain clock. Favourite lacquer colours for collectors and thus for fakers are red, blue, and green.

Prisoner-of-war work

Britain captured about 122,000 soldiers and seamen between 1794 and 1815 when she was almost continuously at war with France and other continental countries. Many of these men were kept in frightful conditions. Yet prisoners made all kinds of objects for sale: chessmen, dominoes, cribbage boards, toys, hats, lace – and especially valued are their models of ships.

Prisoners were at first kept in hulks: ships which were no longer fit for trade or war. Their masts were taken down and they were moored at naval ports such as Chatham, Sheerness, Portsmouth, and Plymouth. British officers and guards lived in huts built on the decks; the prisoners were sometimes crammed into the hulk so tightly that they hardly had room to turn over in their sleep.

Overcrowding became so bad that prisons were built on land. The first was at Norman Cross, near Peterborough; others were on Dartmoor and at Lewes, Dover, Liverpool, Perth, and elsewhere. The one at Dartmoor later became the ordinary prison. Some of the men, to relieve the monotony, fought or gambled; or learned reading and writing, Latin and Greek, tailoring, shoemaking, or carving. Groups of them were formed to make models of ships – one man might be good at the rigging, another at cannon, another at assembly.

The ships can be as large as seven feet long or as small as two inches long. Miniature models can be marvels of finely detailed craftsmanship. Some of the 'ropes' are of wood as thin as silk thread and a magnifying glass is needed to see the smallest of the features properly.

The usual size is between 12 inches and 24 inches long and the usual materials were bone and wood. Rarer are ivory, horn, tortoiseshell, whalebone, tinsel, and mother-of-pearl. The bones came from the prisoners' ration of meat and it had to be cleaned and bleached before it could be used. Generally, wooden models are the best because bone is difficult to work with. The bone ones also tend to be more fanciful and event fantastic; with more guns

Model made about 1800 of an 80-gun vessel; 21 inches (56.5 cm) long. The name on the stern is Foudroyent (French for striking down, terrifying, or crushing). The name was popular for both French and British ships. But many models were named and given a flag just before they were sold: the makers wanted to please the taste of potential buyers. (See p.221)

that the real ship would have had, more masts, booms, and so on, and superfluous detail. Uneven quality of carving on different parts of a model shows that several prisoners worked on it.

Warships are the commonest. The other types include many smaller or less usual craft such as Maltese galleys, feluccas, and Revenue cutters. A special refinement is found in some warships: you pull a cord which comes from the hull, and the guns run out of the ports. This mechanism depends on springs, which after more than 150 years have in many cases rusted away.

The craftsmen could have been French, Dutch, Swiss, Spanish, American, or of other nationalities; but the majority of prisoners were French and the models show features typical of French vessels. Names of famous ships appear on the models, such as the Victory; the men knew what would appeal to the market. Faithfulness to the original is, however, not usual because the men were working from memory or indeed may never have seen the ship they were modelling.

British people bought the prisoners' products at markets held near or inside the prisons. With the money the men were able to buy luxuries and the tools and materials they needed to carry on their work. They even had silkworms to produce silk for the rigging. They probably had primitive lathes. They used drills that were finer than the finest needle now obtainable.

All this detailed work suggests that the men on the hulks were probably not involved in the craft: their conditions were too horrible. Moreover the hulks came to be used for recalcitrant or criminal elements. On the other hand about 5000 officers were allowed out on parole and they lived in far more pleasant surroundings.

It is thought that not all the models in existence were made by prisoners but that other people saw the chance of making money and stepped in. Families with menfolk in the fleet would want to buy a model of one of the ships, even if the accuracy was not good, and £26 and £40 are said to have been paid for specimens. These were large sums for ordinary people at that time.

Models made later in the nineteenth century are from time to time passed off as the genuine thing. A glass case is essential for protection against dust and knocks. Wooden models tend to be less durable than bone, and restoration is a slow and costly business. Restoring a piece oneself offers enormous satisfaction.

Very large numbers were made and many of these have been sold to the United States. The museum at Peterborough has a splendid collection of all kinds of prisoner-of-war work and many other museums have ship models.

Miniatures

George IV was buried with a miniature portrait of his morganatic wife, Mrs Fitzherbert, round his neck. The incident symbolizes people's instinct to possess a likeness of their loved ones; and it sums up a golden age of miniature portraits.

The flowering of the later eighteenth century declined at the beginning of the nineteenth and was soon to be destroyed by the invention of photography.

Enormous numbers of miniatures were produced in the late eighteenth century. The portraits were intimate in scale and intimate in their use, for they were meant to be worn. They were put in rings (for men as well as women), lockets, bracelets, brooches, and snuffboxes, and on chains round the neck.

The artists worked not only in London but also in fashionable watering places such as Bath, in quite small towns, and even in India for expatriates and for princes. Some were 'lightning' operators, taking only a short time to produce a likeness. Others took as many as 50 sittings, wearying their clients. Standard prices varied from a few shillings to as much as 30 guineas, a rather high price for the period.

It was an exacting craft. A magnifying glass was occasionally used and the 'brush' was sometimes the single whisker of a cat. Deteriorating eyesight was an occupational hazard. The usual size until about 1770 was about $1\frac{1}{2}$ inches high but then women's hair styles became taller and taller and miniatures became 3 inches high or more.

Sometimes the artists altered existing portraits to bring them up to date; the women were given the latest fashions of coiffure and military men, on promotion, were given the insignia of their higher rank. Some of the outstanding names are:

Richard Cosway (1742–1821), a short, monkey-faced eccentric and fop who was subject to satire and scandal. He hobnobbed with the Prince of Wales and the Whig aristocracy, and he did the miniature of Mrs Fitzherbert which was buried with George IV. Contemporaries said he flattered his sitters; a more charitable view is that he depicted as well as he could their more attractive features.

John Smart (1741–1811), led, in contrast, a quiet and religious life. His only great adventure seems to have been a stay of nearly 10 years in India, where he worked for the Nawab of Arcot and the Nawab's family. Smart, again in contrast to Cosway, was matter-of-fact about the appearance of his sitters.

Ozias Humphry (1742–1810) began his career in Bath, moved

The Hon. Frederick Sylvester Douglas, by Henry Burch, about 1800; 3 inches (7.6 cm) high. The frame is set with rose diamonds

Opposite page
Scent flask of about 1760, by James Cox. It is 5 inches (12.7 cm) high, and is of faceted blue glass overlaid with gold. The gold is chased with birds, a temple, flowers, and foliage. On one side is a watch and on the other a compass. The base is hinged and forms a snuffbox. (Christie's)

to London, travelled in Italy, and was in India from 1785 to 1787. The Indian trip damaged his health and the Nawab of Oudh failed to pay up; Humphry was embittered about the debt until the end of his days. His sight failed when he was about 50 and he worked on a larger scale and tried full-size oil painting.

Jeremiah Meyer (1735–1789) was born in Germany and came to Britain when he was 14. The Royal Family were his patrons, no doubt because of the German connection, but his work is outstanding on its own merits. He was the first to experiment in this country with the use of ivory as the material on which miniatures were painted. It gave an extra quality to the product.

Richard Crosse (1742–1810) came from a family of landed gentry and probably did not depend on his work for money, but in one year made £960. He was a deaf mute and his life was blighted also by unrequited love for his cousin Sarah Cobley. She refused him about 1778 and he did not see her again until 1807 when she was on her death-bed. Her son, the painter and diarist Benjamin Haydon, has left a moving account of Crosse's grief.

George Engleheart (1750–1829) produced no fewer than 4853 miniatures in 39 years, but still managed to maintain a high standard. His later work shows greater realism and he also produced rectangular miniatures.

Andrew Robertson, a Scot, went to London in 1801 and brought in a fashion for larger, more solid, and richer treatment. The art started to become static about 1820, and the arrival of daguerreotypes, which were cheap, was a grave blow.

Opposite page
Blue glass scent bottles, $1\frac{7}{8}$ inches (4.8 cm) high, and made about 1770. They have gilt metal caps and the original case is shagreen. (Private collection)

Conversation group. Mr and Mrs Smith of Hailsham and Aunt Everard, by Francis Torond; about 1777. On card, 16 inches (40.7 cm) by $24\frac{1}{2}$ inches (62.3 cm) see p. 227

Children, pretty young women, and officers are in general more expensive than middle-aged people. A trend in recent years has been for collectors to be more concerned than formerly with the quality of the painting rather than the name of the artist.

Sometimes false signatures of well-known artists have been added to genuine but unsigned works by others. Retouching of faded areas reduces values, and the buyer should use a magnifying glass. Outright fakes have been made: the trace of a photograph can be seen underneath the paint.

Most miniatures are on ivory. The luminosity of the ivory shows through the transparent colours to good effect. Others are on vellum or card, or in enamels (pigment fused on metal). Ivory is apt to crack, and sunlight fades water colours.

Ivory is highly sensitive to changes in humidity and temperature and is liable to warp or break. The usual medium is watercolour and gum; but watercolour flakes off ivory easily and gum, in humid conditions, is attractive to fungi.

Most miniatures are sealed in lockets. Experience and skill are needed to open them; otherwise locket, glass, and miniature can all be ruined. A miniature, once it is out of its frame, is one of the most vulnerable of art objects. It should be touched as little as possible, and only by the fingertips and on the edge. If it is held on the palm of the hand it may instantly react to the sweat, and warp and lose paint. Ivory miniatures should be held by the top and bottom, where the grain ends; holding them by the sides can cause bending, and thus loss of paint or even cracking.

A young woman, by Richard Cosway, 3 inches (7.6 cm) high

Captain Murray, by George Engelheart, dated 1791; $3\frac{3}{8}$ inches (8.6 cm) high

Silhouettes

Everyone wants to have a likeness of a member of his family or even of himself; and from about 1770 until the invention of photography this need was partly filled by silhouettes. They were comparatively cheap, whereas miniatures were mainly for the well-to-do.

About 300 artists have been recorded, and 20 or 30 of them can be considered in the top rank. Their likenesses are remarkably accurate in many cases, giving a better idea of what the person looked like than some portraits or miniatures. Every large town had its artist or artists at some point and especially such fashionable places as Bath, Cheltenham, and Brighton. Silhouettes of the cheaper sort took a few minutes to produce and cost a shilling. Better quality work was a guinea or more.

Fashion played its part in encouraging business: George III was keen on the medium in spite of his unattractive profile and society followed his lead. Another influence came from a book called *Essays on Physiognomy calculated to extend the Knowledge and Love of Mankind*. It was written by a Swiss pastor, Johann Casper Lavater (1741–1801) and translated into English in 1794. He believed that character could be assessed from people's faces, just as the phrenologists believed that character could be assessed from the bumps of the skull. Moreover, his book was illustrated with many silhouettes, and he believed that silhouettes, concentrating on salient features, were the best means of using his science. Lavater's theories had a huge popularity.

Betsy Sheridan, sister of the playwright, wrote in 1788: "I have been reading Lavater . . . he does not advance the general theory of particular passions and dispositions impressing certain lines of the countenance, but positively insists that a nose or mouth of certain formation almost invariably belongs to a particular character."

The name 'silhouette' came from Etienne de Silhouette (1709–1769), a cheeseparing French Minister of Finance noted for petty tax reforms. He also cut black profiles and the term in its original sense was applied to his hobby to denote cheapness. The artists originally were called profile miniaturists and the likenesses were called profile miniatures or shades. Some were produced from a shadow thrown by a candle on to a sheet of paper; others by machines; others freehand, either cut from paper or drawn or painted. The materials varied: paper, wax, glass, or plaster. Good effects were achieved by touching in hair or dress with gold or other colours, although some silhouettes are quite plain.

Survival of the original frame makes a silhouette much more desirable. Frames are of pearwood, brass, or papier mâché. Another desirable feature is the label which may be found pasted to the portrait. But not all artists used them and the label may in any case have been lost.

Sometimes the subject of the portrait or his family put his name on it. Unless this happened or the sitter is very well known the identification is almost impossible.

Sometimes the artist signed his name. Much information can be gathered from the labels and from advertisements of the time; and distinctive styles make it possible to ascribe examples to a period or an artist. Changes in clothing and hairdressing are a help in dating.

A decline in quality set in about 1820 partly because of production by unskilled silhouettists. But examples of this later period do have a certain charm in their portrayal of fashions and children. The end came for silhouettes, as it did for painted miniatures, with the invention of photography.

Among the notable artists John Miers (1756–1821) is the best known and most prolific of all. His career started in his home town of Leeds in 1781; he worked in Newcastle, Manchester, Liverpool, and Edinburgh; and finally opened a studio in London in 1788. Some of his work is on card but the best is on plaster. Miers trained several other artists.

Isabella Beetham, whose professional career lasted for 37 years, began by cutting from paper but later painted on paper, and finally worked on glass.

Francis Torond, of Huguenot descent, was a master of 'conversation pieces', showing the well-off classes at their ease.

John Buncome of Newport, Isle of Wight, specialized in military men. His uniforms are splendid and accurate; modern prints have been made of his work.

August Edouart worked from 1825 in Britain and the United States. He did portraits of six American Presidents and Vice-Presidents. Edouart folded his paper in two when cutting and thus produced a duplicate.

Finally, as a curiosity, two infant prodigies. Master William Hubard was advertised in 1822 at the age of 15 as: "The celebrated little artist, who by a mere glance at the face! with a common pair of scissors!! cuts out the most spirited and striking likenesses in one minute." Master Frederick Frith, it was announced to the "Nobility, Gentry, and Inhabitants of Tunbridge Wells," was "extraordinarily talented . . . the astonishment of all lovers of the Arts." Both went on to fairly distinguished careers.

A lady, by Mrs Beetham, 3⅜ inches (8.6 cm) high, in a turned wood frame. On the reverse side is the artist's trade label

Papier Mâché

A vast array of richly-decorated objects was made of what appears to be an unlikely material – papier-mâché. Most common are quite small things such as trays, letter racks, spectacle cases, buttons, screens, jars, and boxes of all sorts. But there were also tables, chairs, beds, wardrobes, and cabinets. Even pianos, or rather the casing to hold the working parts of pianos, were made of it.

Papier mâché was highly adaptable, the equivalent of plastic; and it could be richly ornamented in many ways.

The term looks French but was invented in Britain some time in the mid-eighteenth century. The material was at that time made of pulped paper; it was moulded and used for ceiling ornaments, mirror frames, and snuff boxes, among other things. A step forward came in 1772 when Henry Clay of Birmingham patented a process for making heat resistant panels. Layers of paper were pasted together in metal moulds, drenched in linseed oil, heated, and dried.

Clay's papier mâché was suitable for japanning (see page 29) because it could be given a smooth surface and could be dried in an oven without danger of warping. It could also be worked like wood: sawn, dovetailed, and screwed.

This invention created an industry in Birmingham and Wolverhampton. The first way in which the new material was used was for

A tray made by Henry Clay in about 1810. It is 29 inches long and 21½ inches wide. The background is black and the decoration is mainly in gold

the panels of sedan chairs and coaches, where its lightness was important – at least for the chair men and horses. Ann Rushout, a daughter of Lord Northwick, recorded in 1797 that in Clay's factory "they make bottle stands, boxes, tea boards, salver, etc., in great perfection." But trays were his main product. Middle class families did not think their homes complete without papier-mâché trays or nests of trays. Clay made profits of 200 per cent, amassed a fortune, was made japanner to George III and the Prince of Wales, and in 1790 became High Sheriff of Warwickshire. His coach had

The flowering of papier mâché in Victorian times: right, a nest of tables; far right, a work box

panels striped in dark green and chocolate and was drawn by cream-coloured horses.

His patents ran out in 1802; after that he moved to London and ran his business from there. He died in 1812. His factory was bought in 1816 by Aaron Jennens and T. H. Bettridge, whose firm became the biggest makers, had a reputation for quality, and had a big export trade with India and North America. Jennens and Bettridge presented to Queen Victoria, on her marriage, a set of trays decorated with such elegancies as "splashing fountains, formal foliage, and exotic

birds on an apple-green ground." They labelled their products with their name, sometimes adding: "CAUTION: Jennens and Bettridge feel it encumbent on them to appraise the public that only those goods marked Jennens and Bettridge can be relied on as their manufacture."

They first patented in 1825 a method of decorating their wares with mother-of-pearl which, with its shimmering effect, was seized upon for reproducing moonlight scenes: the Houses of Parliament and the Thames, Tintern Abbey, lakes, and waterfalls.

The use of papier-mâché continued well into Victorian times and at its height a vast array of fancy, decorative materials was available as well as mother-of-pearl: ivory, tortoiseshell, stones, paste jewels, enamels, gold leaf, and coloured metallic powders. Other effects were imitations of marble, malachite (a green veined mineral), and the attractive graining of woods such as walnut and maple. National mourning for Prince Albert brought in a vogue for mauve and grey tones.

A lustrous black background is the most common and on it the designs were painted, gilded, inlaid, or applied. The favourite decoration was flowers – at first they were conventional but after about 1830 more realistic. Common too are coaching scenes, landscapes, famous buildings, Chinese men and women in Oriental settings, portraits of royalty and the famous, and reproductions of Old Master paintings. Styles were typical of the age: imitations of the Renaissance, Elizabethan, Gothic, Moorish, rococo, and so on.

Some of the objects now have little use but are all the more interesting because they reveal a different way of life: trays and cases for calling cards, letter scales, voiding dishes (to hold dirty plates at meal times), boxes for fans or gloves, tables for the card game of loo, elaborate writing sets, screens to protect ladies' complexions from the heat of an open fire.

Some furniture was made entirely of paper mâché but was found not to be strong enough: so most specimens are supported by a frame of iron or wood. A piano cased entirely in papier-mâché was not resonant enough.

The trade suffered badly in the 1860s. Jennens and Bettridge closed down in 1864. Fashions changed and the quality of the product declined. Papier-mâché became a means of making merely 'novelty' goods. From this downward spiral it became impossible to recover and by the end of the century the trade was more or less finished.

Fakes have been made, especially of trays, and comparatively plain pieces have been given extra ornament. Dirt is best removed with a damp cloth and a little mild soap, not detergent and hot water. Furniture oil will restore a shiny surface and to some extent replace moisture lost through dry conditions. Chips and breaks can be mended with plaster of Paris stained to the right shade. A coat of varnish can be applied. But repairs are best left to an expert or more harm than good may be done.

Enamel

Gay and dainty trinkets in coloured enamel, made from the 1740s to the end of the eighteenth century, reflect exactly the pretty taste of the time. They can hint, too, at masculine vanity, feminine attractions, and love affairs.

They are often called Battersea enamels, after the London factory where the trade was pioneered in this country. It is a misnomer, because by far the greatest number was made elsewhere in London and in Birmingham, Bilston and Wednesbury in Staffordshire, and Liverpool. Even later productions from the Continent are given the magic name Battersea, although most of them are crude.

The decorations are flowers, portraits (especially of royalty or fashionable beauties), pastoral scenes with maidens and gallants, or mottoes such as 'Esteem the Giver,' 'Pour la Plus Belle,' 'Voyez et Souvenez.'

Another group was made after about 1780 as souvenirs of places: 'A Trifle from . . .' London, Margate, Dover, Tunbridge Wells, and so on. They are not very distinguished in quality.

Just as varied are the kinds of objects. Boxes are the commonest – for cosmetics, sweetmeats, snuff, tobacco, or tea. They could take the form of human heads, birds, animals, or fruit. And there are scent bottles, mustard pots, cream jugs, salt cellars, candlesticks, and étuis (for holding scissors, needles, a pencil, and other useful items.) The colours include blue, pea green, turquoise, pink, yellow, and claret.

These things were made in imitation of costly gold and porcelain boxes from the Continent. British makers plagiarized freely the work of artists because the law of copyright was ineffectual. Sources were books of engravings and mezzotints of famous paintings. Even such important artists as Boucher and Watteau were copied.

Enamel is a tough kind of glass fused with intense heat on a base of copper. It is durable and brilliant and looks like porcelain. The early products of the Georgian makers were simple plaques, but as their skill grew they made more and more elaborate pieces. Paper-thin copper was coated in liquid white enamel and fired in a furnace. Each extra colour needed another application of enamel and another firing.

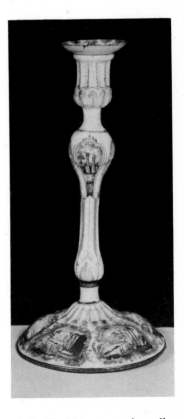

A Staffordshire enamel candlestick, $11\frac{7}{8}$ inches (30.2 cm) high

The process of decorating was soon helped by the use of transfer printing, in very much the same way as porcelain and pottery were decorated (see page 123).

The next stage was generally a retouching of the design with a paintbrush; often this means that the original transfer print can hardly be detected underneath the paint. Transfer-printing speeded up production and cut costs. A lot depended on the skill of the retoucher. But some enamels were done entirely by hand and some transfer-prints were not 'improved' at all.

It was technically difficult to make large pieces or, for example, entire snuff boxes. Small sections of enamel were assembled by means of metal mounts. This required skill and some of the best work is remarkable. The hinges are so well made that snuff and face powder cannot escape.

Mounts had another purpose. The enamel did not cover the edge of the metal, which showed as a dark line; this had to be hidden. And an exposed edge might result in the enamel starting to flake away. The mounts are of gilded alloy or brass. Gilding with a compound of mercury was a danger to health; dangerous too was the arsenic which was sometimes an ingredient of the enamel.

Products of the factory at Battersea are comparatively scarce because it existed only from 1750 to 1756. The promoter, Stephen Theodore Janssen, at that time Lord Mayor of London, went bankrupt and the finished and half-finished stock, copper plates,

Battersea plaque, transfer printed, 4½ inches (11.5 cm) wide. About 1750

and so forth were sold. A French-born artist. Simon François Ravenet, engraved for the Battersea factory many portraits and some mythological scenes. The manager – and inventor of the transfer printing – was John Brooks, an Irishman (c. 1710–after 1756).

Work of high quality was done at various factories, especially in London, until the 1780s when a decline set in. Quantity was preferred to quality and economic pressures meant that care could no longer be devoted to the process. Many of the goods were exported and the industry suffered when war broke out with France and when import duties were imposed by Prussia. Before the end of the eighteenth century the great age of the craft was over.

Reproductions were made in the nineteenth century by the firm of Samson in Paris, which also reproduced English porcelain of the eighteenth century (see page 124). Samson enamels include patch boxes, candlesticks, and tea caddies, are well made, and find a place in many collections. Other enamels have been made in recent years in Britain, for example the series under the name Halcyon Days, but with no intention to deceive. Outright fakes have recently been made on the Continent. Attributing particular pieces to Staffordshire, Birmingham, Liverpool, or London is difficult, and opinions are divided. It seems that some of the best may have been made in London and not in Birmingham as has been believed.

Buttons for a hunting jacket – rare items. They are $1\frac{3}{4}$ inches (4.5 cm) across. About 1760

Snuff boxes

Snuff-taking was a special ritual in the eighteenth century as well as the usual way of taking tobacco. Cynics and satirists mocked the follies that went on: the exaggerated gestures of foppish people when taking snuff, the indulgence of women in the habit, and the large sums of money sometimes spent on the boxes. Yet the social pressures were strong. Fanny Burney, the formidable novelist and diarist, was shocked when she found that Sir Joshua Reynolds used a 'vile and shabby' tin box as well as his more elegant gold one. Great expense and care were devoted to the boxes by the rich and much imagination by rich and poor. Among the refinements, forms, and varieties are:

Tiny musical boxes which play when the lid is opened.
Birds which sing and move their wings, heads, and tails.
Secret compartments to hold the portrait of a loved one or a politically risky Jacobite emblem, or an erotic picture.
Two separate compartments for snuff with different flavours.

The materials were in infinite variety: gold, silver, pewter, brass, copper, wood, onyx, agate and other semi-precious stones, papier-mâché, enamel, ivory, horn, amber, and tortoiseshell. Gold was coloured by the addition of other metals. Copper produced a red hue, silver white, and so on. Sometimes a print was put on the lid, showing a hunting or coaching scene, a portrait, or a caricature.

The shapes, apart from simple oblongs and ovals, are extraordinary. They include coffins, hats, shoes and boots, heads, bellows, books, pistols (these 'shot' the snuff into the nostrils), casks (perhaps for brewers and publicans), and animals.

The Scots had two special kinds. They made snuff 'mulls' which were of horn curled and pointed at one end and had a lid of metal, wood, or bone at the other. Often a cairngorm or other semi-precious stone was set in the lid. The other kind of Scottish box had a hinge of high craftsmanship which fitted perfectly and ensured that the contents did not escape. These were of wood, four or five inches long, and oblong; they were made in Mauchline, Ayrshire, in the first half of the nineteenth century. The special hinge is said to have been invented by an invalid and genius, James Sandy, of Alyth, Perthshire.

Snuff boxes were also used for a more dubious purpose. A costly example might be given to a Minister or official as a kind of tactful bribe or as an acknowledgement of a favour. The French kings gave superb gold boxes decorated with jewels, enamel, or mother-of-pearl to ambassadors or high-ranking officers; these

Box in gold, chased with scrolls and decorated in relief with flowers in multi-coloured enamel; the top has a scene from Aesop's Fables – the fox and the raven. About 1740
Box in gold and set with figured agate. About 1740

could be taken back to an official of the court and exchanged for cash, so that one box might be given on different occasions to several people. The Sardinian Ambassador received the same box three times and sold it three times. Boxes to the value of £8295 15s 5d were given away at the coronation of George IV to foreign dignitaries.

The very elaborate specimens could not be carried about because their jewels might catch in the clothing or they might be damaged by a knock. Nor could they be left on a drawing room table because they were so valuable. It is likely that they were simply locked away.

Small boxes were made for many other purposes in the eighteenth and nineteenth centuries: to hold cachous for sweetening the breath, patches to adorn a lady's cheeks, rouge for heightening the complexions of both sexes. Sometimes the lid pushes on and off but snuff boxes always have hinges.

Tobacco has been alternately praised and abused since it was brought from the New World by the earliest explorers. It was said in the sixteenth century to be a cure for all manner of ailments and was applied internally as extracts, or externally as poultices. James VI and I, King of Scotland and England, was as bitterly opposed to it as are modern medical men. Snuff was alleged to be a cure for toothache, bad eyesight, afflictions of the lung including tuberculosis, headaches, and coughs. But during the decline of the habit this piece of propaganda was recorded:

Snuff box in Staffordshire enamel, 2¾ inches (7 cm) wide

"Doctor, is it true that snuff destroys the olfactory nerves, clogs, and otherwise injures the brain?"

"It cannot be true, since those who have any brains never take snuff at all."

Perhaps one of the factors which brought snuff into disrepute was the excessive rituals which were attached to it. An advertiser in the early eighteenth century offered to teach "The exercise of the snuffbox, according to the most fashionable Airs and Notions, in opposition to the exercise of the Fan . . . with the best plain or perfumed Snuff"

Handkerchiefs were coloured or patterned so that the stains which result from the habit would not show. Lord Petersham (1780–1851) had a different box for every day of the year; when he died he had 2000 lb of snuff which was sold for about £1000.

Changing social customs brought the almost total extinction of the habit. The invention of better matches also made tobacco, cigars, and cigarettes more easy to smoke. George IV had a remarkable collection of snuff boxes (he even had a special room set aside for different varieties of snuff). But Queen Victoria had them broken up to make jewellery for herself. It was a symbolic end. But if society turns totally against smoking the old ways may come back.

Vinaigrettes

Our ancestors understood that evil smells and infection were somehow connected, and they thought that sweet, strong smells would give protection. Judges at assizes carried posies of flowers (this tradition is still carried on). Doctors and clergymen, when visiting the sick, had walking sticks with a special compartment at the top for aromatic substances. Pomanders, little metal caskets or hollowed-out oranges, contained perfumed spices sometimes in a base of vinegar. Then in 1785 a Dr Henry delivered a series of lectures in Manchester extolling the virtues of a new, much stronger, aromatic vinegar which was said to prevent infection and revive ladies after fainting fits.

The idea caught on and soon the first vinaigrettes appeared. They were small containers which held a sponge soaked in the aromatic vinegar, and were carried on watch chains or in a pocket, purse, or glove. They all had certain features in common: a cover, to keep the perfume from escaping when the vinaigrette was not in use, and beneath the cover a grille to hold the sponge in place when the cover was opened and at the same time let the perfume escape.

Snuffbox made for the Prince Regent and given to a friend. It is gold, green gold, and tortoiseshell; the lid is inscribed: 'The Gift of H.R.H. George Augustus Frederick, Regent of England, to John Waiter 1815'.

Many were in silver. Other materials used were gold (very rarely), semi-precious stones such as agate, topaz, or bloodstone mounted in silver or gold, glass, porcelain, pinchbeck (an alloy resembling gold), or even rabbit paws or grouse feet with the container at one end. Continental makers went in for more elaboration than the British.

The width varied from half an inch to four inches. The special charm of the objects is in the high degree of craftsmanship and in the variety of designs. Vinaigrettes are in the shape of books, fish, insects, beehives, purses, birds, animals, fruits, nuts, watches, shells, and helmets; or with minute portrayals of stately homes and public buildings such as Windsor Castle, St Paul's, York Minster, and Lord Byron's Newstead Abbey. Many techniques are found in the decoration: embossing, engine-turning, beading, filigree work, and chasing.

Silver examples were always gilded at the point where the sponge comes into contact with the metal: the vinegar was highly corrosive and would attack unprotected silver. The grilles were often as beautifully ornamented as the exterior with scrolls of foliage, fruit, and flowers, or animals and birds. Family crests and sentimental legends were sometimes engraved on.

The best are generally Georgian and Regency, which are heavy and made with care, whilst the Victorian ones tend to be thin and

Vinaigrette to commemorate Trafalgar and the death of Nelson. The interior is stamped and pierced with a view of the HMS Victory and the words 'Trafalgar Ocr 21 1805'. This piece is 1½ inches wide and was made by Matthew Lindwood of Birmingham in 1805

to display, as might be expected, a decline in the quality of design. It was in Victorian times that vinaigrettes became exclusive to women. A cartoon in *Punch* showed a buxom cook fainting away and saying: "Susan, fetch my my vinaigrette, I've just had an offer from the dustman."

Vinaigrettes inevitably fell out of fashion and were partly replaced by scent bottles of coloured glass. Solid smelling salts came in too. The decline took place in the 1850s.

One of the advantages of collecting vinaigrettes is that, if they are of silver or gold, the hall marks make it possible to ascribe them to a year, place, and maker. (Hallmarks may, however, be missing if the object is set with stones or is so heavily ornamented that no room is left for the marks.) Almost all the vinaigrettes made in this country are from either Birmingham or London, and 50 or more makers are known. Faults to look out for are dents, wear, strained hinges, and replacement grilles.

A favourite maker, whose name adds considerably to a vinaigrette's price, is Nathaniel Mills of Birmingham, who was active in the craft from 1826 to 1850.

The prospective collector may want to know a recipe for the kind of aromatic vinegar that was used. Here is one from an old pharmacopoeia:

Oils of:	Parts
Bergamot	25
Cinnamon	12.5
Clove	100
Lavender	50
Orange	50
Thyme	25

Glacial acetic acid to 1000 parts (all by volume)

Other recipes included musk, camphor, rose, orris (from the iris family), and neroli (from the flowers of the bitter orange). Some, if not all of these exotic oils may be lurking on the back shelves of old-established chemists' shops although their original purposes are probably forgotten.

Samplers

Childhood used to be a fairly serious business, and it cannot have been made less serious by the tradition of little girls doing samplers to show their skill in needlework. Thousands of these memorials of diligence are handed down in families. Some are wonderfully preserved. They give an insight into a totally different way of life.

Opposite page
Miniature of Peter Johnston of Carnsalloch by John Smart. It is $3\frac{1}{2}$ inches (8.9 cm) high, and was painted in 1803. Johnston (1789–1837) was MP for Kirkcudbright. (Sotheby's)

Miniature of Samuel Pepys Cockerell by Richard Cosway. It is 3 inches (7.6 cm) high. Cockerell (1754–1827) was an architect. His mother was a great-niece of Samuel Pepys. (Sotheby's)

Miniature of Anna Aubry, wife of Captain George Aubry, by John Smart. It is $2\frac{5}{8}$ inches (6.7 cm) high, and was painted in 1787. The couple had been married in Calcutta the year before. (Sotheby's)

Portrait of
Anne Botham.
Married at
Messrs. Burgh & Barber
in Calcutta
March 19. 1786.
by
W. Goddard
Chaplain to
Comr. in Chief

The pride of a mother, teacher, or governess was satisfied by these pieces of work; but this was not the only aim. The little girls learned their stitches; absorbed moral and religious precepts; and became familiar with letters and numbers. Some examples show almost incredible skill among children as young as six or seven.

The inscriptions were of course chosen by adults. A sampler produced at school says:

> Oh smile on those whose liberal care
> Provides for our instruction here;
> And let our conduct ever prove
> We're grateful for their generous love.

The young were warned of the transcience of human life:

> Come gentle God, without thy aid,
> I sink in dark despair
> O wrap me in thy silent shade
> For peace is only there.
>
> ———————
>
> There is an hour when I must die
> Nor can I tell how soon 'twill come.
> A thousand children such as I
> Are called to hear their doom.
>
> ———————
>
> Our days, alas, our mortal days
> Are short and wretched too.
> Evil and few the patriarch says
> And well the patriarch knew.

The Lord's Prayer, the Ten Commandments, the Apostles' Creed, hymns, psalms, and chapters of the Scriptures were always favourites.

Pictures also are frequently religious: Adam and Eve with the Tree of Knowledge; the finding of Moses; the flight into Egypt; the sacrifice of Isaac; Herod and Salome with the head of St John the Baptist; the Virgin; Christ; and so on.

More interesting to the girls may have been the ornaments and borders. Lions, stags, rabbits, leopards, crowns, hearts, trees, and human beings were popular. Birds, insects, and flowers are frequent; strawberries, roses, and pinks grow profusely. Sometimes houses are shown. Maps of Britain or England were done in the later part of the eighteenth century.

Samplers began not as proofs of skill to be framed and displayed but as patterns done by adults of different kinds of stitches which the housewife could use for embroidering clothes, cushions, household

Opposite page
A table clock, made in about 1725 by David Hubert of London, with walnut veneering, silver gilt mounts and silver rings on the face. (Private collection)

linen, and other useful or ornamental things. The decoration is in bands or scattered haphazardly. Among the techniques were birdseye, satin, tent and back stitches. These samplers were up to a yard long and nine inches wide. Some have survived from the early seventeenth century, and Shakespeare has references to them, for example in Titus Andronicus ('tedious sampler'). Pattern books were published too, and they provided themes. Some patterns were repeated from generation to generation.

Sampler on canvas embroidered with coloured silks and dated 1780

The popularity of samplers increased during the seventeenth century; the arrival of Methodism in the eighteenth century brought in the serious precepts and religious subjects. The variety of stitches became less important and cross-stitches were almost universal.

A decline in quality came towards the end of the eighteenth century. Moths, light, and damp are the enemies; woodworm attacks the frames; and large numbers must have been lost.

A well designed example avoids clutter and the conglomeration of ornaments, letters, and numbers. The names or initials of the girls and the date are almost always given after the middle of the eighteenth century, but the dates and ages are sometimes lost. The thread may have been picked out: a woman would not have liked to have documentary evidence on show of her age. And dates and even names have been changed, perhaps by dishonest vendors who want to pass the sampler off as being of a different and more valuable period.

Sampler on woollen canvas embroidered with coloured silks and dated 1789

It is hard to say accurately when a sampler was made if it does not carry a date – the patterns were so traditional. No particular local styles have been found, although the places where they were made is sometimes given:

> Ann Stanfer is my name
> And England is my nation
> Blackwall is my dwelling place
> And Christ is my salvation.

This one is dated 1766.

One unfortunate specimen failed in its aim of proving that the young lady was well brought up in domestic virtues. This sampler, slovenly, unkempt, and unfinished, is inscribed:

> This is my Work so
> you may see what
> care my mother as
> took of me.

Bottle Tickets

Small labels to hang round the necks of bottles and decanters and tell the contents have been made since the early part of the eighteenth century. They are called wine labels or, more accurately, bottle tickets, and were not only for drinks but also for condiments and toiletries. An advantage in collecting them is that they are easily stored and displayed because they do not take up much room.

Most are in silver, but others are in plated metals, enamel, tortoiseshell, bone, ivory, mother-of-pearl, zinc, nickel, porcelain, cork, and even with boats' tusks or tigers' claws.

They can still be used: it is decorative to have table wine, on a special occasion, in a decanter with a Georgian silver label. If the wine is 'plonk,' the original bottle is best kept out of sight anyway.

One of the charms of wine labels is that they were often designed for drinks that are now almost forgotten except when they are met with in the pages of eighteenth or nineteenth century novels. Shrub, for example, was a liqueur made in the West Indies; Bronte a variety of Marsala; Buda a Hungarian wine; Mountain a variety of Malaga; Chusclan a dessert wine from the Rhone; Paxarete, similar to sherry and still made in Spain to add to other wines. Collectors are especially keen on the rarer kinds.

Sometimes one finds labels for 'Nig.' It is said that they were used as a disguise for the household supply of gin when gin was hardly respectable. Other labels call it, straightforwardly, Mother's Ruin. Spelling is sometimes eccentric: one finds Clairret, Champaign, and Conac. Designs have a wide variety, from simple oblongs to elaborate ones with cupids, satyrs, goblets, vine leaves, grapes, or foxes.

Labels were invented as a result of a change in social customs. In the earlier part of the eighteenth century people began to prefer wine matured in the bottle, and a greater variety of wine was imported. But the bottles did not have paper labels as they do now, and some way to identify them was needed. One of the earliest silver labels was made about 1735 by Sandylands Drinkwater.

The famous silversmith family, the Batemans, made some which, like all the Bateman productions, are prized. Most beautiful labels were made at the Battersea enamel factory in the 1750s, but many enamelled specimens are modern and of very little value. And some that appear at first to be old Sheffield plate are in fact modern electro-types.

Apart from wines, one can come across labels for eau-de-Cologne, tooth mixture, barley water, vinegar, mustard, lime juice, and zoobditty-match. The last is rather a mystery but may be an Anglo-Indian word meaning a tasty fish sauce.

A variety of wine labels. These are all perfectly genuine; but fakers have been known to delete a common name and put on a rare one instead

Bibliography

General
Collector's Encyclopedia of Antiques
(The Connoisseur, London, 1973)
Collins Encyclopedia of Antiques
(Collins, London, 1973)
Concise Encyclopedia of Antiques
(5 vols) (Connoisseur, London,
1955–60)
Dictionary of National Biography (to
1900) (Oxford University Press,
reprinted ed. 1967–68)
Discovering Antiques (a part publication:
Purcell/BPC Publishing, London,
1970–72)
Kurz, Otto: *Fakes* (Faber and Faber,
London, and Dover Publications
Inc., New York, 1967)
Mills, John Fitzmaurice: *How to
Detect Fake Antiques* (Arlington
Books, London, 1972)
Savage, George: *Dictionary of Antiques*
(Barrie and Jenkins, London, 1970)

Furniture
The volumes of the *Faber Monographs
on Furniture*, general editor Peter
Thornton, give specialized accounts
of the periods from Chippendale's
'Director' to the Regency. A very
useful general book is Ralph
Fastnedge's *English Furniture Styles
1500–1830*, a Penguin book
Cescinsky, Herbert: *The Gentle Art
of Faking Furniture* (Eyre and
Spottiswoode, London, 1931,
reissued 1970)
Chippendale, Thomas: *The Gentleman
and Cabinet-Maker's Director* (Dover
Publications Inc., New York, also
published in Britain, Remploy,
1971)
Coleridge, Anthony: *Chippendale
Furniture* (Faber and Faber, London,
1968)
Edwards, Ralph: *Shorter Dictionary of
English Furniture* (Country Life,
London, 1964)
Edwards, R. and Jourdain, M.:
Georgian Cabinet-Makers (London,
revised edition, 1963)
Evans, Charles: *Antique or Fake?*
(Evans Bros., London, 1970)
Fastnedge, Ralph: *English Furniture
Styles 1500–1830* (Penguin, London,
1969)
Fastnedge, Ralph: *Sheraton Furniture*
(Faber and Faber, London, 1962)
Gilbert, Christopher: *Late Georgian*

and Regency Furniture (Hamlyn,
London, 1972)
Hepplewhite, George: *Cabinet-Maker
and Upholsterer's Guide* (1788)
Humidifier Advisory Service:
Humidification (Bromley, Kent, 1972)
Joy, Edward: *Antique English Furniture*
(Ward Lock, London, 1972)
Joy, Edward: *The Country Life Book of
English Furniture* (Country Life,
London, 1964)
Jourdain, Margaret: *Regency Furniture*
(4th edition, revised by Ralph
Fastnedge)
Musgrave, C. W.: *Adam and Hepple-
white and other Neoclassical Furniture*
(Faber and Faber, revised edition,
1966)
Sheraton, Thomas: *The Cabinet-Maker
and Upholsterer's Drawing-Book*
(Dover Publications Inc., New York,
also published in Britain, Praegar,
1971)

Silver
The volumes of the *Faber Monographs
on Silver*, general editor Arthur
Grimwade, give specialized accounts
of the periods between 1625 and 1795
Banister, Judith: *An Introduction to
Old English Silver* (Evans Bros.,
London, 1965)
Banister, Judith: *English Silver Hall-
Marks* (Foulsham, London, 1970)
Banister, Judith: *Late Georgian and
Regency Silver* (Country Life,
London, 1971)
Banister, Judith: *Mid-Georgian Silver*
(Country Life, London, 1971)
Bedford, John and Austin D.: *Old
Sheffield Plate* (Cassell, London, 1967)
Bennett, Douglas: *Irish Georgian
Silver* (Cassell, London, 1967)
Bly, J.: *Discovering Hall-Marks in
English Silver* (Shire Publications,
Aylesbury, Buckinghamshire, 11th
ed., 1968)
Bury, Shirley: The Lengthening
Shadow of Rundell's (series of
articles in The Connoisseur, London,
1966)
Delieb, Eric: *The Great Silver
Manufactory: Matthew Boulton and
the Birmingham Silversmiths* (Studio
Vista, London, 1971)
Delieb, Eric: *Investing in Silver* (Barrie
and Rockliff and Corgi, London,
1970)

Fallon, P.: *The Marks of the London
Goldsmiths and Silversmiths* (David
and Charles, Newton Abbot, Devon,
1972)
Finlay, Ian: *Scottish Gold and Silver
Work* (Chatto and Windus, London,
1956)
Goodison, Nicholas: *Ormulu: the work
of Matthew Boulton* (Phaidon,
London, 1974)
Grimwade, Arthur: *Rococo Silver*
(Faber and Faber, London, 1974)
Hayward, J. F.: *Huguenot Silver*
(Faber and Faber, London, 1959)
Holland, Margaret: *Old Country
Silver* (David and Charles, Newton
Abbot, Devon, 1971)
Hughes, Bernard: *Antique Sheffield
Plate* (Batsford, London, 1970)
Jackson, C. J.: *English Goldsmiths and
their marks* (Dover Publications Inc.,
New York, 1965 ed.)
Michaelis, R. F.: *Antique Pewter of the
British Isles* (Bell, London, 1954)
Oman, C. C.: *English Domestic Silver*
(A. and C. Black, London, 1968)
Penzer, N. M.: *The Book of the Wine
Label* (Home and Van Thal,
London, 1967)
Phillips, P. A. S.: *Paul de Lamerie*
1968 ed. (Facsimile reprint of 1935
ed.)
Robertson, R. A.: *Old Sheffield Plate*
(Benn, London, 1957, Practical
Handbooks for Collectors)
Rowe, Robert: *Adam Silver* (Faber
and Faber, London, 1965)
Shure, David S.: *Hester Bateman,
Queen of the English Silversmiths*
(W. H. Allen, London, 1959)
Stone, Jonathan: *English Silver of the
18th Century* (Cory Adams and
MacKay, London, 1965)
Taylor, Gerald: *Silver* (Penguin,
London, 1963, 2nd ed.)
Ullyett, Kenneth: *Pewter Collecting
for Amateurs* (Muller, London, 1967)
Ullyett, Kenneth: *Pewter, a Guide to
Collectors* (Muller, London, 1973)

Pottery and Porcelain
The *Faber Monographs on Pottery and
Porcelain*, edited originally by W. B.
Honey and Arthur Lane and now by
Sir Harry Garner and R. J. Charleston,
and the *Illustrated Guides* published by
Herbert Jenkins and edited by
Geoffrey Godden, are invaluable.

One other outstanding book is *English Porcelain 1745–1850*, edited by R. J. Charleston and published by Ernest Benn in 1965

Barrett, Franklin A. and Thorpe, Arthur L.: *Derby Porcelain* (Faber and Faber, London, 1971)

Bedford, John: *Lustreware* (Cassell, London, 1964)

Bedford, John: *Delftware* (Cassell, London, 1966)

Bemrose, Geoffrey: *19th century English Pottery and Porcelain* (Faber and Faber, London, 1968)

Charleston, R. J. (ed.): *English Porcelain 1745–1850* (Ernest Benn, London, 1965)

Garner, F. H. and Archer, Michael: *English Delftware* (Faber and Faber, London, 1972)

Godden, Geoffrey: *Illustrated Encyclopedia of British Pottery and Porcelain* (Barrie and Jenkins, London, 1966)

Godden, Geoffrey: *The Illustrated Guide to Lowestoft Porcelain* (Herbert Jenkins, London, 1969)

Godden, Geoffrey: *British Porcelain, an Illustrated Guide* (Barrie and Jenkins, London, 1974)

Godden, Geoffrey: *Caughley and Worcester Porcelains 1775–1800* (Herbert Jenkins, London, 1969)

Godden, Geoffrey: *Handbook of British Pottery and Porcelain Marks* (Barrie and Jenkins, London, 1972, 2nd ed.)

Hillier, Bevis: *Pottery and Porcelain 1700–1914* (Weidenfeld and Nicholson, London, 1968)

Holgate, David: *New Hall and Its Imitators* (Faber and Faber, London, 1971)

Honey, W. B.: *Dresden China* (A. and C. Black, London, 1954, new edition)

Honey, W. B.: *English Pottery and Porcelain* (A. and C. Black, London, 1969)

John, W. D.: *Swansea Porcelain* (Ceramic Book Co., Newport, 1957)

John, W. D.: *Nantgarw Porcelain* (Ceramic Book Co., Newport, 1956)

Kelly, A.: *The Story of Wedgwood* (Faber and Faber, London, 1962)

Klamkin, Marian: *The Collector's Book of Wedgwood* (David and Charles, Newton Abbot, Devon, 1971)

Lane, Arthur: *Style in Pottery* (Faber and Faber, London, 1948, reissued 1973)

Lewis, Griselda: *An Introduction to English Pottery* (Art and Technics, London, 1950)

Mankowicz, Wolf: *Wedgwood* (Batsford, London, 1967 new ed.)

Morley-Fletcher, Hugo: *Meissen* (Barrie and Jenkins, London, 1971)

Morley-Fletcher, Hugo: *Investing in Pottery and Porcelain* (Barrie and Rockliff and Corgi, London, 1970)

Nance, E. Morton: *The Pottery and Porcelain of Swansea and Nantgarw* (London, 1942)

Reilly, R.: *Wedgwood Portrait Medallions* (Barrie and Jenkins, London, 1973)

Sandon, Henry: *Illustrated Guide to Worcester Porcelain* (Herbert Jenkins, London, 1969)

Savage, George: *Porcelain through the Ages* (Penguin, London, 1961, new ed.)

Savage, George: *Pottery through the Ages* (Penguin, London, 1959)

Tames, Richard: *Josiah Wedgwood* (Shire Publications, Aylesbury, Buckinghamshire, 1972)

Towner, Donald: *English Cream-Coloured Earthenware* (Faber and Faber, London, 1957)

Watney, Bernard: *Longton Hall Porcelain* (Faber and Faber, London, 1957)

Clocks, Watches and Barometers

Bird, Anthony: *English house clocks, 1600–1850* (David and Charles, Newton Abbot, Devon, 1973)

Britten, F. J.: *Old clocks and watches and their makers* (S. R. Publs., London, 1973, 7th ed.)

Cuss, T. P. Camerer: *The Country Life Book of Watches* (Country Life, London, 1967)

Cuss, T. P. Camerer: *The Story of Watches* (MacGibbon and Kee, London, and Philosophical Library, New York, 1952)

Goodison, Nicholas: *English Barometers and their makers* (Cassell, London, 1969)

Joy, E. T.: *The Country Life Book of Clocks* (Country Life, London, 1967)

Quill, R. H.: *John Harrison, the man who found longitude* (John Baker, London, 1966)

Symonds, R. W.: *Thomas Tompion, his Life and Works* (Spring Books, London, 1951)

Symonds, R. W.: *A History of English Clocks* (Tiranti, London, 1947)

Ullyett, K.: *In Quest of Clocks* (Spring Books, London, 1950)

Ullyett, K.: *Watch Collecting* (Muller, London, 1971)

Ullyett, K.: *Clocks and Watches* (Hamlyn, London, 1971)

Miscellaneous

Armstrong, Nancy: *A Collector's History of Fans* (Studio Vista, London, 1974)

Bedford, John: *Bristol and Other Coloured Glass* (Cassell, London, 1964)

Bedford, John: *Old English Lustre Ware* (Cassell, London, 1965)

Benton, Eric: *English Painted Enamel Toys in the 18th century* Article in Art in Virginia, Vol 14 No 3 (winter 1974) published by the Virginia Museum

Blair, Claude: *Pistols of the World* (Batsford, London, 1968)

Colby, Averil: *Samplers, Yesterday and Today* (Batsford, London, 1964)

DeVoe, Shirley S.: *English Papier Mâché of the Georgian and Victorian periods* (Barrie and Jenkins, Lodon, 1971)

Freeson, Ewart C.: *Prisoner-of-War Ship Models* (Nautical Publishing Co., London, 1973)

Foskett, D.: *British Portrait Miniatures* (Spring Books, London, 1969)

Haynes, E. Barrington: *Glass through the ages* (Penguin, London, 1959)

Hickman, Peggy: *Silhouettes* (National Portrait Gallery, London, 1972)

Hughes, Therle, and Hughes, Bernard: *English Painted Enamels* (Country Life, London, 1951)

Kirk, John L.: *History of Firefighting* (Castle Museum, York, 1960)

Jervis, Simon: *19th century Papier Mâché* (Victoria and Albert Museum, London, 1973)

Penzer, N. M.: *Paul Storr, the last of the Goldsmiths* (Spring Books, London, 1971, new ed.)

Reynolds, Graham: *British Portrait Miniatures* (A. and C. Black, London, 1952)

Ruggles-Brise, Sheelah: *Sealed Bottles* (Country Life, London, 1959)

Rush, James: *The Ingenious Beilbys* (Barrie and Jenkins, London, 1973)

Toller, Jane: *Antique Papier Mâché in Great Britain and America* (G. Bell, London, 1962)

Vince, John: *Fire Marks* (Shire Publications, Aylesbury, Buckinghamshire, 1973)

Whitworth, E. W.: *Wine Labels* (Cassell, London, 1966)

Wills, Geoffrey: *Antique Glass for Pleasure and Profit* (John Gifford, London, 1971)

Wills, Geoffrey: *English and Irish Glass* (Guinness Superlatives, Guildford, 1968)

Glossary

This section contains not only references to the contents but also (1) definitions of technical terms, (2) additional material which is technical but which the reader may want to have available, and (3) words and phrases which the reader may come across in auction catalogues, magazine articles, or elsewhere and which may be unfamiliar.

Acanthus The acanthus plant is fairly common in southern Europe. A stylized version of its leaves was used as decoration in ancient Greece and Rome for architecture and metalwork, for example in the capitals of Corinthian columns. The form was used on silver in the 17th century and during the late 18th and early 19th centuries, and on furniture.

Agate ware Pottery made to resemble the striped mineral. Two kinds of agate ware were made. One is an ordinary body covered with coloured slip; the other is striped throughout the body from mixing stained clays.

Anchor escapement See escapement.

Anthemion ornament Stylized honeysuckle flowers or leaves or date palm branches. It originated in ancient Greece and was used in the late 18th and early 19th centuries on silver and furniture and in interior decoration.

Arcanist Someone possessing or claiming to possess the secret (arcanum) of making porcelain, especially in the early part of the 18th century when the knowledge, newly discovered in Europe, was valuable.

Argyle A vessel to keep gravy warm, nowadays suitable to make tea for one. They are in silver or Sheffield plate and often look like tea pots. The gravy is kept warm by putting a hot iron into a socket; or by putting hot water into a lining of the vessel.

Astbury ware Lead-glazed earthenware made in the mid-18th century by John Astbury and others.

Astragal Small moulding, semi-circular in cross-section. The term is used in architecture as well as the applied arts. This kind of moulding was much used in neo-classical silver. Also the name for glazing bars in glass-fronted furniture.

Ball-and-claw foot A foot for furniture, especially on CABRIOLE LEGS, and also in silver vessels. Talons or claws round a sphere; Oriental in origin. Ball-and-claw feet on furniture were fashionable from about 1710 to about 1760.

Ball foot Plain spherical foot for furniture; late 17th and early 18th centuries.

Balloon clock Shaped like a hot-air balloon; mid-18th to early 19th centuries.

Baluster A pear-shaped bulge, originally an architectural term. The shape is found in for example tankards, candlesticks, glasses, and furniture. It also means, in furniture, a support for a rail but the shape can take various forms.

Banding An inlaid border in furniture, sometimes done in a contrasting wood; for example satinwood on a mahogany body. Crossbanding is where the wood is cut across the grain, straight-banding along the grain. Feather banding or herringbone banding is where the grain is at an angle.

Bannock rack Like large toast rack; in silver. Most are Scottish and date from the late 18th century, but bannock racks are rare.

Baroque The style prevalent in the late 17th and early 18th centuries; forerunner of the ROCOCO. Baroque is a heavy, flamboyant version of Renaissance classicism; it has vitality and even vulgarity.

Bead moulding Ornament on silver. Resembles a row of beads.

Beetham, Mrs Isabella (born 1750) Silhouettist. Her husband was an impoverished actor who became a successful businessman and inventor; he took out a patent for a washing machine. He died in 1809, when she sold the washing machine business and retired. She generally painted on the underside of convex glass.

Biscuit porcelain Unglazed porcelain with a matt finish; often used for figures and groups and also for plaques and vases.

Black basalt (also spelled basalte) A hard, unglazed stoneware developed by Josiah Wedgwood in the 1760s. The ingredients were clay, ironstone, ochre, and manganese. It was developed from Egyptian black, a traditional ware of Staffordshire.

Bleeding bowl Shallow bowl with one handle, for letting blood in medical treatment. In silver, pewter, or delftware.

Blue john A beautiful fluorspar mined in Derbyshire. Blue, yellow, and purple. The name is derived from the French *bleu-jaune* (blue-yellow). Matthew Boulton mounted vases of blue john in ormolu.

Bonbonnière Small box for sweets or for cachous (breath fresheners). Sometimes in fanciful forms such as a human head or an animal.

Bocage Foliage and flowers in porcelain as background for porcelain figures. Also in earthenware.

Bone ash Calcined and ground bones, an ingredient of porcelain to give stability when the object is being fired. Bone ash and hard paste porcelain are the basis of standard British bone china, which was introduced by Josiah Spode II about 1800. Burning the bones gets rid of gelatinous matter; the residue contains a high proportion of lime and phosphates. The factory at Bow used up to 40 per cent or even more of bone ash in its body. The result of adding bone ash is a heavier, less translucent porcelain. Chelsea adopted the ingredient in about 1755; when Duesbury bought the Chelsea factory he obtained the recipe at the same time. Lowestoft, perhaps linked in its beginnings with Bow, used bone ash; Longton Hall never did.

Bracket foot Foot on furniture cut to resemble a wall-bracket; from early 18th to mid-19th centuries.

Breakfront Term in furniture – a central section projects from the side sections, for example in a large bookcase.

Britannia metal An alloy of tin, antimony, and copper devised about 1770; a substitute for pewter and Sheffield plate. Usually shaped by SPINNING which is cheaper and easier than casting. (Pewter had to be cast and thus began to be ousted.)

Bumping glass English drinking glass of the 18th century with a thickened foot. The custom was to bang the glass on the table at toasts; thus the thickened foot. Also called firing glasses, because, it is said, the noises of the banging resembled gunfire.

Bun foot Foot in the form of a sphere slightly flattened at the top and bottom. From mid-17th century.

Bureau Desk with a sloping flap which comes down and rests on supports. From late 17th century.

Bureau bookcase Bureau with a bookcase on top.

Cabochon In furniture, a decorative motif like a cabochon gem(i.e. cut and polished but not faceted). Often on the 'knee' of a cabriole leg.

Cabriole leg Curved leg in furniture, based on animal's leg.

Canterbury Term in furniture for two types of article. (1), a stand with three transverse divisions to hold cutlery and a curved end for plates; late 18th century. (2), a stand for holding music books, sheet music, and suchlike; from early 19th century.

Chatelaine Ornament for men and women, worn at the waist and in the form of a panel of chains. To chatelaines were attached seals, keys, étuis, watches, etc. 18th century.

China clay and **china stone** See PETUNTSE.

Coaster Small circular tray or stand for wine bottle or decanter, to 'coast' the drink along the table. From late 18th century. In silver or Sheffield plate, with wooden base. Underneath is green baize to protect the table. *Variations* Double coaster is for two bottles or decanters; wine waggon has wheels.

Commedia dell'arte Italian popular improvised comedy which flourished from the 16th century to the early 18th. Influence felt all over Europe; ancestors of the Punch and Judy show and of some elements of the pantomime. Characters included the Doctor, amorous and gullible; Pantalone, full of reprimands, tirades, and advice; the Captain, a braggart and coward; and lovers.

Commode A low chest of drawers.

Console table Side table, often without legs but with a bracket support fixing it to the wall. From late 17th century.

Cosway, Richard (1742–1821) Miniaturist. Patronized by the Prince Regent from 1785 and became flamboyantly wealthy until illness made him give up work in 1806. A charac-

teristic of his miniatures is a blue sky in the background, with white clouds.

Cut-card work Ornament on gold or silver articles. A sheet of metal was cut in a pattern and soldered on. Fashionable from the mid-17th to early 18th centuries.

Cut fruit painter Identity unknown; decorated plates from Worcester, Chelsea, and Bow, with fruit (sometimes cut), leaves, birds, and insects.

Cylinder escapement See ESCAPEMENT.

Detent See ESCAPEMENT (dead beat).

Earthenware Pottery fired until the particles of clay begin to fuse together. Can absorb water and thus is usually glazed, which gives the surface an impermeable skin.

Ebonizing The staining of wood black to imitate expensive ebony. The technique was used for example in the making of bracket clocks.

Enamel Glass, coloured with metallic oxides, which is fused to the surface of glass, pottery and porcelain, or metal.

Engine-turning Engraving by machinery on ceramics and metals. Wedgwood used it. Patterns include fluting, chevrons (zig-zags), and chequers. Replaced enamelling on snuffboxes about 1800.

Engelheart, George (1752–1829) Miniaturist. Pupil of Sir Joshua Reynolds; did many portraits of royal family; retired 1813.

Engraving On glass – by a wheel or by a splinter of diamond; the finest examples are of the 18th century on, for example, Jacobite glasses and ale glasses. On metal – the removing of a sliver of metal by means of a sharp tool called a graver.

Entrée dish Covered serving dish, generally in silver or Sheffield plate. Various shapes.

Epergne Centrepiece for the table designed to save (*epargner*) diners the trouble of passing dishes to each other. The dishes were for bread, fruit, sweetmeats, and so on; epergnes can also have sockets for candles and containers for condiments.

Escapement *Verge* The earliest form, used on bracket clocks until about 1800 and on watches well into the 19th century. A wheel with teeth standing up on the rim (thus called crown wheel) engages staff or verge. *Anchor or recoil* For pendulum clocks only. More accurate than the verge

type. Anchor-shaped bar engages teeth of escape wheel. *Cylinder* Invented 1695, perfected by George Graham. For watches only. Slotted hollow cylinder, often of ruby, the vital part; recoil is minimized. *Lever* Invented by Thomas Mudge about 1765. The most successful type of all, and used to this day. For watches. Recoil and friction are minimized. Not unlike anchor escapement with two jewelled pallets (small flat projections) giving alternately locking impulse. *Grasshopper* Invented by Harrison. Name derived from jumping action, which reduced friction between escape wheel teeth and pallets. *Dead beat* Pallet faces, curved, stop the teeth without forcing them back; this reduction of recoil was a modification of the anchor escapement and was devised by Graham.

Etui Small case for personal necessities such as scissors, needles, and pencil. During the 18th century was often hung from a chatelaine. Materials for étuis are very varied – precious metals, porcelain, leather, etc.

Ewer Large vessel for pouring liquid. By the 18th century it had become mainly for ceremonial use although the basic form remained.

Festoon A garland of flowers, fruit, or drapery, suspended from each end and dipping in the middle. A common ornament on, for example, neoclassical silver. Also called swag.

Fiddle-back The back of a chair in a shape resembling the outline of a violin. First used in the late 18th century.

Fiddle pattern Shape of stem in forks and spoons. Somewhat resembles the outline of a violin.

Filigree Ornament made from silver or gold wire. Birmingham was an important centre of the manufacture during the 18th and 19th centuries.

Firing glass See BUMPING GLASS.

Flatware Objects in gold, silver, Sheffield plate, pewter, or electroplate in flat form; for example, dishes, plates, and salvers. Also knives, forks, spoons, etc. (See also HOLLOW-WARE.)

Flat chasing A form of decoration in silver, in low relief.

Flaxman, John (1755–1826) Designer and sculptor in the neo-classical style. Josiah Wedgwood I and Rundell, Bridge, and Rundell employed him. For Wedgwood he did chessmen and reliefs and figures in jasper ware; for Rundell the Shield of Achilles and the

Trafalgar Vase. The Trafalgar Vase was inspired by a Greek original and 66 examples were made for presentation to the senior officers who had been at the battle.

Flute A tall and slender drinking glass. The bowl is cone-shaped.

Fluting Parallel grooves, semi-circular in section, used on silver, glass, and furniture. The grooves are generally vertical but can be curved or slanting. (See also GADROONING).

Flux Substance, in the manufacture of glass, porcelain, and enamels, to reduce the melting point and help in fusion.

Fob Pocket in the breeches, on the right, for watch; on the outside hung seals or chatelaine.

Frog mug Contains a model of a frog which is revealed as the contents are drunk.

Fuddling cup Several vesseals joined together usually by hollow handles; to drain one, you have to drain all. Made in the late 17th century and in the 18th.

Gadrooning Parallel flutes or lobes in relief, on silver, furniture, glass, etc. Generally vertical but can be curved or slanting.

Gesso Compound, used in furniture, of size and whiting. Is gilded, painted, and carved. Pronounced jesso.

Gallery Railing or parapet, in furniture, round a tray or the edge of a shelf or table. Also in silver ware.

Gilding Applied by various methods. *Gold leaf* – not durable. *Lacquer gilding* – gold leaf, powdered and mixed with lacquer; not durable. *Oil gilding* – gold leaf mixed with oil and resin; more durable but dull. *Fire gilding* – gold and mercury mixed to form an amalgam; mercury then driven off by heat; used on bronze, brass, silver, pottery and porcelain, and glass – durable. *Honey gilding* – gold leaf and honey mixed and painted on surface; moderately durable.

Giles, James (1718–after 1780) Gilder and painter of glass and porcelain; worked in London. He or his workshop decorated Bristol glass and porcelain from Worcester, Bow, Longton Hall and Plymouth. Certain distinctive styles can be traced in the work and his artists have been nicknamed, for example, the Cut Fruit painter.

Glaze The 'skin' of most pottery or porcelain. Stops liquid from being soaked up by the body of the article and gives a chance for decorative effects. The texture and colour can be varied according to the chemicals and temperature used.

Gouache Watercolour paint with white added to give opaque effect; much used in miniatures.

Grandfather clock See LONG CASE CLOCK.

Grandmother clock Small version of grandfather or LONG CASE clock; about 4 feet high or less.

Green, Guy See SADLER, JOHN.

Gridiron compensation 'Gridiron' of brass and steel rods, to compensate for changes in temperature. Aim is similar to MERCURY COMPENSATION

Ground colour Background colour on pottery and porcelain.

Guilloche Interlaced ribbon-like bands sometimes enclosing circles or rosettes. On silver, ceramics, furniture, and other objects.

Hanoverian pattern Shape of stem of cutlery. The end of the stem is rounded, flat, and slightly upturned. The stem tapers away from this towards the bowl or prongs. First made about 1710.

Highboy American chest of drawers, on a LOWBOY.

Hollow-ware Vessels in gold, silver, Sheffield plate, pewter, or electroplate: for example mugs, beakers, and bowls. (See also FLATWARE.)

Humphry, Ozias (1742–1810) Miniaturist. Worked also in Italy and India. His eyesight began to fail and he began to do larger works in crayon. He gave up work in 1797.

Husk ornament Stylized representation of corn husk used as a decoration on furniture and silver.

Imari pattern A design for porcelain incorporating chrysanthemums, birds, discs, and vases of flowers. Painted in red, blue and gold. Also called brocade pattern because of its rich effect. It was originally Japanese and acquired its name because the Japanese porcelain of this pattern was exported to Europe from the port of Imari. The factories at Chelsea, Derby, and Worcester used the pattern.

Inlay Pieces of wood, ivory, mother-of-pearl, or metal set into a ground material to form a picture or pattern. Seel also MARQUETRY and PARQUETRY.

Japanning European version of Oriental lacquer but quite different. In Europe, resinous substances were dissolved in alcohol, stained in various colours, and applied to furniture or papier mâché. Japanned metal was also made especially at Pontypool and Usk.

Kaolin See PETUNTSE.

King's pattern Design for cutlery based on the fiddle pattern, but also enriched with scrolls, shell, and anthemion motifs. First used in the 19th century.

Knee-hole Term in furniture; a recess in the front of a desk, dressing table, etc., to allow someone to sit at it with his knees going underneath.

Knife box or knife case A container, common in the 18th century, for holding knives. Materials are wood or a covering of SHAGREEN Shapes are vase-like or rectangular; the rectangular ones often have sloping lids. The knives stand upright in slots. Knives boxes were often attractively ornamented, for example with inlaid fan patterns and metal fittings.

Knop Decorative feature on many kinds of objects in many kinds of material; for example, the ends of spoons, the stems of 18th century drinking glasses.

Ladder-back or slat-back In chairs. The back is formed of horizontal slats.

Lantern clock An English type, of brass driven by weights; to go on a wall. The whole is topped by a bell. Made in the 17th and early 18th centuries.

Lever escapement See ESCAPEMENT.

Library steps Often ingeniously disguised, for example as a cabinet, or incorporated in another article of furniture, for example a table or chair.

Loading Use of resin, pitch, or other substance to give extra weight in for example candlesticks. Objects made in thin silver or Sheffield plate were flimsy and needed loading.

Long case clock Also called grandfather clock. Followed the introduction of the pendulum in the 17th century. Up to eight feet tall in the late 17th century; made throughout the 18th and 19th centuries and to some extent in the 20th. Style generally follows furniture, for example in the wood used.

Loo table For the card game of loo; usually with a round top. Early 19th century.

Loving cup Term now applied to any two-handled cup. Originally, it is thought, a wedding or an anniversary gift. Often have initials or inscriptions. Also used for communal toasts at banquets.

Lowboy Chest with two drawers; on legs, usually cabriole. For bedroom, as dressing chest, or for dining room, as side table. An American term.

Lund, Benjamin Brass founder who became manufacturer of porcelain. He was a partner in a factory in Bristol which made porcelain from 1749; the business was bought by the Worcester Porcelain Company in 1752. He had a licence to mine soapstone, an ingredient of soft paste porcelain, near the Lizard, Cornwall.

Lustre (1) Pendant of cut glass used from the 18th century to ornament chandeliers. (2) Form of decoration on pottery – a sheen derived from the use of metals.

Lyre back Open back of a chair resembling the classical Greek lyre. Robert Adam introduced the form about 1775 and it was used also in furniture of the Hepplewhite, Sheraton and Regency styles.

Mackintosh service Made at Nantgarw for The Mackintosh of Mackintosh and decorated in London, 1817–1820, with large birds and, in the distance, landscapes.

Marks on pottery and porcelain Unreliable guides to place and time of manufacture. Marks on silver and gold were fairly strictly controlled in Britain; this was not the case with pottery and porcelain. Plagiarism, fakes, and forgeries are common.

Marquetry Decorative technique in furniture. Pieces of wood, metal, bone, ivory, or tortoiseshell are inlaid on a sheet of veneer; this is applied to the basic body of the furniture (the carcase). Vulnerable to changes in humidity. See also PARQUETRY.

Marrow scoop or marrow spoon Has a long narrow 'bowl' for scooping the marrow out of the bones. Silver or Sheffield plate. Made from late 17th century to early 19th. Examples from early 18th century are in the form of two elongated scoops of different widths; each scoop can also serve as the handle. Single-bowl scoops were also made.

Matting Tiny dots on silver, giving a textured rather than a smooth appearance. Applied with a punch or special hammer. Much used in the 18th century on cups, bowls, tankards, etc.

Mazarine Dish strainer, in silver or Sheffield plate. Fits into larger dish and is pierced with holes to strain such foods as boiled fish.

Meissonier, Juste–Aurele or **Juste–Oreille** (about 1693–1750) Designer, architect, goldsmith and artist; based in Paris but born in Italy. An influential pioneer of the ROCOCO style.

Mercury compensating pendulum Variations in the length of the pendulum produce variations in the time it takes to oscillate and thus in the timekeeping. Warmth expands the metal and lengthens the pendulum. A means of avoiding this was to have a container of mercury on the pendulum; expansion of the pendulum was compensated by the mercury expanding and rising in its vessel. This changes the centre of gravity.

Meyer, Jeremiah (1735–1789) Miniaturist, born in Germany; studied for a short time in studio of Sir Joshua Reynolds, became miniaturist to Queen Charlotte and enamel painter to George II. One of the pioneers of using ivory for miniatures.

John Miers (1756–1821) Silhouettist. Worked first in the North and then in London; his sitters included Mrs Siddons the actress and Robert Burns.

Mills, Nathaniel (worked 1826–1850) Silversmith in Birmingham who specialized in boxes and vinaigrettes; his mark adds to the price of an item. Used engine turning and views, in high relief, of buildings.

Molinet or stirring rod Wooden rod for stirring the contents of a chocolate pot; inserted through an opening in the lid. Chocolate pots rarely have their original rods.

Monteith Large bowl of silver, pewter, or ceramics; with notched or scalloped rim. Originally for cooling wine glasses which were hung from the notches; the bowl contained water or ice. Later examples in silver have sometimes a detachable rim so that the bowl could be used for punch. First appeared at the end of the 17th century.

Moonlight lustre Purple decoration with a mottled effect used by the Wedgwood factory from about 1810.

Mote-skimmer, mote spoon, or **strainer-spoon** Spoon with holes in the bowl and a spike at the end of the stem. Thought to be for straining tea and for poking tea leaves from teapots, which had a strainer at the bottom of the spout. Other theories have been put forward about the use of these spoons.

Mourning jewellery Worn in memory of a dead person; sometimes with a lock of his or her hair.

Muffineer Caster of silver or Sheffield plate for sprinkling sugar on muffins; from late 18th century.

Nelson or **Trafalgar chair** With nautical motifs such as rope, anchor, and dolphin; to commemorate Trafalgar (1805).

Neo-classical Style based on those of classical Greece and Rome. The movement was inspired by excavations at Pompeii and Herculaneum, begun in 1738. Artists and scholars spread the ideas through illustrated books. The chief exponent in Britain was Robert Adam. Neo-classicism emphasised straight lines rather than the curves of the rococo. Classical motifs were universally used – ACANTHUS, ANTHEMION, PALMETTE, vase shapes, tripods, FESTOONS, and so on.

Nottingham ware Salt-glazed stoneware with brown surface and metallic sheen. Developed in Nottingham in the late 17th or early 18th century. Decoration usually cut into the body (incised).

Nutmeg grater Small silver box to hold a nutmeg and a steel grater; in many kinds of shape. Mid-17th to mid-19th centuries.

Old English pattern Design for cutlery. Quite plain. The end of the stem is rounded and turns downwards. From mid 18th century.

O'Neale, Jeffreys (or **Jeffrey**) **Hamett** (1734–1801) Irish-born artist and painter of porcelain. Worked at Chelsea and Worcester, and for William Duesbury and Josiah Wedgwood. Also exhibited miniatures at the Society of Artists, 1763–1766.

Onslow pattern Design for cutlery. The end of the stem has a scroll; the stem has also a series of ridges.

Ormolu Gilded brass or bronze; especially used for ornamental mounts on furniture. From the French *or moulu* (ground gold).

Ottoman Originally in Britain an upholstered bench, often with a back; from late 18th century. Also a circular or polygonal stuffed seat, often with buttoned upholstery, and with a back rest.

Outside decorators Painters who decorated ceramic wares, especially porcelain, bought from the factories in the plain white form. The decorators added enamel colours and gildings.

Ovolo moulding Pattern, especially on silver, of repeated oval shapes.

Oyster veneer Cross-sections of wood applied as a decorative veneer; cut from the root or small branch. Woods include lignum vitae, laburnum, olive, walnut, and fruitwoods. Mainly late 17th century and early 18th centuries.

Pair case Watch case, the standard form in Britain from about 1650 to about 1800. The inner case contains the movement and has a glass front; round it is the outer case which has no glass and often has ornament.

Palmette Ornament or classical origin and derived from the branches of the palm tree; popular in the late 18th century.

Pap boat Silver vessel for giving semi-liquid food to infants; has a spout and is narrow and boat shaped. 18th and 19th centuries.

Parcel gilt Partly gilded. Gilding was sometimes ornamental and sometimes useful; salt for example corrodes silver and salt cellars often have gilding on the inside.

Parquetry Veneer in a geometrical pattern. See also MARQUETRY.

Partners' desk Large desk for two people sitting opposite each other. Popular from about 1750 to about 1800.

Patch-box Small container for patches – pieces of taffeta worn as beauty spots by both sexes in the 17th and 18th centuries. Examples from the late 18th century sometimes have a mirror in the lid and compartments for different kinds of cosmetics.

Patera Motif in low relief sometimes resembling a flower. Used especially on neo-classical silver and furniture.

Patina The mellow surface of silver or wood acquired by generations of use and polishing; a valuable attribute which is lost through over-cleaning.

Pearlware Creamware with lead glaze tinted with cobalt; introduced by Wedgwood in 1779. Much was made between 1790 and 1820, for example at Leeds.

Perfume burner or pastille burner Container with pierced cover for burning perfume pastilles to sweeten the air of a room. In silver, pottery or porcelain. The ceramic versions were, from the mid-18th century, sometimes in the form of castles, cottages, or other buildings, or of animals. The perfume was often used after a meal to get rid of the smell of food.

Petuntse One of the ingredients of the true or hard paste porcelain. The other ingredient is kaolin; both are decayed forms of granite. (The English terms are china stone and china clay.) Petuntse melts at 1300–1400 °C, binding the kaolin into a solid mass. (See also PORCELAIN.)

Pie-crust border Scrolled or raised border on 18th century furniture or silver; rather like the edge of a pie crust.

Pie crust table For tea; mid-18th century; usually in mahogany and on a tripod. The outside of the top has a pie-crust edge.

Pier glass Elongated mirror to go between windows. From late 17th century.

Pier table To go between windows; often of console type. From late 17th century.

Plate Items made of gold or silver. Also applied, inaccurately, to Sheffield plate and electro-plate.

Pole screen Screen for protection against draughts or the heat of a fire. Can be adjusted: it is mounted on a pole (hence the name) and is usually on a tripod base. Popular in the 18th century.

Pontypool ware Japanned metal ware made at Pontypool, Monmouthshire, between 1680 and 1822. Boxes, trays, etc. Designs include chinoiserie, rustic scenes, sporting scenes. Imitated at Wolverhampton.

Porcelain Two types, hard paste ('true') and soft paste ('artificial'). Hard paste cannot be marked with a file and the glaze is thin and brilliant. Soft paste can be marked with a file and the glaze is somewhat uneven. The enamel colours on hard paste lie on the surface; on soft paste they often sink in. See section on Plymouth and Bristol porcelain.

Porringer Vessel for food or drink, with or without a lid and with one or two handles. Made in silver, pewter, Sheffield plate; often the term is applied to a form like a two-handled cup.

Privateer glass Drinking glass engraved with picture of a privateering ship or with, for example, a slogan such as 'Success to the Constantine'. Most were made in Bristol between about 1756 and 1770. Rare.

Putti Chubby naked boys; a common decorative feature on many kinds of objects.

Quaich or quaigh Scottish drinking vessel in silver or, rarely, pewter. In the form of a bowl with two flat handles.

Queen's pattern Design for cutlery. Resembles King's pattern but has palmette on the back of the bowl instead; curlier edges on the stem; and rosettes. From 19th century.

Quizzing fan Fan of the 18th century, with transparent panel or holes so that the user could observe with modesty and in secrecy.

Race cup Prize in a horse race; of gold, silver, or silver gilt. An important part of the silversmith's business from the mid-18th century to early 19th.

Rat-tail spoon With 'spine' of metal going up the back of the bowl to give strength.

Remontoire A mechanical device in the movement of a clock or watch. It transmits the driving force, which is generally too powerful and varying, into a delicate, uniform, and constant force. This is necessary for precision. Remontoire is usually denoted by a periodical rewinding of a subsidiary spring, as often as every 30 seconds or as infrequently as every hour. John Harrison used the device but it is mainly found in French pieces.

Rent table Kind of library table with a polygonal circular top; the top in many examples revolves. Drawers marked with letters of the alphabet, etc., for filing. Made from about 1750 to about 1800.

Rococo Style of decoration with asymmetrical but balanced curves, especially C-scrolls, and S-scrolls; rocks, shells, flowers, and leaves; water and icicles. Originated in France in the early 18th century, spread throughout Europe and to America. Flourished in Britain until about 1770.

Rosso antico Red stoneware first made by Wedgwood; style inspired by classical red pottery.

Rummer Heavy drinking glass made from about 1770 to about 1850. Various shapes.

Rundell, Philip (1743–1827) Retailer of silver and shrewd businessman. Born and served apprenticeship in Bristol and moved to London in 1767. Bought plate and jewellery for low sums from refugees of the French revolution; this was altered and sold by his partner John Bridge at large profits. The firm in its heyday dominated the trade.

Rundell, Bridge, and Rundell
Firm of silversmiths and jewellers in London with agents on the Continent, the Middle East and Russia.

Sadler, John (1720–1789) With Guy Green, ran a business in Liverpool for the decoration of ceramics by transfer-printing.

Samson, Edmé, et Cie Ceramic firm established in Paris in 1845. Has manufactured reproductions of the output of many factories; most of the porcelain productions are in hard paste (see PORCELAIN).

Settee Seat with arms; for at least two people. Sometimes with upholstered seat and back; sometimes the back resembles several chairs linked together. Popular in 18th and 19th centuries.

Settle Bench for several people; has high back and arms or sides; often the base is a chest. The seat is hinged and forms the lid of the chest. For the less wealthy classes.

Shagreen Leather or fish skin, often stained green or black.

Slip Clay mixed with water so that it becomes rather runny; applied as decoration to pottery.

Smart, John (1741–1811) Miniaturist. Also worked in India. His works usually have a plain background colour.

Sofa Upholstered SETTEE.

Spinning A method of forming silver and other fairly soft metals into small hollow-ware. Flat metal is spun at high speed on a lathe and is forced onto a shaped block of wood. The metal takes the shape of the wood. The process was rather like the way a potter 'throws' clay on a wheel. Spinning was quicker and cheaper than some other methods such as casting.

Stirring rod See MOLINET.

Storr, Paul (1771–1844) Silversmith whose products were often of lavish kind. Worked with and for Rundell, Bridge and Rundell. His styles revived rococo and classical Roman. Many pieces for royalty and aristocracy.

Stothard, Thomas (1775–1834) Painter, book illustrator, and designer of silver (e.g. Wellington Shield).

Strainer-spoon See MOTE SKIMMER.

Stretcher Rail between the legs of furniture, to give extra strength.

Stringing Long and thin inlay on veneered furniture.

Sugar tongs Device of silver for picking up lump sugar. Two forms:

(1), like pair of scissors, from late 17th century; (2), elongated U-shape with spring effect, from 1760s. Also called sugar nippers.

Tallboy Tall chest of drawers like two chests one on top of the other. Also called chest on chest or double chest.

Tambour Flexible lid of wood such as on a rolltop desk. Slats of wood are fixed to cloth; the lid rolls out of sight when not in use. Popular from 18th century onwards.

Taperstick Implement for holding taper; resembles small candlestick. In silver, porcelain, or glass.

Tatham, Charles Heathcote (1772–1842) Architect and designer. Advocated 'massiveness' in the design of silver and influenced taste in this respect. Also advocated good craftmanship in silver.

Tea caddy For keeping tea in. The term dates from the end of the 18th century; until then, called tea canister. First made at end of 17th century.

Tea kettle Vessel in silver or Sheffield plate for holding hot water. Should have original stand and spirit lamp. From early 18th century.

Tea urn Vessel for holding hot water; in silver, Sheffield plate, or japanned metal. Supplanted tea kettle. Water usually kept hot by hot iron in a special compartment.

Theed, William (1764–1817) Sculptor; worked for Josiah Wedgwood I and for Rundell, Bridge and Rundell as a designer.

Time Solar time, according to the sun, is not constant throughout the year; the time shown by clocks – mean or apparent time – is an adjustment of solar time to give days of equal .ength. Equation clocks show the difference between solar and mean time.

Torond, Francis (1742–1812) Silhouettist. Of French origin; worked in Bath and London. His best known work is of people in groups, i.e. conversation pieces.

Toy 18th-century term for small, fairly costly trinket. For adults, not children – e.g. snuffboxes, miniature furniture, sweetmeat boxes, scent bottles.

Trafalgar furniture Furniture with nautical themes made to commemorate Trafalgar (1805). See NELSON CHAIR.

Transfer-printing Method of decorating enamels or ceramics. The design is inked on paper and then transferred to the surface to be decorated. A cheap and quick method, often in one colour, mostly blue.

Trembly rose painter Unidentified painter who worked at Longton Hall porcelain factory.

Tunbridge ware Objects made of wood in the form of mosaic. Done in Tunbridge Wells, Kent, from 17th century.

Tureen Dish for soup (large) or sauce (small). In silver, Sheffield plate, pottery, or porcelain. From early 18th century.

Tyg Large vessel in pottery for communal drinking. Has at least three handles: each drinker uses one of them and thus has part of the rim for himself alone. 17th and 18th centuries.

Usk ware Japanned metal ware made 1763–1862, at Usk; similar to Pontypool.

Veneering Method of ornamenting furniture etc. Thin pieces of costly and attractive wood glued to body or carcase of cheaper wood. Also used: tortoiseshell, ivory. The wood used for the veneer may have an attractive grain which can be displayed by halving, quartering, and so on.

Verge escapement See ESCAPEMENT.

Verre eglomisé Decoration of gold or silver foil on glass.

Vitrine Glazed cabinet for displaying ornaments. From mid-18th century.

Waster Fragments of pottery or porcelain thrown away at the factory because the piece has been spoiled in the manufacture. Excavations of wasters have provided evidence about what was made where.

Windsor furniture Windsor chair the commonest. Made in many parts of the country from 17th century on. Different woods used for different parts of the chair. Many variations of backs. Centre of production from early 19th century was High Wycombe, Buckinghamshire.

Wriggle-work Decoration on pewter, mid-17th to mid-18th centuries. Engraving tool was pushed along the surface and at the same time rocked or wriggled from side to side.

Index

No separate references are given to illustrations where they are alongside the text. Where the illustrations are separated from the text, the page number appears in italics.